"This World Is Not My Home"

A VOLUME IN THE SERIES
African American Intellectual History

Edited by
CHRISTOPHER CAMERON

"This World Is Not My Home"

A CRITICAL BIOGRAPHY OF AFRICAN AMERICAN WRITER CHARLES WRIGHT

W. Lawrence Hogue

University of Massachusetts Press
Amherst and Boston

Copyright © 2023 by University of Massachusetts Press
All rights reserved
Printed in the United States of America

ISBN 978-1-62534-707-7 (paper); 708-4 (hardcover)

Designed by Sally Nichols
Set in Minion Pro and Scala by Westchester Publishing Services
Printed and bound by Books International, Inc.
Cover design by adam b. bohannon
Cover photo: unknown photographer, *Charles Wright at his typewriter
at Handy Writer's Colony.* From *Sepia* (December, 1957).
Courtesy of the University of Houston.

Library of Congress Cataloging-in-Publication Data

Names: Hogue, W. Lawrence, author.
Title: "This world is not my home" : a critical biography of African
American writer Charles Wright / W. Lawrence Hogue.
Description: Amherst : University of Massachusetts Press, [2023] |
Series: African American intellectual history | Includes bibliographical
references and index.
Identifiers: LCCN 2022045023 (print) | LCCN 2022045024 (ebook) |
ISBN 9781625347077 (paperback) | ISBN 9781625347084 (hardcover) |
ISBN 9781685750084 (ebook)
Subjects: LCSH: Wright, Charles, 1932–2008. | Authors, American—
20th century—Biography. | African American authors—Biography. | LCGFT: Biographies.
Classification: LCC PS3573.R532 Z68 2023 (print) | LCC PS3573.R532 (ebook) |
DDC 813/.54 [B]—dc23/eng/20221125
LC record available at https://lccn.loc.gov/2022045023
LC ebook record available at https://lccn.loc.gov/2022045024

British Library Cataloguing-in-Publication Data
A catalog record for this book is available from the British Library.

A portion of chapter three was previously published as "Exposing Limiting, Racialized
Heterological Critical Sites: An Existential Reading of Charles Wright's *The Messenger*,"
in *African American Male, Writing, and Difference: A Polycentric Approach to
African American Literature, Criticism, and History*
(Albany: State University of New York Press, 2003). Used by permission.

CONTENTS

FIGURES

ACKNOWLEDGMENTS

I am extremely grateful to the many people and institutions that aided my work on this critical biography. First, I want to thank the libraries that gave me access to their collections and archives: the New York Public Library; the Norris I. Brookens Library at the University of Illinois, Springfield; the Morris Library, Southern Illinois University; Kent State University Libraries; the archives at the University of Texas, Austin; and the special collections at the University of Delaware.

In addition, I thank Clarence Major for permission to quote from his papers, archived at the Elmer L. Anderson Library, at the University of Minnesota, Minneapolis, and especially for the opportunity to consult an unpublished interview between himself and Charles Wright. At the height of the pandemic, Cecily Marcus was of tremendous help in getting me the unpublished interview and letters between Clarence Major and Wright. I thank Kaylie Jones, the daughter of James Jones, for permission to quote from correspondence between Wright and her father, archived in the James Jones Papers at the University of Texas, Austin. I also thank Edward Field for permission to quote from his unpublished Moroccan letters. I want to thank my research assistant Damon Puckett for locating and gathering the pieces from Wright's column in the *Village Voice*. Finally, I thank Brian Halley, executive editor, who guided the manuscript through the peer-review process; Rachael DeShano, managing editor, who with kindness and generosity shepherded the manuscript through the production process; and the editorial staff at UMass Press for seeing it through to publication.

PREFACE

Locating the African American novelist Charles Wright was an arduous task, and critically defining him and his literary works were equally as difficult. They resisted categorization. In 2001, I published an article about Charles Wright's first published novel, *The Messenger*, and subsequently expanded it into a chapter in my 2003 book, *African American Male, Writing, and Difference*. Before long I began receiving queries from students and scholars about Wright's whereabouts. Though he was rumored to be alive, he had not published a novel since 1973. Did I know anything more? I had no answers, but the questions did pique my interest. What had happened to Charles Wright? Why did he stop publishing? If he really were alive, where was he?

I first encountered Wright's fiction in the late 1970s, as a graduate student in the Modern Thought and Literature Program at Stanford University, and was immediately taken by it. As a literature professor, I regularly taught his novels in my undergraduate and graduate courses on contemporary African American fiction. By 2003, I had spent almost twenty years with his work, and my literary interest in him was serious. Now, with others asking questions, I began to entertain the idea of tracking him down and interviewing him. My plan was to write a long critical article exploring his life and works. I also wanted to know what had happened to him after the 1970s. Why was he no longer writing and publishing fiction? The sources I consulted told me that he was, indeed, still alive, though I was also hearing wild stories about his disappearance into Mexico. But no one could tell me where he actually lived. Then, in about 2005, Robert Phillips, then one of my colleagues at the University of Houston, told me that while he was attending a writer's conference on the East Coast, he had seen a distinguished-looking gentleman. This, he had learned, was the novelist Charles Wright, now living in a retirement home somewhere in New Jersey. I followed up on this information but was not able to locate him. Later I discovered that Wright was actually living in a retirement home in the East Village. Apparently he was even listed in the New York City telephone book.

In 2003, Mercury House in San Francisco had published a new paperback edition of Charles Wright's novel *The Wig*, with an introduction by Ishmael Reed; therefore, in the fall of 2007, I contacted Reed, asking for information about locating Wright. He never responded. In December 2008, I emailed the director of Mercury House, Jeremy Bigalke, and inquired about Wright. Bigalke eventually informed me that Wright had died during the previous October. He put me in touch with Charlotte Sheedy, Wright's literary agent in New York, who supposedly now held the copyright to *The Wig*. But Sheedy told me that the copyright had reverted to Wright, and I was back to where I had begun.

Several years passed before I took up the search again. While reading Wright's obituary in the *New York Times*, I noticed that the writer had gained much of his background information from a Jan Hodenfield, with whom Wright had apparently lived for more than twenty years, from the mid-1970s through the mid-1990s.[1] Hodenfield had been the editor of the *Downtown Express* from 1990 to 1993 and was a former contributor to the *New Yorker* and the *New York Post*. Searching for a contact, I tried googling him, to no avail. Then I reached out to the *Times* obituary writer, who agreed to help but then discovered that Hodenfield had passed away on July 21, 2012. I had run into another dead end.

Another year went by. In the summer of 2013, I traveled to New York and ventured up to Harlem to interview the novelist William Melvin Kelley. I asked him if he knew Charles Wright. He said yes but not personally. He was not able to provide me with any information. Then in November, while eating sushi in Houston with the writer Allen Gee, a former student and at that time a creative writing professor at Georgia College (he is now at Columbus State University in Georgia), I shared the tale of my frustrating search for Wright. The issue had become more pressing, I told Allen, because the French publisher of Éditions Le Tropode had recently contacted me. He wanted to translate and publish *The Messenger* in France and wanted to know who held the copyright. Here was another person eager to promote Wright's work, another person equally at sea about how to do so.

I told Allen about Jan Hodenfield as well as two other linked names—Lynn Hodenfield and Hallie Hodenfield. I had not been able to contact any of them, nor did I know their relationship. Allen confidently assured me that his own literary agent knew everything and everybody in New York City; he would see what he could find out. Within a month Allen had located Hallie Hodenfield, who turned out to be the daughter of Jan and Lynn, and had introduced us via email.

According to Hallie, Charlie, as she called him, had lived in her family's apartment in Brooklyn for many years. Hallie told me that Wright had played a crucial role in her and her brother's upbringing, and she agreed to sit for an interview, along with her brother. In addition, Hallie shared the contact of Phelonise Willie, a friend of Wright's for more than thirty years and a co-executor of his estate. Finally, she urged me to contact her mother Lynn, who had known Wright for many years, and would be an excellent source. But Lynn stepped in and canceled the interviews with Hallie and Tor.

Later that summer, I requested a personal interview with Lynn, with whom I had previously communicated. She emailed me the following reply:

> Renewed interest in Charles Wright's life and work has been coming from various directions of late. Therefore, we are trying to assess the different avenues in order to ensure that Charles' legacy is appropriately maintained. Your interest is greatly appreciated, and I know Charles would feel the same way, so, at such time as our deliberations as a family yield more concrete results, I will surely be in touch.[2]

Of course, Lynn never got in touch with me, and neither she, Hallie, nor Tor ever granted me an interview. In the fall of 2019, as I was completing the first draft of the manuscript, I sent her another email, requesting an interview and access to any of Wright's papers she might have in her possession. She never responded.

Therefore, I moved on to Phelonise Willie. I had first contacted Willie in 2014, telling her that I was writing a long critical article on Wright and requesting an interview. In her response, she was very protective of him. She had been angered by the *New York Times* editor's obituary of Wright and assured me, "I have a vested interest in promoting Charles' work." She continued:

> So, I am interested in anyone interested in Charles. I was wondering when the world would remember his existence. However, as his good friend I'd like to know a bit of the direction the description . . . will take . . . . When Charles died there was an obituary written about him, ironically by a close friend of his, I despised! Charles was no saint. . . . What I don't want is inaccuracy. Charles was many things but most of all he was just human. He had a great mind, a lot of charm & talent, and like most of us a lot of faults. That obituary made him seem pathetic. While I don't believe in glossing the truth, I won't be part of any account that is not compassionate.[3]

Willie wanted to know how I had gotten her name and how had I come to know about Wright. She wondered what direction my article would take, and she wanted to see "the research [I had] already published on Charles."[4]

I have already mention that I was introduced to Wright's fiction at Stanford. But my interest in his work went beyond the classroom. In those years, as I was developing a focused interested in American and African American literature, I began to visit local bookstores, searching for relevant books. In a store in downtown Palo Alto, I was approached by a mild-mannered, elderly man. His name was Eugene White, and he gave me his card, inviting me to visit his archive, the Fern P. White Collection of Black Creative Writing, located in East Palo Alto. The collection had been named after his daughter, who had been killed in a car accident.

Several weeks later, my dear friend Susan Ross and I visited White's collection, which was housed in a building two or three doors down from his residence. For years, White, who worked in the shipyard in San Francisco, had been acquiring what he called "creative" fiction by African Americans from around the world. I was absolutely stunned by his collection. In the late 1970s and early 1980s, many African American literary texts were out of print, so it was here that I saw, for the first time, copies of Charles Wright's *The Messenger* and *The Wig*. Because Mr. White would not let me purchase copies from him and I did not want him to just give me books, Susan and I hit upon an idea: if we brought African American writers who were visiting Stanford to see him and his collection, would he give us spare copies of out-of-print novels? He agreed. Therefore, when Alice Walker and Ernest Gaines visited my freshman seminar, we took them to see White's collection. Both were immensely impressed, and Walker even borrowed a text by Roi Ottley. When Toni Cade Bambara came to lecture for a week, we took her to visit White's collection. We also took Sylvia Wynter, the department's chair of African American studies, and the novelist Ishmael Reed to visit White's collection. These visits gave White enormous joy. He was being recognized and acknowledged for his efforts.

What I acquired from these visits were out-of-print African American texts, including Wright's novels. For me, reading *The Messenger* for the first time was similar to reading Richard Wright's *Native Son* for the first time. In high school, *Native Son* had introduced me to the political, economic, psychological, and social landscapes that explained the African American subaltern and the American racial world. Now, *The Messenger* showed me a familiar human interiority. It was a truly modern experience, one involving an African American, working-class intellectual who was struggling with issues of being as he lived among other African American outcasts. I sensed that Wright, like James Baldwin, was a self-taught intellectual who was a vagabond, an existential cipher, a bluesman, a person who was sexually fluid and who lived according to his own rules. He had no desire to conform to the middle-class, white norm. I found the novel enlightening and very attractive. Later, I read *The Wig* and was equally impressed.

Wright was extremely well read in contemporary western literature. Bisexual, working-class, and intellectual, he traveled the world both physically and imaginatively, through life and fiction, crossing social, class, and sexual boundaries. Unlike Baldwin, he was at home among the socially rejected; and in his fiction, particularly in *The Messenger*, he gave the people of that world validity and meaning. To him, these outcasts, who lived by their own non-middle-class and non-Christian rules and values, were worthy of poetic portrayal. They justified the world according to their own logic. Of course, as I would later learn, his attraction to this social milieu became a problem not only for elite Manhattan editors but also for liberal New York reviewers and critics, all of whom were framing literary taste and value for the rest of America. They were not accustomed to seeing outcast African American characters as complex human beings, with agency and a distinct subjectivity.

In reading and teaching Wright's novels, I worked to define his artistic and literary worth outside of the middle-class, puritanical, enlightenment values that dominated American literature. I eventually decided that he was an American modernist, whose subject was the urban subaltern African American but who also dealt with racial oppression, sexuality, and the issue of being. Wright had immersed himself in the work of modernist writers such as Ernest Hemingway, F. Scott Fitzgerald, William Faulkner, Nathanael West, Djuna Barnes, Jean-Paul Sartre, Albert Camus, and Katherine Ann Porter. I also sensed that he was a fan of Black music, especially jazz and the blues, and of Black vernacular language. This assemblage, I thought, was what had produced the working-class writer Charles Wright and his work. But, more importantly, as I critically and literarily positioned Wright, I concluded that he had begun his modernist writing with James Jones and Ernest Hemingway, early influences from the Handy Writers' Colony. But he ended up writing in and extending/challenging/transforming/playing with the western existential and satirical genres. He incorporated experimental and postmodern elements, sufficiently altering these genres to deal affirmatively with the subaltern class, homosexuality, Black language and Black music, and racial oppression and ultimately creating something different. This became my critical approach to Wright's fiction.

But, I also wanted to place him within a critical African American tradition. The mainstream American critic Edward Margolis has highlighted a certain restrictive representation of Black literature, claiming that "by and large there is an absence of humor."[5] In fact, an absurdist, satirical tradition has a long history in African American literature and culture. Until recently, however, it has been marginalized, suppressed, or ignored by both white and Black critics. In an interview with Joseph Henry, Ishmael Reed discusses a long-standing, visible tradition of "fantasy, humor, and satire" in African American life and culture: a persistent, non-western form of satire that "gets back at [its] exploiters."[6] "If you look at our [African American] tradition all the way back to the plantation," he notes in an interview with Mel Watkins, "you see that satire and signifying are widely used. It's a way of subverting the wishes of the people in power."[7]

Historically, according to Reed, Black satire was a subversive countertradition to mainstream American traditions, which tended to represent African Americans in devalued terms. As some of the first moderns in the West—physically and spiritually dislocated, homeless, and subalternized—they used satirical elements and strategies such as humor, laughter, irony, and wit to survive, deflect, and undermine oppressive and dehumanizing living conditions. Laughter, humor, and satire were ways to get through the pain and hardship and difficulty of living while Black in America. These satirical features have always been a part of African America's culture and art, appearing in slave narratives, folklore, working-class culture, the blues, and literature. Yet this tradition was mostly ignored by critics during the modern postwar era.

Only recently have African American scholars and literary critics turned their gaze to these features in African American life and literature. Darryl Dickson-Carr's seminal *African American Satire: The Sacredly Profane Novel* was the first full-length study of African American literary satire, engaging narratives and texts from slavery to the present and constructing a satirical literary tradition in African American literature. This critical text placed certain neglected African American texts (among them George Schuyler's *Black No More*, Rudolph Fisher's *The Walls of Jericho*, Ishmael Reed's *The Terrible Twos*, Paul Beatty's *The White Boy Shuffle*, and Darius James's *Negrophobia*) within a heterological critical site where they were illuminated and clarified, making them come alive. Dickson-Carr also did a wonderful job of satirically rereading canonical texts such as Ralph Ellison's *Invisible Man* and breathing innovative meaning into them.

With the publication of his groundbreaking *Spoofing the Modern: The Role of Satire in the Harlem Renaissance,* Dickson-Carr extended and deepened the satirical literary tradition he established in *African American Satire.* He traced satire in the margins of nineteenth-century fiction writers such as Charles Chesnutt, Paul Laurence Dunbar, and Pauline Hopkins, explaining how this tradition became prominent in the fiction and nonfiction of the 1920s Harlem Renaissance. Nonetheless, African American literary scholars and intellectuals did not give it much attention. Why? Was it because satire questions hegemonies? Was it because satire was viewed as overtly political? I am not sure I know the answer to these questions. However, I do know that African American satire did not compete with either the hegemonic African American racial uplift narrative (which was easily accommodated by the political and literary norms of mainstream American society), the return to the African past, or African American protest literature, all of which were advocated by white critics. Charles

Wright belonged to this satirical tradition, altering and subverting the mainstream existential and satirical approaches. Hence, his Black, modern, humorist novel was excluded from larger consideration.

After I sent Phelonise Willie a copy of my article and my book, she warmed up to me. Eventually she became comfortable about sharing her knowledge of Wright, describing their friendship and offering invaluable information. She gave me the names of people such as Larl Becham and Mary Jacobs, who had known him in New York. She told me that Wright had met James Baldwin and Langston Hughes, that he had corresponded with Norman Mailer and Clarence Major, that he had spent time in Mexico and Tangier. With some guidance from Willie, I began to research the archives of American writers whom Wright might have known or corresponded with. I found letters between Wright and Hughes at Yale's Beinecke Library. At the Harry Ransom Center at the University of Texas, Austin, I discovered several letters between Wright and Norman Mailer and between Wright and the British novelist Rupert Croft-Cooke, who had met in Tangier in the 1960s. I read Croft-Cooke's discussion of Wright in his travel book *The Caves of Hercules*. Also at the Harry Ransom Center, I read correspondence between James Jones and Wright. Learning that Wright had befriended the American novelist Alfred Chester in Tangier, I found Chester's papers at Kent State University. I read the correspondence between Chester and the poet Edward Field archived at the University of Delaware, in which the two had discussed Wright in the context of Tangier. Later, Field permitted me to read his unpublished manuscript on Chester, which also contained extensive conversations about Wright.

I sought out other sources. Learning that Clarence Major had been a friend of Wright's, I searched his archived papers at the University of Minnesota and located letters between the two. Knowing that Kay Boyle had written a blurb for Wright's first published novel, I examined her papers at Southern Illinois University and found a correspondence. Examining the Handy Colony Collection at the University of Illinois, Springfield, I discovered correspondence between James Jones and Wright and, most importantly, between Wright and Lowney T. Handy, director of the colony, detailing Wright's arrivals and stays. Included in the collection were articles published in *Ebony* and *Sepia* about Wright during his stay at the colony. I talked with the superintendent of education in New Franklin, Missouri, where Wright had attended elementary school, and with Rhonda

Chalfant, the president of the NAACP in Sedalia, Missouri, where he had attended junior high and high schools. She knew people who had known Wright, and they became sources.

I located, interviewed, and had long conversations with the late Mary Jacobs, who had befriended Wright in Tangier and later in New York City. I discovered that Jacobs possessed a nine-hour taped conversation between herself, Wright, and Alfred Upton, recorded in June 1981. I later traveled to New York to listen to those tapes. Finally, I drew on the pieces that Wright had published in his *Village Voice* column "Wright's World" between 1967 and 1973. Many later became the foundation for his fiction/nonfiction book *Absolutely Nothing to Get Alarmed About*.

After reading a review of Boris Kachka's *Hothouse*, a history of Farrar, Straus, and Giroux, where Wright published all of his novels, I emailed the book's author, who pointed me to the thousands of pages by and about Wright archived at the New York Public Library. This gold mine includes three decades of correspondence, from the 1960s through the 1990s, between Wright and the press.

I examined census data in Missouri to learn about Wright's family, particularly his maternal grandparents. I had several telephone conversations with Steve Cannon, the author of the wonderful novel *Groove, Bang, and Jive Around*. Along with Ishmael Reed, Cecil Brown, and David Henderson, Cannon visited Wright at the Hotel Albert after the publication of *The Wig*. In 1993, when HarperPerennial reissued Wright's three novels in one volume, Cannon and others organized a reception for him. I had several telephone conversations with the poet Abba Elethea about the friendship between Larl Becham and Charles Wright. I visited the Schomburg Center for Research in Black Culture in Harlem and had interviews and conversations with Clarence Major and Wilfred Samuels.

From these sources, along with my readings of his three published novels and his short stories, I constructed this critical biography of Charles Wright. I have not been able to talk about his complete oeuvre, for I could not account for the lost novels, plays, and short stories; the "unfinished" texts; the "sketches that he himself abandoned"; the lost letters; the "reported conversations, transcriptions of what he said made by those present at the time, in short, to that vast mass of verbal traces left by an individual at his death."[8] As a result, this book contains many gaps and silences. Still, I hope it will serve as a beginning for other scholars who are pursuing Wright and his work.

Charles Wright was known not because of his life but because of his fiction. Therefore, I have focused on close readings of the texts, their production and critical reception, and how they emerged out of Wright's life. The project is a critical effort that endeavors to illuminate some fruitful dialogues between Charles Wright's life and his literary work. By not adhering too closely to biographical details, I hoped to be loyal to his texts and to the work of his life: creation, encounters, becomings, and productions. I bent the genre to offer a scholarly reading of the novels rather than to suggest *a* reading, as is the expectation in conventional biographies. Wright was embodied in his writing, and he was born again and again, along with his literary texts, within personal traumas, anti-Black racism, encounters with literature, social and political issues, the literary institutions within the ideological state apparatus, and friendships with other writers.

"This World Is Not My Home"

CHAPTER ONE

A Tumultuous, Traumatic Missouri Childhood

In the late nineteenth and early twentieth centuries, Missouri citizens lived under the regime of white supremacy. Jim Crow laws created and reinforced Black social and economic inequality by structurally and legally denying African Americans access to the vote as well as to adequate jobs, wages, education, health care, and housing. Only the lowest-level employments, such as domestic service and fieldwork, were open to Blacks. In and outside of cities, Blacks were segregated in the workplace and lived in grinding poverty.[1] The Great Depression of the 1930s made their economic and social position even worse, as whites now took over many of the unskilled jobs that Blacks had once held. For African Americans, every aspect of life was racialized.

Charles Stevenson Wright was born on June 4, 1932, in racially segregated, Jim Crow New Franklin, Missouri, located on the Missouri River, just north of Boonville, home of his parents, Dorothy Hughes and Henry Hill Wright. Dorothy (October 17, 1912–August 18, 1936) was the eldest of three sisters, all of whom would die young. Anna Rose (January 9, 1915–September 19, 1931) died of pulmonary tuberculosis.[2] Nannie (July 19, 1919–September 12, 1920) died of "whooping cough."[3] Charles was four years old when his mother died. At that time, he came to stay with his maternal grandparents, Charlie Hughes (born in 1873) and Dora Jordan Hughes (born on July 31, 1881). Charlie was a day laborer, working at odd jobs to support his family.[4] Both of Wright's grandparents would play crucial roles in his tumultuous childhood.

Wright's father, Henry Hill Wright, was born on March 25, 1880. Dorothy was his second wife; his first was Rosie Spence (December 9, 1888–October 1932). That marriage produced one daughter, Florence Etta Wright Parks, born on January 23, 1911.[5] After Rosie died of cancer, Henry married Dorothy; and when she died, he married for a third time to Martha Hill Wright. Henry died on March 27, 1953, at the age of seventy-three.[6]

Charles Wright's first vivid memory was of himself, at the age of three, listening to a St. Louis Cardinals game with his father. This was the same year that the Hughes Chapel Methodist Church, named after a great-uncle who was a famous Missouri preacher, moved down into the Black section of New Franklin. But the relationship between father and son quickly soured, soon becoming disorienting and unhappy. He also recalled a visit from his grandfather on a hot August day in 1936. Charlie Hughes, who was "wiping his forehead with a red bandana handkerchief," asked the young Charles if he wanted to get ice cream, obviously trying to distract his attention from his sick mother. Charles agreed, knowing that something was wrong. When they returned home with the blackberry ice cream, they found his mother dead.

Dorothy's death was devastating. When, as a nineteen year old, Wright wrote of that loss, he "remember[ed] the day as if it were only yesterday."[7] According to Phelonise Willie, he "always regretted not knowing his mother longer and better."[8] The attachment theorists John Bowlby and Mary Ainsworth write that "the death of a mother results in lifelong struggles for the individual," and this was certainly true for Wright.[9] A young child, they say, uses his mother as a "secure base to depart from and return" to in his "exploration of the world." When that base is absent, the child can develop "trauma and troubling behaviors in adolescence and adult life."[10] Thus, at the age of four, Wright's world fell apart.

It had been his mother's stated "wish" that if something were to happen to her, her son would live with her parents, although her husband's middle-class family was more financially stable. Charles later recalled that the Wrights "expected [him] to be a minister or teacher or work for the Civil Service, but none of these things interested [him] in the least."[11] Therefore, by 1940, seven-year-old Charles was living with Charlie and Dora Hughes in New Franklin. Though his father lived nearby, he seldom saw him. Henry remarried; and when the United States entered World War II, he enlisted in the army. After serving his tour, he returned to New Franklin. With few employment opportunities available, Henry found work as a fire builder at the steam railroad shop and as a railroad porter.[12]

Henry's detachment affected Charles for the rest of his life. He wrote, "Although we were never together and my father never showed me any kindness, I loved him." This thwarted affection initiated a traumatic relational pattern that Wright reprised throughout his life. He was convinced that his father did not love him. Yet because he was emotionally starved, he needed his father's love. When the boy met his father and stepmother on the streets of New Franklin, the father "never" spoke. In the presence of his wife, he simply ignored the child. But if Charles encountered his father "by himself," Henry "would always speak." These mixed signals were confusing, "proof" that his "father did not love him."[13]

According to the psychologist Erik Erickson, when a person does not experience love in early childhood, "significant needs for love and trust continue to be present in life's challenges."[14] Charles Wright's early experiences allowed him to internalize a sense of disempowerment that, as an adult, repeatedly led him into problematic and damaging relationships. Patterns linked to his mother's death and his father's rejection repeated themselves throughout his life.

Young Charles was also caught within the tensions of his extended Wright and Hughes families. For instance, knowing that the families of soldiers were eligible for government stipends, Dora Hughes, his grandmother and guardian, applied for his father's allotment. This created a rift between Dora and the stepmother. But the process was painful in other ways as well. When Dora went to the service office to apply for the allotment, the "gray haired woman would ask: Has he [the father] ever done anything for the boy? Does he even recognize the boy as his son"?[15] Dora's answer was no, and she eventually won the stipend.

To psychologically survive these early traumas, Charles turned inward. Knowing that he was powerless, he became aware of power dynamics and, in response, worked to distance himself from people. Among peers who seemed to be enjoying "normal" childhoods, he felt alone and abandoned. He suffered from what has been called reactive attachment disorder, which included withdrawal, distrust, and the inability to form healthy social relationships. He later wrote:

> I had a feeling about things and people. This feeling has always made me think things out for myself. I have always been my own best friend. When most children are at the age of innocence enjoying a normal childhood, mine was crushed in. I understood and really didn't understand what was happening. This is coupled with a still unhappy life . . . [which] has made me give up hope.[16]

He assessed his problem as "learning to much too fast, without . . . taking time to think." He knew, from an early age, that he "must take a long hard look at Charles Wright," and this became a lifelong literary project.[17] As a traumatized person, Wright had suffered "damage to the basic structure of the self," and he used his fiction to examine and pursue that self.[18]

In New Franklin, Wright attended public school in a red, one-room building until the age of fourteen. It was a segregated school, with about twenty-five students.[19] He remembered being "taunted by his classmates for being yellow" in skin tone, an experience that reinforced his marginalization and alienation.[20] In a later conversation with Clarence Major, Wright recalled a strong sense of racial dehumanization. When he and his "best buddy" stopped after school to watch some workers build a bridge, the white men "used to have us to fight . . . and he was my best friend and we would fight, and they would give us money each evening. . . . you know . . . that the Blacks are to entertain . . . for the amusement of the whites."[21] This memory, which sounds like a scene from Ralph Ellison's *Invisible Man*, shaped how Charles responded to white people in his adult life.

But there were bright moments. One was his relationship with the artist James Dallas Parks (August 25, 1907–August 17, 1983), who was married to Florence, Charles's half-sister.[22] James became a father figure to Wright during these early years. Born in St. Louis, he taught at Lincoln University, a historically Black institution in Jefferson City, eventually becoming head of the art department.[23] Parks had been a student of Thomas Hart Benton, a renowned painter and muralist who was at the forefront of the Regionalist art movement. Despite Parks's encouragement, however, Charles showed no aptness for painting. "At eight, I knew I couldn't draw decent stick figures. Then and there, I gave up my art career."[24]

His half-sister Florence was also a support. A 1929 graduate of the Lincoln Lab School, she attended Lincoln University before marrying Parks in 1934. The two lived for many years in Jefferson City, where she owned and operated the Blue Tiger Restaurant from 1936 to 1946, ran Lincoln's campus bookstore from 1946 to 1971, and worked as a clerk at the Missouri capitol from 1971 to 1973. Young Charles was close to Florence, whom he referred to as his cousin. As late as March 1965, while he was living in Tangier, he wrote to his editor at Farrar, Straus, Harold Vursell, informing him that if anything were to happen to him, his belongings should go to her or "if she is dead" they should go "to her son."[25]

During these confusing early years, Charles Wright turned to reading and writing. With painting out of the question, he was searching for answers and meaning, and he was encouraged in these pursuits by his grandmother, with whom he had bonded. Reading exposed him to creations, encounters, reactions, and becomings—those hallmarks of his own mature fiction. When he was alone and in pain, he wrote for himself, seeking what the cultural studies scholar GerShun Avilez calls "psychic and emotional safety."[26] In school, when asked to write about his "summer vacation," he wrote instead about "what [he] saw and what [had] happened to [him] that summer" when his mother died. He "was very proud" of what he had written, but his teacher thought the subject was too off-putting.[27] Without support or reinforcement, Charles withdrew into himself again and stopped trying to write.

Then, on March 14, 1944, his grandfather Charlie Hughes died at the age of seventy-five. For the next several years (until his father's World War II allotment came through), Wright and his grandmother lived on welfare, though occasionally she was able to find work as a housemaid in a private home, which was one of the few employment options available to her. He later wrote, "There was nothing my grandmother could do but apply for public assistance. It was a pittance in every sense of the word. Sometimes she did day-work for white families in the valley of New Franklin," but "not too many white families could afford full-time servants not to mention part-time help."[28] In 1945, when Wright was fourteen, the pair left town and moved in with Dora's mother, Emma Hollands Wynn, who wanted them "with her in Sedalia."[29] Here he was happy, at least for a time, and he remained deeply connected to his very religious grandmother. She had great influence on him, and a representation of her appears prominently in *The Messenger*.

As a "dreamer," Wright saw the move to Sedalia as "heaven." "I had just come from a village of around 1,144 people to a small city of around 25,000 people." Though he had "always loved playing baseball," there had not been enough boys near New Franklin to "play regular types of games." But Sedalia had organized baseball, with enough players to fill two teams. This was a delight for him. Nonetheless, he still felt like "a shy, dumb country boy, [and] I started drawing farther into my shell."[30]

Between 1945 and 1947, Charles attended Sedalia's segregated Black Hubbard High School, which served Blacks from the five surrounding counties.[31] Initially, he was "one of the most popular kids in school—a leader."[32] He even tried out for the basketball team, but "between [the ages of] 12 and 14 different events in his personal life happened and he withdr[ew] into his shell and beg[an] to keep these things within," becoming "a quiet and secretive person."[33] Displaying what might now be diagnosed as a schizoid personality disorder, he felt extremely alienated from himself. Knowing that he was different, he became a loner, an outsider to both the white and Black worlds, not exactly fitting in socially with his high school classmates. Wright's first autobiographical novel, *The Messenger*, also suggests this was the period when he began dealing with his homosexuality. He hitchhiked to Kansas City and had sexual encounters with men, something that was not condoned in either the Black or white worlds of Sedalia.

"The detached nature" of an adolescent child, writes John Bowlby, is "connected to early separation from family members."[34] Again, feeling his powerlessness and his desire to "manage" the world, Charles, to emotionally protect himself from the pain of his traumatic past and, perhaps, from his repressed homosexuality, distanced himself from his classmates. To compensate, he escaped into reading. Wright haunted the Sedalia public library, reading the work of Ernest Hemingway, Truman Capote, Richard Wright, Thomas Wolfe, John Steinbeck, William Faulkner, Carson McCullers, and other modernists. He read all of the volumes of *Best American Short Stories* and the O. Henry Prizes. This reading further produced creations, encounters, and becomings. His impulse to create reemerged, and he tried painting again. His high school English teacher assigned him to write short stories, and he used them as a way to talk to himself, to invent companions, to fill the void. Art became a "means for addressing material and psychic injury."[35]

One night, as Wright walked past a gas station, a sailor said hello to him, and the two had a short conversation. This encounter became the source of his first short story, "So Long, Pal," about a soldier with a limp. Wright had been reading Hemingway's "Indian Camp," in which young Nick, his doctor father, and his uncle visit an Indian camp and Nick confronts suffering and death. Wright was impressed by Hemingway's method and technique. He later recalled "discovering . . . his method, which was very simple and everything and shocking, and he did have that genius for presenting horror and tragedy in such a quiet, understated way, that had a much more powerful effect."[36]

"So Long, Pal" was "well received by his classmates" and his teacher. The story was his first use of a real-life situation to spark his imagination, a pattern he would continue to follow in his career. More and more, Charles was feeling that the adventure of literature was the life for him. "I began to understand about people and [got] excited over what I read. This I thought was the life I wanted."[37] Reading and writing became the way the alienated and confused Wright connected to the life he saw around him and to the life he lived.

In his junior year, Wright dropped out of high school before hitchhiking to California. Now the fifteen-year-old spent long days in the library and at the local railroad station, where, according to a story he told the Hodenfield family, "he would read magazines in their bound stacks . . . because he knew that once they got to the local drugstore, he wouldn't be allowed to look at them."[38] Restless and adventurous, he often hitchhiked to Kansas City. During one of those visits, he was "picked up by this white couple" and he had sex with the wife.[39] (This incident would later end up as a scene in *The Messenger*.) Before long, he hitchhiked to California, taking a route through Albuquerque. Finding himself lost, he showed up at a hotel outside Albuquerque, and the owner put him up for the night. The next day, Charles hitchhiked farther west, stopping in San Bernardino, California, and asking a Seven-Day Adventist couple for a drink of water. They obliged, and he ended up staying with them for two and a half months. In fact, they wanted to adopt him. Already, he was using his charm, intelligence, and survival skills to his advantage. He spent some time in Los Angeles before hitchhiking back to Missouri, stopping again outside Albuquerque, "where he might have left a Mexican woman with a child."[40] He caught a ride with a trucker, who dropped him off in Blue Springs, Missouri, where a family from Sedalia recognized him and gave him a ride back home.

Wright "hung out" in Sedalia until 1951, when he was drafted into the army.[41] During this time, his great-grandmother Emma Wynn died, and the family's money problems increased. Wright returned to high school and withdrew a second time. He recalled leaving school "a few months before he would have graduated. [He] couldn't afford to graduate." He had had an insurance policy worth $500, which was supposed to mature when he turned eighteen, allowing him to finish high school and go to college. "But something happened to its value." Therefore, instead, on the night of his high school graduation, he walked up the railroad track smiling. He always smiled when he was in trouble; it was one of the ways in which he dealt with life. "I think I was smiling and laughing life in the face. But it became harder to smile."

Walking was one of the ways in which Charles dealt with his restlessness. "I used to take walks at night. I'd start up the railroad track [in Sedalia] and end up on a side street off downtown which in turn lead me back to the tracks and home. . . . I would walk and think and dream."[42] But these walks also revealed the town's racism:

> I had to come through a white residential district before I reached the side street. Some one noticed me, and cars would always follow me home. Later the police picked me up. After I told my story and they didn't find any weapons, . . . they let me go. They warned me: if [you] want to walk—walk in [your] own neighborhood. The reason I didn't walk there was [because] I didn't want to meet anyone [I] knew.[43]

Before going into the army, the eighteen-year-old Wright worked "setting pins at a bowling alley," where he dealt with more racism. But he clung to his dream of becoming a writer, and many of these personal experiences became part of his fiction. Then, in a 1950 issue of *Life*, he learned about a new writing colony in Marshall, Illinois, founded by Lowney Turner Handy, her husband Harry Handy, and the novelist James Jones.[44] Wright took a chance and wrote to Lowney Handy, expressing his desire to write and his doubts about his abilities. "I have hesitated a dozen times or more before writing you this very long letter. But I have finally decided to do so." He told Handy that he had written some stories:

> I have not tried to publish them because I think they aren't good enough. At times when I get discouraged and there is no one I can turn to, I ask myself: what's the use? Then the unfinished stories are put away. Ever since I was small, I've had a feeling about things and people. This feeling has always made me think things out for myself. I have always been my own best friend.[45]

Clearly, despite his troubled childhood and his insecurity, Charles was a risk taker. He had an independent spirit but was willing to seek help with his writing. In the same letter, he told Handy:

I would still like to write but I think I may need a little professional training. I could take a writing course and work during the day. But how could I get started. Would they accept me on the basis of my stories and an exam (If I passed since I didn't finish high school). . . . I am independent. I would want to work my own way—so if I failed, I would only be in debt to myself. At present I am unemployed. . . . Again and again, I said that the only sensible thing to do is join the army. It would give my life a since of direction.[46]

After some months of correspondence, Lowney asked him to attend the Handy Writers' Colony. Later, Charles Wright spoke of this experience with a reporter at *Sepia* magazine. "I just took a long chance and wrote to her. We exchanged letters for six or eight months and then she told me to come on down here."[47]

On arriving at the colony, students received "two heady morsels of inspiration: a copy of the best-seller *From Here to Eternity*, clearly a successful literary text within the institution of popular American literature, and a guided tour of author James Jones's sumptuous $85,000 red wood and limestone home."[48] Wright remembered his first days at the colony in the summer of 1951: "Lowney treated me real nice, but the second day she chewed me out for feeling sorry for myself. She has often told me she feels Negroes and Jews are their own worst enemy. 'We all give the enemy the gun to shoot us with,' is the way she puts it."[49] Wright soon resisted Handy's discipline, further displaying his independent streak. But she kept confronting him because she did not think he was working hard enough. Sometimes he was "goofing off because [he] couldn't stand the pressure."[50] At other times, he was doubting that he was cut out to be a writer.

Wright encountered other problems at the colony that year. Lily-white, conservative Marshall had only one Black man, the barber Squab Wilson, in permanent residence. When he refused to cut Wright's hair, James Jones had to intervene. Ironically, Wilson, a friend of Lowney Handy's father, was afraid of losing his white customers at the colony if he cut a Black man's hair. Jones, however, informed him that the writers at the colony would boycott his shop if he did not. Vincent Tubbs, a reporter for *Sepia*, drily concluded, "Under such a threat from one of the town's richest and most famous citizens, Wilson found himself with a new head of hair to cut."[51]

Wright returned to Sedalia feeling as if he had undergone a transformative experience. In a letter to Handy, he said, "Even though I was there only a month I learned a lot. More than I've ever learnt before. Considering that I was such a mixed up, confused kid, it was a completely new and happy experience for me. Meeting the new and different people. . . . I only wished I could have fulfilled my part of the deal." The colony had had a profound effect on him, introducing him to a new social and intellectual situation and pushing him to look at Sedalia more critically: "I found the old town quite different. Also the people. I have begun looking at them in a more objective and [with a more] honest point of view." He struggled to describe his feelings: "There is so much I want to say in this letter, but I can't find the right words to describe my emotions."[52]

After this first visit into the world of writing fiction, Wright was restless in Sedalia. In a letter, Handy reminded him that one of the highpoints of the summer had been his "out line or idea for a novel," so he decided to write a "few scenes and send them to [her] and see what [she thought] of them." This became a common pattern between the two.[53] Eventually, Wright made other visits to the colony, for he was determined to become a writer and he saw the place as a vehicle. But how much did he know about the profession he wanted to enter? What did he know about getting published or about the institution of literature? Not very much.

In "Ideology and Ideological State Apparatuses," Louis Althusser discusses how western societies reproduce the relations of production by which they function. The state is thought of primarily as the "State Apparatus,"—that is, as the sum of the institutions: the government, the administration, the army, the police, the courts, and the prisons.[54] All are relations of power, practices and actions by which the ruling class maintains its economic dominance and enforces its rule. For Althusser, the state also contains an "Ideological State Apparatus" comprised of distinct and specialized ideological institutions that work together to maintain the order of the state and its values and that have their own agenda and internal cultures: religious, educational, family, literary, media, legal, political communication, and cultural.[55]

The literary and educational institutions include the specific institutions of literary production and distribution: publishing houses, editors, bookstores, and libraries. Mainstream/hegemonic teachers, publishers, editors, and reviewers seek their own definitions of the literary experience in all texts that come to their attention. They evaluate literary texts by pointing out their contribution to knowledge and explaining how they reproduce certain values, conventions, and perspectives. They certify those literary texts that speak the discourse better, that conform to the established literary standards and criteria. They exclude or marginalize those texts that do not conform in subject or perspective.

The cultural apparatus also encompasses a range of secondary supporting institutions—among them literary academies, English departments, literary criticism, review journals and magazines, the concept of literature, granting and awarding agencies—whose function is more directly ideological. These secondary supportive institutions are also concerned with the definition and dissemination of certain codified literary standards, conventions, stereotypes, and assumptions, which they want to keep alive in the public's mind. In the modern form, literature has come to mean, as Raymond Williams notes, "taste," "sensibility," and "discrimination."[56] These terms become the unifying concepts of modern American literature.

This concept of modern literature, produced historically and ideologically in the West, generates these established literary conventions, stereotypes, and assumptions. More importantly, this concept is about selling books. In the case of the African American, it is also about selling images, determining which will be sanctioned and promoted before the American public. Historically, the African American has been defined as a devalued other, as a victim, without complex subjectivity or an interior, and the literary apparatus has sought these images in the texts that come before it. The published and sanctioned images of the African American are to serve the white norm. And as Richard Jean So points out in *Redlining Culture*, throughout the postwar era, from the 1950s to 2000, the period when Wright wrote his fiction, "how race gets represented in the [mainstream] novels . . . remains unchanged or continues to benefit the racial status quo—whiteness."[57]

It has been the task of most African American writers to refute or rewrite this simple, devalued representation of the African American, highlighting the tension between Black writings and the publishing industry. Therefore, in 1951 and again in 1956, when Wright attended the Handy Writers' Colony and later engaged with publishers, editors, and reviewers in New York, he was confronted with this concept of literature, its image of the African American, and how it affected his literary work and his representation of the African American.

The colony bought into many of the values and definitions of the institution of literature in the ideological state apparatus. Founded informally in 1943, chartered in 1951, it was built on the outskirts of Marshall in eastern Illinois, about twenty miles west of Terre Haute, Indiana. Lowney Handy was a Kentucky native and the wife of an oil executive, whose life changed in 1943 when she met a deeply troubled soldier, James Jones, who wanted to be a writer. She soon took Jones into the family home—encouraged him, mothered him, loved him, and badgered him while he learned to write fiction.[58] He became the model for the colony's writers, the model for how Handy approached her apprentices, including Wright.

The colony reflected her unorthodox philosophy and forceful personality. Handy believed she could teach anyone to write. She was a transcendentalist, drawing wisdom from Hindu sources and the theosophical texts of Madame Blavatsky and Annie Besant and, like most mainstream modernists, rejecting middle-class materialistic values.[59] A few of her apprentices were deadbeats, but many were indeed talented. She was not afraid to give renegades, castaways, African Americans, and Japanese Americans a chance.[60] "All of my people are lonely to desperation," she stated in a *Sepia* article about the colony.

Before they began on their own work, students spent a considerable amount of time copying texts word for word. Most were by mainstream American male writers such as Hemingway, Faulkner, and Fitzgerald. The purpose was to encourage students to absorb the material thoroughly so that it could emerge in new thoughts. She said, "When these fellows come here, they are full of ego or torn up with complexes. They are burdened with all kinds of problems. The copying makes them forget themselves, develops concentration and forgetfulness. I have them copy until they have learned to concentrate and sit at their typewriters every day."[61] But the copying process was really an indoctrination into certain ways of thinking about and writing mainstream western literature. Only when students had progressed to her satisfaction were they permitted to work on their own manuscripts.

Instead of encouraging her students to read widely, Handy had them read from a list of approved literary texts. Instead of having students critique each other's work, she alone read and commented on the work in progress. Her students, completely subsidized, lived in Spartan accommodations, and she controlled their lives, yelling and cussing and, at times, behaving irrationally. The students copied or wrote in the mornings and worked at various odd jobs and played sports on the grounds during the afternoons. Students built rock walkways throughout the camp. "Too much mental work is not good," Handy said:

> It must be balanced with physical work. . . . Good writing comes from feeling you are on a desert island. . . . I always tell every incoming student that this is the loneliest profession in the world. The job I try to do is to encourage people to go on. Books are written out of nothing. We begin here without ideas, but there is hope, and where you have hope, and enough belief in the person themselves, to start, you've got half the battle won.[62]

Handy preferred to work with male students who had seen some of the worst of what life had to offer, but she also taught several women, most of whom had also experienced difficulties. She wanted her male students to avoid marital entanglements; she felt they could satisfy their urges with sex workers.[63]

Her husband, the oil executive Harry Handy, and Jones, her first student, financed the colony. In 1951 Jones published *From Here to Eternity*, a sensational bestseller that earned him more than $500,000 and was made into a movie. An article in *Life* promoted and mythologized the colony, Jones, and Handy's methods.[64] Harry gave his wife $400 a month to support her school, which was in session from April to September. Jones put about $65,000 of his royalty into the nonprofit, which expanded and grew in reputation from 1951 to 1957.[65] Then, in 1957, Jones, who had been Handy's secret lover, married Gloria Mosolino and broke with his mentor, who opposed his marriage. The colony managed to survive for several more years, and Handy did develop several talented writers. About seventy students came for long or short stays, and ten of them published novels and short stories, including Wright.

He was an ideal student for Handy: poor, insecure, with little formal education and a strong desire to write. He emphatically believed that the Handy Writers' Colony was the best thing to ever happen to him, regardless of its philosophy of writing. Somebody was giving him a chance to learn to do what he wanted to do: write. It was the "biggest break [he] ever got."[66]

After his first short stay at the colony in 1951, Wright served in the army for two years, spending 1952–53 at Fort Leonard Wood in the Missouri Ozarks and 1953–54 in Korea. He viewed his years in the service positively:

"Drafted, indifferent to the military. I thought that I'd emerge as Heming-way's Black stepson. It never entered our minds to burn draft cards. Either you went or copped a good deferment."[67] In an interview with John O'Brien, he said, "The army was a fantastic experience, and I don't regret it at all."[68] He recalled the trip overseas:

> Fear curdled our Korea-bound ship. Insane inspections, standing on the deck in the wind and rain. Vomit peppering stair wells, heads—we were very religious and attended the Catholic and Protestant services with the same marvelous indifference and would have attended morning Voodoo services. We were tired of standing in the cold and rain. We wanted to sleep during the services.[69]

To deal with their fear the soldiers tried "to stay high most of the time. We didn't know a goddam thing about Korea and took pot with us. . . . And always the fear, the nightly cries. Fear was alien to me. But when we waded ashore at Pusan something grabbed me and would not let go. This was not basic training."[70] The army and Korea were totally new experiences for Wright, more encounters, becomings, reinventions that would eventually appear in his fiction.

On his first night in Pusan, Wright went AWOL, going into town to learn more about the people and the country. This curiosity became a characteristic of Wright the writer. Eventually he relaxed, realizing that there was no fighting, only an uneasy truce. "We began to believe that we would not die in a strange, small country called Korea." As a member of the combat construction engineers, he helped build "roads, schools, latrines, Quonset huts, and Quonset hut service clubs that buckled under the spring thaw. We were the carbine-toting heirs of a situation that we did not completely understand."[71]

In the army, Charles Wright remained a loner. He looked much younger than his age—"Black and little and skinny"—and he saw himself as the "strange one, the one that was different."[72] These feelings of marginality and sensitivity were not new, but now he recognized that, to survive in the army, he had to become a politician. To protect himself, he presented a tough exterior. He "prided himself on being fast and getting everybody's position before they knew his. And as a defense . . . he could push their buttons or he knew exactly where they came from and he could put them in their place."[73] Wright learned how to read people and situations, a skill he used for the rest of his life. "He learned to deal effectively with people, developed a heightened degree of shrewdness and toughness, became a cook, and was about to travel to [other parts of] Korea just prior to its pacification in July 1953, and near the end of his foreign tour of duty, he was given a leave in Japan."[74] He thought being the chief of the supply depot was the best role he could have found in the army, and his experience in Korea became the source of his first novel.

In December 1954, Charles was released from the army, and he returned to Sedalia and his grandmother, declaring, "it is good to be back, and I am quite happy." After Christmas, however, he decided to go away and "get a job, as there are no jobs around here." While in Korea, he had continued to correspond with Handy, telling her that he was "trying to write this little thing" and that he would send it when he had "finished part of it."[75] In early January 1955, he moved to St. Louis. He stayed there for two years, his living expenses paid in part by a "twenty-six week Armed Forced stipend (and a thirteen-week extension), which provided a modest salary to former soldiers seeking civilian employment." The "remainder of his income" came "from his work as a stock boy." Racism prevented him from "finding work well-suited to his talents."[76]

During these years, Charles returned to the Handy Writers' Colony for a second time. This time, another African American writer was also in residence: William H. Duhart, who was from Chicago but had come to the colony from a prison in Wisconsin. Wright also met Charles S. Robb for the first time. Robb was from Summit, New Jersey, and had hitchhiked to Illinois in 1955, hoping to gain admission to the colony. He had spent the first half of the year as a student at the University of Pennsylvania but had left because he wanted to become a writer. At the colony, Robb was too shy to make many friends, but Wright was an exception. The two began a turbulent, up-and-down friendship—like all of Wright's friendships—that lasted for most of their lives.

At the colony, Wright's looks and intelligence stood out. Handy wrote, "[Everybody] talked about how handsome and how good looking and intelligent and keen, smart appearing you were. We talked of you often and although this isn't the kind of romantic love you've been seeking—we love you here." What she adroitly detected was his need for "someone to love" him, and she came to fulfill that need.[77]

Wright returned to St. Louis determined to become a serious writer of fiction.[78] But, as was typical, he couldn't quite pull himself together.

He left his army trench coat at the colony and wrote to ask Jones to send it to him.[79] He asked Handy for $50 for food. She told him, "Stop kidding yourself. You don't want $50 you want to come here and write a great book, a terrifically (perfect) beautiful novel . . . and you want me to make you come and make you write it, to beg you. I know how neurotic . . . you are. . . . I work with this phase in these boys here all the time."[80] She decided not to send him the money, quoting him Shakespeare instead: "I must be cruel in order to be kind." Later, she changed her mind and sent him $10, asking him to come back:

> I . . . sent it because I like you and believe in you and figured you were in the process of discovering yourself. I know you will make a great writer when you learn or mature or grow up enough and I wanted to be in on the ground floor. To know that I helped has been all I wanted, and the bill is in full payment when you write. In fact, that is the only way you can every pay me back . . . you or anyone else. I gamble on literature. I didn't gamble on Charlie Wright. But as a means of making literature, I admire and like you as I would a beautifully manufactured piano.[81]

In St. Louis, Wright first read James Baldwin's *Go Tell It on the Mountain*, published in 1953 and sent to him by Jones. He liked the novel but thought Baldwin had remained distant from his subject. Seeking confirmation, he wrote to Handy:

> Yesterday I read . . . Baldwin and I like him, though with reservations. I, there is no doubt of his sincerity and his intellect but maybe I, and now I'm speaking merely as a [N]egro, I got the feeling that there was some thing quite cold about this young man and that he was in his tower or his small room far removed from the people he wrote about and while he saw it all, saw it well and wrote it well, he was aloof from the people he wrote about.[82]

This became the distinction that Wright would make between his fiction and Baldwin's. Although the two wrote about the same urban African American social milieu, Wright refused to be "aloof from the people he wrote about."

In her response, Handy asked if it were a "lack of sentimentality" in Baldwin's novel that "you've called coldness?"[83] Great writers, she thought and taught, eschew sentimentality and embrace coldness. "To be a great writer, you will contrive problems, upsets, paradoxes, and twists that will be a constant surprise to the reader." She believed that paradoxes were essential and that "the best way to handle a paradox is to start in before you write to build or concoct situations that are not routine. . . . Because once started, then next doesn't follow in sequence, this is the trap too many writers fall into, they have typed their characters and they continue to keep them within the type." Handy said that "a good writer never tells anything. He shows."[84] She objected to safety and confinement: great fiction must have "big deep problems" and "real suffering and agony," and its characters should be outside the law.[85] In other words, she was emphasizing the hallmark of modern American literature—alienation and fragmentation.

In early 1955, Wright met the blues singer Ruby Brown, who eventually became the model for the character Ruby in his autobiographical novel *The Messenger*. Again, we see how a real-life experience served as a catalyst for his fiction. He wrote to Handy:

I have been thinking about Ruby Brown, a comely [N]egro with a beautiful half white half [N]egro boy, she loves and hates him at the same time. She would be her worse enemy regardless of whether she was white or [N]egro. Slowly she is going down drinking herself crazy thinking about her old lover and making a living hell for herself and everyone around her. At present she's singing at a place in East St. Louis at a very low type of place, the type of place where even [N]egro maids and porters go "slumming." . . . The place is called the "Hole." And you walk down the dirty rick[e]ty wooden steps and the smells of body odors and stale beer and cigarette smoke and the foul smells of the toilet that never flushed, momentarily took your breath away. There were a couple of naked light bulbs in the ceiling and the table and chairs were unpainted and a potbellied stove stood in the corner with the coal dumped out on the floor. In the center of the room is a raised platform where a piano player and an alto saxophone and bass and drummer are always playing the blues. Then you hear some one humming in a rich huskey [sic] voice and you turn and see a high yellow woman walking toward the stage. Her face is taut like a mask but the skin is soft and there is a sort of guarded look about her suggested from her wide pouting mouth and that cold impersonal look her eyes that could look a hole through you and yet they were warm curious eyes which perhaps gave her the auria [sic] of mystery. She walks toward the stage dragging her feet, her hips, moving, rolling gracefully like waves and there was the promise of excitement underneath her tight black dress. But man you'd better just dream and admire Ruby at a distance because there was nothing you could do for her and she did not give one good God damn about you. She sings [the] blues in the authentic style that only a [N]egro can sing them. She was disgusted and world weary and felt like her heart and soul were about to drop to the floor. And although, she was up there singing only for herself and the people listening were along only far [sic] the ride, she touched us, rather reached us, because true blues regardless of the words were always about troubles, troubles all the time. Misery. Rotten misery. And we all know about those things from the moment we came from our mothers' womb and took our first breath and sucked in the evil smelling air of a world into which we were born but might never be a part of. I turned my back on her and ordered a double whiskey straight and downed it in one swallow. The whiskey burned my insides and brought me back to earth. Ruby was my sister and I fought like hell to keep back the tears.

Clearly, Wright identified and empathized with this blues life that Ruby embodied. He ended his letter to Handy with "I hope you get the idea and [that] I've made myself sort of clear. Now I want to hear from you and whatever you say I am man enough to take it."[86] This insight into the blues life and the wisdom/truth it possessed—joy and pain and suffering—colored Wright's construction of African American urban, subaltern life. He knew about these "things." It, along with his experience of Korea and his grandmother and sex with the wife of the couple in Kansas, found its way into *The Messenger.*

Wright wrote to Handy, "What ever you say [about this description of Ruby Brown] I am man enough to take it." Still insecure about his writing skills, he craved her "help and above all [her] criticism": he felt he had "so very much to learn and if he ever expects to become a good writer, [he] must be able to take all the slaps on the back."[87] In her response, Handy told him that she thought Wright's portrait of Ruby was magnificent: "I wish I knew her." But she pushed him to go further: "How wise she must be. . . . it made me think you were drawing a picture of me as I wish I were. . . . how weary I am singing this song here in this camp. . . . how stinking life is . . . and yet if you are good you rise above the bad smells and you laugh at life. . . . you are missing something by not REALLY GETTING TO KNOW YOUR SISTER BETTER if this is the truth." Handy felt that Wright's portrait of Ruby was judgmental and sentimental, that he should see Ruby's life as a triumph over a bad situation and should be learning from her. In her view, Wright was revealing himself as an immature moralist who believed in good and evil. She wanted the *I* of the narrative to grow and mature as a result of his encounter with Ruby's story:

To get back to Ruby . . . to write a real true story . . . [N]egro blood has nothing to do with this . . . you must learn to write coldly and leave all that out . . . and then the greatness will be there . . . but write this boy suffering . . . and his suffering . . . and his suffering partly an act is a kind of solace to him. Write the book, so that the boy hears his sister but nobody with him knows . . . and this sister . . . she's truly the suf-ferer because she hasn't the ability to feel as the boy does. She's inar-ticulate with her misery . . . only in song.[88]

Notably, Handy's focus was on the speaking/narrating *I*—his condition and how he was responding to Ruby. This was one of the crucial lessons that she taught Wright, one that fitted well into his existential fiction. His *I* observed, was aware, experienced epiphanies, and grew.

As his fiction would eventually reveal, Wright absorbed Handy's absurdist, existential lessons; he could "laugh life in the face" and move beyond "good and evil." But her conventional, western approach to writing fiction also created problems for him. Handy did not think his work should deal socially, politically, and morally with race: "Negro blood" should have "nothing to do with this." In her view, high literature aesthetically tran-scended race, gender, and class; Wright should "leave all that out" or risk becoming judgmental and sentimental. Yet he did not know how to sepa-rate his writing from race. "A long time ago, I used to think about the color problem all the time. The more I thought, the more confused I got. Then I tried to put it out of my mind, though it never really left me because it was part of me."[89] Race had everything to do with his life, and his fiction would wrestle with this conflict.

Handy urged Wright to write non-sentimentally "about the . . . [Black] side of the coin."[90] So he began, under her tutelage, his first novel, which was about Korea and war. Handy pressed him to imitate the white male moderns who had written war fiction. She wanted him to "keep the power strong, by writing it factual and cold."[91] As models, she offered him scenes from Jones's *From Here to Eternity* and his short story "Christ in Concrete," which dealt straightforwardly with brutality and violence. She referred Wright to Stendhal's *Waterloo* and Leo Tolstoy's *War and Peace* as examples of great works that dealt with war in a cold, non-sentimental way. Wright responded to these models and learned from them.

Handy wanted Wright to write about the people he knew best, the Black people of the street—but not about their culture and history, or racial oppression, or victimization, what she called "over-writ[ing]." Rather, she wanted him to write about them as individuals outside of their racial milieu and class and morality. She lectured him about not becoming a Negro writer or a moral writer but a mature writer, someone who could get "outside the social mores":

> But if you get outside and object to society mores and rules of convention and racial and environmental teaching . . . you soon learn that GOD IS IN EVERYTHING. . . . If you'd talk to Ruby (if real) in your letter she'd tell you much the same. . . . They hate themselves for breaking the laws (social mores) and then they start hating bad smells . . . and hating all kinds of things. . . . society is a bunch of lies and delusions."[92]

Although Handy was a tough critic, she remained supportive:

> Your writing is magnificent. Emotional. TRUTHFUL . . . full of color . . . POWER. . . . It has originality, fire, anger, love of people, perception . . . and intuitional knowledge . . . Depth . . . all of the things that makes the finiest [sic] writing. But you are held back by lack of technique. . . . I believe in you. . . . Have always believed in you since the first day you wrote to me . . . since you came into my camp. Never, not once since then have I stopped believing in your eventual development . . . *your one day greatness*. . . . I just know. It all depends upon your discovering yourself.[93]

Here, she was identifying an inner conflict that would plague Wright throughout his writing career. It was the contradictory conflict between whether Charles Wright wanted to be a great writer (or not). Did he want to put in the necessary hard work to learn the craft and technique that would allow him to be a great writer? He was "driven by equally compelling forces in opposite directions."[94] I am not sure Wright was consciously aware of the clash between the two equally compelling forces. Certainly, he was not conscious of the underlying tendencies behind these forces. Would he be able to resolve the conflict? Or would they become two gestures happening simultaneously without resolution, thereby challenging logocentric thought? Being insecure about himself and his writings and needing the love of others, Wright had difficulties resolving this conflict. Thus, we can understand why Handy and her philosophy of writing had a lasting impact on Wright's becoming a fiction writer. After he moved to New York, he kept in touch with her and would periodically revisit her at the colony.

CHAPTER TWO

The Struggle to Become a Writer
in New York City

In the fall of 1956, at the age of twenty-five, Charles Wright moved to
New York City, after living for several years in St. Louis. Most of his
clothes were still at the colony, and he wrote several letters to James
Jones, asking him to send them. He told Jones that "[a] lot ha[d] been
happening to [him in New York]. But [he was] fine. [He was] learning
and [was] holding on." Always he asked Jones to say "hello" to Handy.[1]
In many ways, the colony was his beginning, his anchor in becoming a
writer. Therefore, he continued to write to Handy for advice and reinforcement. "I like hearing from you," he later wrote to her, "because there
is always something new to learn from your letters. I save all of them and
would like your permission to quote from them and perhaps use you in
a book. . . . Charles Robb and I were talking the other day about you,
saying that one of these days, the world will realize the great things you
have done."[2]

New York was where Wright would make his mark as a writer, but his
early months there were difficult. He struggled to find a job, cope financially, and adjust to life in the city. After being jailed for fighting, he wrote
to Handy, asking for money. She refused: "You are there in New York to
learn a lesson, one you refused to learn here. You insist on being an iso-
lationist, you don't want people to be nice to you. . . . You want to be your
own boss. You think a great deal of Charles Wright and you are angry
because all the world doesn't stop their own living and spend their times
in adoration in the babe." Handy thought Wright's problem was the
lack of love for self, which was true because he had always wanted but
never received love from his father. Because of this lack, he had begun
to drink and act out, a clear sign of repressed trauma. Handy wrote:

Self-love, self-pity . . . which is why you drink . . . sorrow, hatred, fears
are all the result of not being loved enough. . . . You've got to get over
a little of it . . . but unless you can stop thinking a little about yourself,
you're not going to turn out as much of a writer. And unless you can
stop suffering, being hurt . . . because the world don't stand and wait
at your door . . . getting drunk and getting in jail . . . to me is no more
than overeating. . . . For God's sake . . . grow up. . . . I'm sick of your
adolescent whining. Your suffering touches me not at all.[3]

As Handy pointed out, Wright's drinking was a symptom of other problems—his troubled childhood, his inadequate education, his working-
class background, and the burden of his homosexuality—but it became a
part of his personality, his friendships, and his day. In time it became who
he was. Trauma in a person over time can look like personality.

Wright settled into a place at 366 West 29th Street and got a job as a
messenger at Rockefeller Plaza, which helped him get "to know New York
City from Park Avenue to Harlem to Brownville in Brooklyn."[4] It also
reinforced what he already knew about being a Black man in America.
One day, as he was making a delivery in Manhattan and admiring the
neighborhood's Victorian houses, a policeman stopped him. The cop
thought Wright had no business in this area and took him to the station.
Wright recalled to Clarence Major, "His experience at the station was
quite unpleasant and whereas it did not make too much of an impression
on him at the time, as the years went on the experience contributed to his
bitterness or awareness of the white world."[5]

Wright remained concerned about his grandmother back in Sedalia,
who was getting old and sickly and was "about to move out of the damn
house that was about to fall in on her. . . . [He had] been sending her
money."[6] But in 1950s New York, he gradually found his element, living
the life of a true bohemian and a working-class intellectual. He read vora-
ciously, listened to jazz and the blues, and hung out in the Village with
beat writers and artists. There was always a good chance that "two writers [would run] into one another at a bookstore."[7] As Jack Kerouac once
noted, *beatniks* were "characters of special spirituality who didn't gang
up but were solitary Bartlebies staring out the dead wall window of civi-
lization."[8] Hanks Bar in the Village became one of Wright's steady hang-
outs. Yet he remained a loner, a Bartleby. After meeting "a young lady,"

he thought about changing his "lifestyle and get[ting] one of those nice little houses and buy[ing] a proper suit and tie," but did not.[9] He could not enter into that kind of existence. Throughout his life he returned again and again to his grandfather's lament: "This world is not my home." "If the latter is true," he later said, "then what a trip. What a hell of a vacation."[10] Because there was no God or grand narrative to give his life meaning, he existentially took responsibility for his own existence and lived as if he were on a perpetual vacation.

In New York, Wright continued his up-and-down friendship with the writer Charles Robb, whom he had met at the colony and who had moved to the city at about the same time. Briefly they lived together on 49th Street in the East Village. But the two did not always get along, often because the opinionated Wright felt a need to assert his superior position as a writer. In later years, when he was depressed about the reception and sale of *The Wig*, he blamed Robb: "I've been extremely disappointed in the people I know. It would be a terrible life if I had to spend it here talking to only one person: Charles Trabue Robb."[11]

Wright continued work on the war novel he had begun under Handy's tutelage, now titled *The Highest Tension*, even as he immersed himself in the bohemian, sexually fluid world of the Bowery, the area of lower Manhattan where he would come to spend most of his time. Between the 1940s and the 1970s the Bowery was the city's skid row, but it was also a multiracial and multicultural community, home to Blacks and Puerto Ricans and Chinese and whites. Accepting the other, Wright became intimate with the Chinese community. After the 1970s it began to gentrify, which Wright wrote about in *Absolutely Nothing to Get Alarmed About*. Middle- and upper-middle-class suburban white youths moved in, and poor people and racial minorities were forced out. At this time he also established a life-long friendship with the dancer Larl Becham. Becham had begun his career at the Katherine Dunham School of Dance in New York and later toured the United States and Europe as a featured dancer in the Dunham company.[12] He became director of the Eartha Kitt Dance Foundation, which in 1958 offered free dance lessons to the people of Harlem. After leaving the Dunham troupe, Larl mostly worked independently. He was a dancer-choreographer in the Paris production of *Deux Anges Sont Venus* and appeared in the Metropolitan Opera's production of *Quanga* and the Broadway productions of *Emperor Jones* and *The Josephine Baker Show*. In later years Becham toured Europe, India, Ceylon, Egypt, Canada, and the United States with the Larl Becham Dancers and became the director-choreographer in residence at La MaMa in Manhattan.[13] Now, in these early years, Becham introduced Wright to the ins and outs of the sexually fluid world in New York City, revealing the "unnecessary boundaries between man and woman, Black and white, gay and straight, [and] the vernacular and the expert."[14] It was at one of these dance classes at La MaMa that Wright, accompanying Becham in the 1970s, met Phelonise Willie. The two became life-long friends. Willie told the story that upon meeting Wright and realizing that he was a writer, she was "intrigued and confessed [to him] I wanted to write." He asked her to write "30 pages by such and such a date."[15] Wright also became a friend of the Cuban American avant-garde, lesbian-focused playwright and director Marie Irene Fornes, who was a leading figure of the Off-Off Broadway movement in the 1960s. But I am getting ahead of myself, as I am trying to construct a version of Wright's life and make sense out of Charles Wright the beginning writer in New York City.

In the summer of 1957, Wright, now age twenty-six, returned for another stint at the Handy Writers' Colony, his novel *The Highest Tension* in hand. The other writers in residence that summer included William H. Duhart, Charles Robb, Neal McMahon, and Eugene Nelson. They lived in barracks-style dormitories—six-by-nine-foot rooms containing beds, desks, and typewriters. All students received full scholarships, with cigarettes and spending money provided.[16] They wrote or copied every day from 5 a.m. to noon and spent the afternoons doing yard work, swimming, and reading. Students took turns preparing meals, which they ate in The Ramada, a rustic pavilion with a kitchen, dining room, and lounge. There were no newspapers or radios available, and students were forbidden to discuss ideas or literature. Each day, they went to bed at 8 p.m.[17]

Wright's novel *The Highest Tension* was written very much in the shadow of James Jones, and G. P. Putnam's Sons had already shown interest in publishing it. Though Wright had revised it twice before arriving at the colony, it was now "ripped to shreds by the camp's tyrannical mentor."[18] Handy made Wright retract the manuscript from Putnam's, telling him it needed more work. "She said I was hamming up some of the clinch

FIGURE 1. Charles Wright reading *From Here to Eternity* by James Jones, one of his influencers. *Sepia* (December 1957). Courtesy of the University of Houston.

scenes. Told me I was acting like a kid who was out to shock somebody, and it was a shame that I didn't write enough dirty words on outhouses."[19] He accepted her "advice," emphasizing that he did not "want to ever disappoint" her or himself.[20] Yet he also rebelled against some of her methods. Wright knew that Handy was very good at teaching "dialogue," "narrative," and "the technical side of writing," but he thought the editor at Putnam's would have worked with him and eventually taken the novel if he could have "gotten James Jones away from Scribner."[21] The editor was not successful in his endeavors. Therefore, he did not publish Wright's novel. However, aspects of Wright's experience in the Korean War appeared in *The Messenger*.

Even as Handy pressed Wright and other Blacks to write about Black life, she "attempted to purge Negro students of racial bitterness."[22] She claimed that the colony was free of racial and religious bigotry: "A man is a man," she told a *Sepia* reporter, "and that's all there is to it."[23] Yet when it came to evaluating major Black male writers such as Richard Wright, Langston Hughes, Chester Himes, Frank Yerby, and William Gardner Smith, she was not always a shrewd, informed, and intelligent critic: "I've

FIGURE 2. Charles Wright and William Duhart piling rocks at the Handy Writers' Colony, a task intended to be physical exercise. *Sepia* (December 1957). Courtesy of the University of Houston.

read some of them. Hughes, of course, and Richard Wright. I think Richard Wright suffers from the actual, concrete things that harm a writer most: politics, women, drink, money and ambition. He has been ruined by an obsession with social harm and injustice, like Norman Mailer, and has become a pamphleteer."[24] Such comments entirely overlooked the artistry of Richard Wright's fiction. Of Frank Yerby, who wrote about Black people but not about the problematics of race, she said, "[He] may remain a popular writer but will never produce a classic." In her view, Yerby's fiction fell into a "class of writing which she calls 'wishful thinking.'"[25]

Handy felt that African American writers should learn to write about whites just as "men should learn to write about women."[26] In short, she wanted them to create writing that was removed from the racial, and the political, that did not deal with "social harm and injustice," that was "universal" in the western white male sense. She objected to certain content, subject matters, and aesthetic discourses because they differed from her definition of modern literature. In her critiques, Handy held Charles Wright to the precepts of New Criticism, which emphasized the utter autonomy of each literary work, totally rejecting political, social, and racial contexts in any discussion or writing of a text. New Criticism, reinforced by Althusser's notion of the ideological state apparatus, had reached its apex in the late 1940s, as the United States launched the Cold War and entered McCarthyism. Although its influence had begun to decline by the end of 1950s, it still held sway among English departments, publishing houses, and review journals. Even into the 1960s, the critic Aijaz Ahmad was noting that the "great majority of teachers and critics . . . continued to function . . . as if nothing much has changed since T. S. Eliot and the 'New Criticism.'"[27]

Yet there was something terribly limiting and exclusionary about New Criticism and Handy's definition of modern literature, something essentially male and Eurocentric. When Handy talked about universals, she was talking about the forms, values, and aesthetics of contemporary, upper-middle-class, western, white men, who reproduced and reinforced a hegemonic, western definition of literature. By defining all African American literature as social or racial protest, she assumed that canonical writers such as Faulkner and Hemingway and the problematics of their characters existed outside of historical, social, and gender situations. She believed that the high literature of white male canonical writers had, in the words of Jeffrey R. Di Leo, "no connection with critical citizenship or democratic values let alone current critical commonplaces such as race, class, gender, and sexuality in their full intersectional complexity."[28] Of course, Hemingway, Faulkner, and their compatriots very much belonged to and wrote out of historical, gender, racial, sexual, and social situations, even as they brought "richness to individual lives."[29] Yet because Handy did not acknowledge this, she was not able to deal with the fact that African American writers such as Charles Wright also belonged to such situations.

At the end of the summer of 1957, Wright returned to New York City, this time to an apartment at 199 Second Avenue. He brought with him a revised version of *The Highest Tension*. But that November, his grandmother became ill, so he hitchhiked back to Missouri to care for her. On his return to Sedalia, Charles was able to stop drinking and focus on Dora. He avoided his high school classmates and spent a great deal of time reading, frequently visiting the public library.[30] But Dora did not recover; she died on January 26, 1958, at the age of seventy-seven, "after a long terrible period of suffering."[31] Charles hitchhiked back to New York City in the winter snow and became sick with something he thought might have been tuberculosis. He did not go to the doctor, however, for he feared that diagnosis would be confirmed.

Wright was devastated by the death of his grandmother, who had replaced his deceased mother in his life. She was the only family he had ever had, and the only person he felt had ever loved him. Later, describing his connection to his grandmother in *The Messenger*, he wrote, "We were not only connected by blood; we were friends. Whatever had happened to us, whatever thoughts crossed our minds . . . could not destroy the love we bore for each other."[32] With her death, he was reexperiencing the traumatic, relational pattern of separation from someone he loved. As Bessel van der Kolk has written, "trauma is not just an event that took place sometime in the past; it is also the imprint left by that experience on the mind, brain, and body."[33] In a letter to James Jones, Wright said, "I am now just realizing she is dead and discovering that, I am alone, a man without a family, so to speak. I've been trying to tell myself, Hell, I can make it, nothing can get me down, which maybe it [won't]."[34]

During this difficult period, Handy—a friend and teacher who gave him good and valuable advice on his writing—did not offer the support and sympathy he craved: she didn't "send a card—her word, [at] a time when I needed a few words of wisdom to carry me through the bad time."[35] Instead, she told Wright, "Your grandmother brought it [her hard life] on herself. . . . We make our own niche, carve our own graves, build the cross we carry up Cavalry . . . and you are too indoctrinated with her defeatism to ever get very far in this world."[36] Obviously, she did not understand the limited options available to a poor, uneducated, unskilled Black woman during the first half of the twentieth century. Wright, disappointed by her response, declared that he would break with her completely and not "return to the Colony" in the upcoming year.[37]

For the next several years, he floundered, often jobless and broke. He told Jones, he "couldn't buy a box of matches to light [his] Camel cigarette with" and asked for a loan of $200 to help him regain his footing.[38] In the fall of 1959 and into the early 1960s, Wright was living with Robb, and they occasionally reminisced about Handy and the colony. Robb wrote to her, "The other day Charles and I were out hoofing around and went down to the docks and sat a long time talking about Norman Mailer and William Styron's new book." They mused over how "much better things might've turned out for those guys if they'd had somebody like you":

> Truly Lowney I had no idea how precious you are. Recently I worked in a club to which belonged the crème de la crème of New York society. . . . Yet not one could hold a candle to you. . . . When I think of all that you gave me and how it was squandered. You were brainy, fun, terrifically well read, a storehouse of anecdotes, a terrific cook, a spark plug, a battler. They don't seem to make the girls like you anymore.[39]

For a while after his grandmother's death, Wright "didn't even think about writing."[40] Eventually, however, he began working on a new novel, though even after a publisher expressed interested, he was apprehensive about his abilities: "Sometimes I wonder if it is worth it, or that maybe I am not strong enough or something is wrong with me."[41] In time he was able to regain focus, to rediscover his drive to "become a good, if not a great writer." At the same time he recognized "that desire to hurry up and get in print" because "there is that Bitch-Money that has always got me by the heels."[42] Money would always be a demon for Wright, but he also struggled with concerns about the kind of writer he wanted to be. The more he thought about the "color problem," the more confused he became.[43] He was aware that race was part of him, but it was not all of him. He would have to work out this conflict.

Eventually, Wright found a steady job; now he "just went along, worked every day and lived." He was paying $4 a week for a one-room apartment on West 49th Street, and in a letter to Handy (with whom he had reconciled) he said, "Am working and writing. Working on *Tension* and [a] novel about grandmother and also on one like *Gatsby* and *Sun Also*

Rises."[44] He told her that he had submitted *The Highest Tension* to Crown Publishing. But while the editor read it twice and thought that there was something valuable in it, he did not accept it for publication.[45]

In addition to revising *The Highest Tension*, Wright worked on the new novel about his grandmother, about "facing that last horrible winter with her."[46] He also began a third novel, initially titled *Traveling Light*, which later became *Blackbird*. It centered around a Black-white love affair in the Village, a topic sparked by what he was observing in New York City. He wrote to Handy:

Hundreds of Negro-white romances in Village and it can't be all love. Mostly Jews and Negro but a lot of the others too. Interesting too. How many Negro-Jew[ish] show business marriages? Lena Horne and Lennie Haydon, Harry Bel[a]fonte and his Jew[ish] wife. Dianne Carroll and her Jew[ish] husband]. Dorothy Dandridge and her Jew[ish] nightclub owner. Richard Wright was the first of course years ago with his Jew[ish] wife. So what do you think of all this jazz?[47]

In *Blackbird*, Wright defined this interracial relationship sexually. The protagonist Joey is a Black sex worker who is having an affair with an upper-middle-class white woman, and Wright recognized elements of himself in his character. He told Handy, "So much of Joey . . . is me. But, at last, I can face Charles Wright and I can smile at him."[48] Wright knew that the novel's subject matter would make publication difficult in the country's current racial climate. He also knew that some Black and white readers would not like it. "I will have to fight time and life and the NAACP and all those terrible little people, the moralist, those righteous thinking [people]."[49] He told Handy, "I get so sick of all that shit in the papers about the race thing. . . . The white man is afraid of the [N]egro because in a hundred years or maybe sooner, everyone (almost everyone) will be the color of me. And the colored people are becoming nothing but piss poor imitations of the white man."[50] Eventually Gold Medal Books expressed interest in buying the paperback rights to *Blackbird*, but the book was never released.

In the summer of 1960, Wright took a job as a houseboy on Long Island and used that setting as the background for a hundred-page fragment of a novel. He added another fifty pages to the novel about his grandmother, but it, too, trailed off. Later that summer, he restlessly hitchhiked to St. Louis, decided to stay, found a job, and saved some money, intending to write over the winter. He initially moved in with his friend Ken; but when he told Ken, "I'm not looking for sex or love," his disappointed friend threw him out. Although Wright was as "hard up as hell then," being in the cold and with no money, he could not "help but laugh. It was a good shock and another lesson on the ways of people." This was another experience in which Wright, though desperate, laughed in the face of life. He thought the experience might be "good material for a queer novel I'll have to write and there hasn't been an honest queer novel written yet. And I feel no one could do it better than I."[51] He began to talk again about his novel *Blackbird*, which now had become *No Regrets*, and he continued reworking *The Highest Tension*. But none of these beginnings were ever finished or published. In the end they were gaps and silences in the oeuvre of Charles Wright.

Still by 1961, he was seriously writing again, working not only on these older pieces but also on *Diamonds from These Bones*, another attempt to write about a Black male sex worker: "the book is me."[52] Wright wanted Handy to help him revise *Diamonds from These Bones*, but she did not like his use of the first-person narrator and declined to spend time on it. Therefore, he asked James Jones to read the "opening section and give [him] some advice, become [his] editor on this."[53] He also sent it to Crown Publishing, which declined it. The book was too hot.[54] It was clear Wright needed help, and he did not have anyone else to turn to.

Wright's writing career seemed to have stalled; he was at an impasse. Handy had distanced herself from him, and Wright was insecure not only about his writing ability but also about how to get published. It is unclear if he was just ignorant of the politics of literary publishing or if he was simply refusing to play the game. In New York City this was the heyday of the Black literary avant-garde: Amiri Baraka and the Black Arts Movement; the Umbra writers David Henderson, Cecil Brown, Steve Cannon, Ishmael Reed, and Abba Elethea.[55] There were writers' workshops in Harlem. There was the beat movement. But Wright did not take part in any of these literary gatherings. Naturally distant and reclusive, he had also been tutored in the white male tradition of radical individuality, alienation, and fragmentation. He did not know how to enter into these other communal worlds.

Sensing Wright's problem, Charles Robb believed Wright needed a mentor, someone to give him advice and guidance. Therefore, he wrote to Norman Mailer, asking if he would read his friend's nearly completed novel, *Diamonds from These Bones*, the story of a "Manhattan Negro buck" who has "an affair with an upper middle class white girl by hustling himself." Robb described Wright as

> [a] young Negro buck without a high school diploma who has never looked I'm sure at Strunk E. B. White and probably never will. His use of homosexual Negro argot may throw off the uninitiated. He has been a pet (though so far unpublished) of the Lowney Handy–Jim Jones writing Colony. His race has surely been a deterrent in what should be at the least a noteworthy career.

Wright had been shopping the manuscript, Robb told Mailer, but publishers had told him that it was "not the sort of work our house would want to handle." The people at those presses, Robb emphasized, reproduced form, subjects, and images that sell. They were not sure they could buy and sell what Wright was offering. These publishers who were rejecting Wright's manuscript, Robb further told Mailer, "are not of his social background [and] could not judge him for selling out if he does." He believed that what "Wright needs is a group of established writers whose work he respects to stand behind him at this time. He is not capable of being Christ on the mountain, although the publishers are quite definitely the Devil from their silk suits to their cashmere jock straps." Robb asked, "Would you send Wright some word of encouragement? I am sure he would let you read the MS if you are interested."[56]

Mailer was interested and asked Robb to send him the first section of Wright's manuscript, though he warned "it will take me about a month to get around to reading it."[57] The novel, now titled *No Regrets*, was a first-person account of an affair between a Black beatnik from the East Village and an upper-middle-class white girl whom he has impregnated.[58] Mailer praised the opening section and promised to send Wright "a letter telling you in more detail what I like specifically and don't like." He then asked if the two had met "a few years ago when I was living on East 55th street."[59] In a return letter, Wright thanked Mailer for "liking the first part and for reading it. It took me a day for it to sink in and I needed that."[60] Wright was completely in awe of Mailer, a reaction obviously born out of "a neurotic need for affection, provoked by anxiety and aimed at feeling safe with others."[61] Wright's childhood needs from his father were reproduced in a new light.

Mailer did ask for the rest of the novel, but in October 1961 he told Wright that he had not "had a chance to read the second part yet nor will I be able to for at least another month because I'm far behind on a lot of things. Can you wait that long? or would you rather have the manuscript back? Let me hear."[62] Wright told Mailer, "Take [your] time. I trust your judgment."[63] Mailer responded immediately with "I'll get to it as soon as I can. If you haven't heard from me in a month, drop me a card in reminder."[64] On December 19 Wright reminded Mailer that he had not "heard from him."[65] By January 1962, Mailer still had not read and responded, but he did tell Wright, "I wasn't trying to put you on when I said I liked the first part because I did and I think I would even look forward to reading the next installment."[66] He again promised to read the novel "within the next month."[67]

Despite these delays, Wright remained warmly patient with Mailer, even as he continued to receive rejections from publishers. Then in March, Mailer wrote to say that he had finally read the "second installment." He liked it, but he warned Wright that he did not think he was "going to have an easy time getting this [book] published," given the subject matter. He advised him to

> cut it everywhere you can, cut out all the repetition and the rants which are thematically repetitive, all the bitterness which is shapeless, . . . the places where the story stops. . . . if you get it typed well, then I think you [will] have a good fighting chance because . . . you[r] writing . . . is true and it's damn readable, and I think at the least you'd get a soft cover publisher to go along with you. . . . There's a lot that's wrong with your writing and most of what's wrong with it is your cockiness and your self-righteousness, so if you . . . start thinking of yourself as a better writer than you really are, you're just going to write a lot of shit and waste everybody's time. Stay modern and write clean.[68]

Though brutal language, Mailer was echoing some of the criticisms offered by Handy, who also told Wright repeatedly to focus on craft and technique. Later, he warned Wright to keep a carbon copy in his possession because he did not "want ever to have to look a man in the eye and say I lost his one and only [manuscript]."[69]

Wright was considering submitting the manuscript to Corinth Books, and asked Mailer for advice. Mailer responded, "Hold out, keep writing it and don't worry about a publisher until the book is done."[70] He also told him not to try to self-publish: "If you write it well enough and, as I said last time, neatly enough, you'll get a publisher somewhere or other." He also admonished him, "Don't write stoned. Writers are not supposed to feel like fighters in the second minute of the tenth round."[71] Wright saw the wisdom of Mailer's advice: "don't push and be a goodie-goodie boy. Just be yourself."[72]

Mailer asked to see the full revised manuscript, promising to forward it to an agent. Then, in October 1962, Wright sent Mailer a copy, holding onto another himself. But somehow both men lost the only two copies in existence. Later Wright told "this story with [a] good-natured shrug,"[73] Again, Wright laughed in the face of life's adversities. The lost manuscript did not get him down.

In 1961–62, Wright was living at 117 West 49th Street and working as a messenger, making $40.59 a week. He continued to read voraciously, primarily books by modernist novelists such as Mailer, Hemingway, Fitzgerald, Marguerite Duras, James Joyce, Jean Rhys, Laurence Durrell, Samuel Beckett, Jean-Paul Sartre, Albert Camus, Katherine Anne Porter, Djuna Barnes, and especially Nathanael West, one of his favorites, whose literary values and definitions of literature he internalized. He devoured the *New York Times* and *Esquire*. He listened to the blues and jazz, and the influence of this Black music, along with some of these modern writers, began shifting his writing away from the style promulgated by the Handy Writers' Colony.

He was also meeting other writers. While working as a messenger, he ran into Kay Boyle in "the office part of The Museum of Modern Art." Later, in a letter, he recalled, "I asked if you were Kay Boyle and you said yes and you must be a writer." Boyle was charmed that someone so young had recognized her. "You must be a writer," she said, "how else could you know this face?"[74]

In the meantime, Wright continued to try to attract the attention of publishers. He would write twenty-five to thirty pages and then send them out, hoping for a royalty advance that would allow him to finish the novel. At one point Wright had sent a sample from *No Regrets* to Roger Straus of Farrar, Straus, and Giroux, "arguably the most influential publishing house of the modern era." It was "home to an unrivaled twenty-five Nobel Prize winners and generation defining authors like T. S. Eliot, Flannery O'Connor, Susan Sontag, Tom Wolfe, Joan Didion, Philip Roth, and Jonathan Franzen."[75] However, like other large New York publishing houses of the era, it "remained largely white in both demographics and content," and it published mainstream fiction that reproduced racial stereotypes.[76] Roger Straus was known to have "set the intellectual tone [in publishing] of postwar America." The scion of two powerful families, the Strauses and the Guggenheims, he was not an intellectual; he had never finished high school. His abilities were "more attuned to commercial than literary publishing." Although he had "boundless optimism, a tolerance for risk, and just enough of a personal financial cushion to keep from falling over the brink," he was also cautious.[77] Straus did not want to publish No Regrets, but he did want to meet the young man who had written it.[78] When he returned the manuscript on February 5, 1962, he said, "Why don't you write about what you do? You must have seen a lot."[79] That was on a Thursday. By the following Monday, Wright had delivered thirty new pages to Straus. By the end of the week, he had a contract for The Messenger, which would be published in the summer of 1963.

In taking Straus's advice to assemble his autobiographical novel, Wright drew together and transformed into art aspects of his personal life, including his Missouri childhood, the death of his mother, his relationship with his grandmother, his time in the army, his distant relationship with his father, and his life as a writer and messenger in New York.[80] Through art and with these experiences, Wright created new objects and new forms of perception, offering experiences fundamentally dissimilar from the everyday ordering of sense. He wrote to Mailer, telling him about the acceptance and promising to "dedicate [The Messenger] to you," though he said, "Your famous name doesn't have anything to do with it. I always do things for people I admire who are honest and have guts."[81]

In the late fall of 1962, Wright submitted the full manuscript of The Messenger to Farrar, Straus and left for his first trip to Veracruz, Mexico. His intent was to relax, to wait for the galleys, and to write. He returned to New York in January with a new novel, Toward Morning, which he shared with his editor, Harold Vursell. After reading a section, Vursell told him he had "made a good start. You have established three characters quite clearly, and I know a great deal about their milieu, about who and what they are."[82] But the editor also had concerns. Suspecting that Wright had been doing drugs in Mexico, he warned, "You will mar your talent seriously—if not completely destroy it—if you continue to rev up your body and your brain with all kinds of stimulants. In the end, it is self-defeating. . . . What you have to work for is conscious control of your writing talent."[83] Yet already drugs and alcohol had become a mainstay, helping Wright "spontaneously dissociate" from his traumatic past and "obliterate [his] growing sense of helplessness."[84]

While *The Messenger* was in production in early 1963, Straus and Vursell, as was customary, reached out to prominent writers—in this case, Norman Mailer, Philip Roth, James Jones, Mary McCarthy, Lucy Freeman, William Styron, Joseph Heller, Henry Miller, Kay Boyle, W. H. Auden, James West, Lillian Smith, Herbert Gold, Frederic Wertham, and James Baldwin—sending them galleys and asking them to comment on the novel.[85] Because the novel's homosexual subject matter and construction of subaltern Black life did not fit neatly into either mainstream modern literature or Black protest literature, the two were hoping for positive endorsements. In those years, Farrar, Straus was "a place uncommonly tolerant of gay men [and themes] in various stages of openness, from Vursell to Giroux to Michael di Capua."[86] But the press was still not sure how to publish and market Wright's novel. Straus and Vursell were afraid that, if famous writers did not endorse the book, "reviewers will be afraid of its contents, coming as it does from a man with [no] name." As Vursell argued, mainstream reviewers, who also belonged to the ideological state apparatus, were a "gutless lot" who would shy away from writing a serious review unless "they ha[d] a recommendation by a writer of importance behind which to hide."[87]

The reactions to Wright's galleys were telling. Mailer, supposedly one of Wright's earliest mentors, wrote that he would "take a look at *The Messenger* as soon as I can. Speak to you then."[88] Straus wrote back to Mailer, saying, "You are a pal in re *The Messenger*, and I look forward to hearing from you."[89] Mailer finally responded with "It's a good book but it doesn't go far enough," declining to write a blurb. Vursell called this "chicken shit."[90] Gold was too busy planning for an upcoming book and a "trip to Europe, and other obligations" to read Wright's.[91] Roth was occupied with his own writing; "all I can say is that I'll try" to look at the galleys, but he never did.[92] Miller was out of the country; therefore, his wife returned the galleys to the publisher. Auden, McCarthy, Styron, Jones, and others did not respond at all. Smith wrote a screed. Although she thought *The Messenger* "was the work of a talented man; a man who has sort of blotted up the contemporary jargon," she did not think it had literary merit or wisdom. "He tell[s] us about one little sex perversity after another—what a mess Henry Miller started 34 years ago!" In a tone reminiscent of Lowney Handy's, Smith concluded, "Just because he is a Negro, he should not be given special consideration as a writer. This is not a false sentimentality[;] that is not good for Negro or white. He must be considered as a human being. . . . It is heartbreaking to see 'race' ruin these young men." Smith blamed Baldwin for being a bad critic and thus "a sad sight to me."[93] In his response to her letter, Vursell agreed that "young writers" did not have "wisdom" and that they should "have a different feeling about sex." Though he did advocate "special treatment" for Black writers, given their history in the United States, he found himself apologizing to Smith because she was not able to "speak for the book."[94]

Clearly, Smith, like Handy, understood nothing about African American literature. She could not discern Wright's accomplishments in *The Messenger* or appreciate Baldwin as a critic. She was parroting the hegemonic values and definitions of mainstream American readers that had erased Black life and kept Henry Miller's fiction out of the country for thirty years. Smith's puritanical, Eurocentric lens, with its hierarchies of aesthetic greatness, had narrowed her notions of literature. She was unable to view *The Messenger* from the standpoint of its own cultural logic or reason, or even from an intelligent American perspective; and this is notable, given that the novel, in style and genre, was heavily influenced by American and European modernism.

Both the editors at Farrar, Straus and the writers who were asked to read Wright's galleys operated from a naturalized white discourse: a visible but unmarked cultural identity in which they saw themselves as the primary subject. This made it very difficult for them to view *The Messenger* on its own merits, or even within the modernist tradition, because its subject matter did not reproduce that discourse. Instead, in responding to the novel, they reacted to a racial identity that had been "marked as deviant" and behaved as if that marker could be ignored or erased.[95]

Historically, Farrar, Straus had published few books by African Americans. By the early 1960s its list included Owen Dobson's poetry collection *Powerful Long Ladder* (1946), William Gardner Smith's novel *Last of the Conquerors* (1948), and Sammy Davis, Jr.'s, memoir *Yes I Can* (1965) which Farrar, Straus had difficulties putting together.[96] Over the course of the decade it would publish Henry Van Dyke's novels *Ladies of the Rachmaninoff Eyes* (1965) and *Blood of Strawberries* (1968) as well as Carlene Hatcher Polite's novel *The Flagellants* (1967). But when *The Messenger* was released in 1963, the press had not yet learned how to publish and promote a Black-themed book that did not conform to Black stereotypes, that gave agency to Black outcasts, and that had a homosexual theme and a bisexual main character. Wright's characters were not the predictable Black victims of brutal white men; they were not yearning for respectable middle-class security or housekeepers exhausted by working for white families. Instead, they were individuals in possession of their own complex lives.

Vursell wrote to Wright about the responses from some of the writers he had contacted : "None of them [are] showing much understanding of what you have written.... Almost nobody can come to a book clean. They all read it with fixed preconceptions of what it is going to be. Let's hope— but don't count on it—that somebody will read what you have written and not what he *thinks* you have written."[97] No mainstream American writers in the early modern era, including the ones contacted by Farrar, Straus, could imagine complex Black subaltern life beyond the dominant society's victimized representation and negative stereotypes, especially a Black book that was different, that instead challenged and reconfigured the representation of subaltern African Americans. They could not imagine an African American writer creating a working-class, intellectual African American subject who was concerned with existential being, his own ontology, rather than with race exclusively or the white gaze.

Still, not only did Lowney Handy offer to help promote *The Messenger*, but James Baldwin, Kay Boyle, and Lucy Freeman came through with strong endorsements. In a letter to Vursell, Baldwin wrote:

> It's a very beautiful job. . . . It sometimes seems to be scarcely a book at all, but a *happening*: it seemed to me that I could hear the music, smell the smells, knew all those streets and all those people. . . . He's caught the New York laconicism behind which so much anguish growls, and almost the exact shade of that awful half-light in which so many people are struggling to live. And he doesn't judge them; he accepts them; perhaps it's for this reason that the distance between ourselves and the people in this book seems so minimal. And, no matter what the city fathers may say, this *is* New York; this is the way we live here now. Charles Wright is a terrific writer, and I hope he goes the distance and lives to be 110.[98]

In her response, Boyle told the editor:

For some time now, a new and ruthlessly honest literature has been emerging from the lonely horror of the junkie and homosexual world of New York. Charles Wright's *The Messenger* is the most recent and in many ways the most moving of these statements from our contemporary lower depths. . . . Wright's book . . . is important as fresh, unencumbered writing and important as social comment as well. It is not just one more book about perversion, and about the Negro's place in the society of outcasts. It is a courageous and heartbreaking document in which even the most transient figure takes on and retains a terrifying life.[99]

Both Baldwin and Boyle said they had read the novel in one sitting, and Freeman was equally impressed. She called the book "a poignant portrait of a young man without a country or even a city":

[This] is a sad, tragic tale he tells, full of sound and fury but signifying much. [Wright] mirrors what countless other young men and women, white as well as Negro, feel today as they try to fill the emptiness of their lives with a constant search for pleasure in pads, seeking insensibility through liquor, and drugs, and sex. There is one difference, however, between Mr. Wright and most of the others—*he* is a fine writer. He is able to deftly draw with only a few words a scene, a character, an act.[100]

Freeman saw *The Messenger* as a profoundly American novel.

With these three responses in hand, Farrar, Straus now had sufficient "firepower" to market *The Messenger*.[101] Its publicity department sent copies of the Baldwin's letter along with galleys to literary agencies, journals, clubs, and elsewhere and was able to attract attention. For example, Edith Kiilerich of A/S Bookman Literary Agency in Copenhagen said that when her client from the Danish press Hasselbalch, which was about to publish a translation of Baldwin's *Another Country*, read his comments about *The Messenger*, he became "particularly interested in this book."[102]

In April, as *The Messenger* entered the final stage of production, Wright returned to the Handy Writers' Colony, seemingly at Vursell's urging. New York had wound him up very tightly. He arrived tense and sick, hoping that the place would give him peace of mind and allow him to escape the pressures of New York. His goal was to live simply, do some outdoor labor, and write. He settled into one of the trailers on the grounds, and Vursell forwarded him a copy of Baldwin's letter, which he called "wonderfully perceptive and generous. This letter will help us a lot."[103]

Jon Shirota arrived at the colony after Wright. He was the only other student in residence and was advised by Handy not to get too friendly with Wright: "She was afraid I would go on a binge with him, raise hell, and not do any writing." But in the days that followed, the two did get together during mealtimes in The Ramada, and Handy eventually relaxed her rules on drinking, even supplying bottles of vermouth. Shirota recalled that Wright was drunk most of the time. But about two weeks after Shirota's arrival, he and Handy saw Wright at the Marshall bus station with his bags. She commented, "I knew he wouldn't be sticking around any longer. His book is coming out and he's got ants in his pants."[104]

But even in New York the colony stayed with him. As Wright was walking in Rockefeller Plaza, he saw a "young man and woman looking in a window":

> She was holding his arm, smiling quietly, while he talked. She was dressed well, good clothes, but . . . this young man appeared tacky. He was well built, like a boxer. Tan . . . , blond and wore a well-tailored grey pin stripe suit and dark glasses. There was something almost distinguished about him. Yet the couple did not make a complete picture. [They looked] like a photograph, half developed, or locked in an old trunk for years, yellow, old, lost in the brisk . . . sunshine of April. [The couple was] James Jones and his wife.

Wright and Jones had "a small conversation"; but as Wright later told Handy, "Jim seemed ill-at ease. He asked about my writing and when I had heard from you. . . . He was not his old self and like I said seemed ill at ease. So, I very quickly end[ed] the talk by saying how good it was to see him and started on my way."[105] Like Wright, Jones had left the colony and begun a new life in the city.

The Messenger was published in the summer. It was not reviewed by elite outlets such as the *New York Times* or the all-powerful *New York Review of Books*, and the *New York Herald Tribune* trashed it. Wright was livid, and Vursell had to prevent him from writing an angry letter in response. He told Wright, "When you go into the marketplace [you] lay yourself open to understanding, misunderstanding, and all kinds of expressions of stupidity. I know your rage (I felt it myself when I read the *Herald Tribune* review) but we have asked for it: you are writing the book, we in publishing it. . . . This book will come out all right. Relax a little."[106] Wright backed off.

Farrar, Straus had sent press releases and copies of *The Messenger* to *Ebony* and other subsidiaries of Johnson Publishing, the *Amsterdam News*, the Associated Negro Press, the Global News Syndicate, and "major Negro newspapers around the country."[107] Generally, however, African American critics and reviewers ignored it. Most were not willing to accept Wright's focus on bisexuality/homosexuality and his reconstruction of subaltern Black America. Baldwin was the only out queer Black critic who championed the book, and even he, in his comments, did not focus on the text's homosexuality. An editor at *Negro Digest* did speak somewhat positively of *The Messenger*, hailing Wright as "yet another bright star rising into the literary firmament." He called the novel "simple" and "readable," though he regretted that the protagonist's "friends are an unlovely lot, mostly socially estranged people on the edges of solvency and respectability." Nonetheless, he admired "some quite tender and moving scenes, all the more profound because they are drawn with such natural subtlety."[108] L. M. Meriwether, writing for the *Los Angeles Sentinel*, argued that "the charm of this book" lay in the way in which Wright "has captured the nothingness which afflicts a growing segment of our population. He has recorded their headlong flight into the twilight world of perversion and moral turpitude with a ruthless candor."[109] Like most mainstream critics and reviewers, these readers had lapsed into a sociological rather than artistic examination of the text. As Wright acknowledged to Handy, the "Negro press did not really get my message and were very cool."[110]

Still, there were hopeful signs. A writer for the *Atlantic* responded to the novel's power:

> Sparse and quiet in style, less a novel than a series of vignettes, the book carries the reader immediately and easily into the bustle, the sights, sounds, and smells of the streets of New York. . . . As a novel, it is very slight, but manages nevertheless to carve out a pretty large slice of New York life; and it is all done with an economy of means that would be admirable in an older writer. . . . Mr. Wright is that rare thing, a natural writer, and it is to be hoped that this novel is a portent of many fine things to come.[111]

In the *Library Journal*, Milton Byam wrote, "[*The Messenger*] presents its portrait with scalpel incisiveness and spare wit. The point of each incident is made with pin-prick sharpness."[112] Citing the failure of a "sizeable number of novels written in the past ten or fifteen years about the relationships between urban Negroes and white," Whitney Balliett, writing for the *New Yorker*, said,

> *The Messenger* . . . stands firmly on a middle ground untouched by its predecessors. . . . Wright mixed his anger and experience and insight and allowed them to cool and harden into the dispassionate omniscience essential to novelists. That done, he began to write, and in a plain, clear style that reflects this emotional and intellectual sureness.[113]

Writing in the *Reporter*, Nat Hentoff argued,

> Unlike Kerouac and his boyish emulators, Wright views the microcosms of the disaffiliated with a total lack of sentimentality. . . . Charles Wright may not yet have "found" himself, but he has an advantage over the more self-adulatory Beats in that he knows who he is not. As a writer, he has developed a deceptively simple style that is clearly the result of honest distillation of experience and hard-won craftsmanship.[114]

Yet even though several mainstream critics briefly mentioned *The Messenger* within the context of existentialism, none went so far as to develop an existential reading of the text.[115]

The editors at Farrar, Straus were surprised and relieved by the relatively positive critical reception. In a letter to Wright, Vursell admitted that the review coverage "had been better than [he] would have dreamed possible for a first novel, given the subject matter of yours."[116] Rupert Croft-Cooke, whom Wright would later befriend in Tangier, thought *The Messenger* "was a fine [book]" and should "meet with great success."[117] After reading the novel "while on a boat cruise to Greece and Israel," Langston Hughes wrote several letters to Wright, telling him that he had "found it a most interesting and effectively written little book indeed. I hope you will write many more such beautifully done volumes."[118]

With such favorable responses in hand, Farrar, Straus staff member Paula Diamond shopped the rights of *The Messenger* to European presses. Several publishers in Europe and South America expressed an interest, and ultimately paperback editions came out in the United Kingdom, France, and Brazil. The response in those markets was outstanding. Ernest Hecht of Souvenir Press in London sent Diamond a sample of reviews from the *Illustrated London News*, the *Oxford Mail*, *Books and*

Bookmen, the *Daily Worker,* the *Halifax Daily Courier,* the *Northampton Evening Telegraph, Men Only, Time and Tide,* the Sunday *Times,* and the Sunday *Telegraph.* All spoke to *The Messenger's* style, Wright's "quiet control of the writing," his "fascinating narrative." "The bundle of sensations here depicted," wrote the *Times* reviewer, "are immediate and undeniable." Writing in the *Illustrated London News,* E. D. O'Brien said, "If anyone had told me that I should be moved by the beauty of a book dealing with the life of a young coloured man in New York, drifting between junkies and homosexuals, I should have regarded him as insane. Yet there is just that remarkable quality of Charles Wright's *The Messenger*."[119]

In June, the U.S. Information Agency requested permission from Farrar, Straus to include *The Messenger* in "In the Author's Words," a government-sponsored program featuring a "voice reading [a] selected excerpt through which we endeavor to impart the flavor and style of the book."[120] In May 1964, Fawcett Publications brought *The Messenger* out in paperback, paying Farrar, Straus $3,500 for the rights and beating out Monarch Books, which had offered $3,100. The writer Terry Southern wrote a blurb for the Fawcett edition, calling it "an exceptionally fine novel of insight and originality, yet without a shade of exaggeration of the shameful truth behind it."[121] With a print run of 15,000 in 1964, *The Messenger* sold quite well in paperback; and though it did not make Wright wealthy, the book remained in print until the end of the 1970s.[122] In 1965, Souvenir Press submitted copies of *The Messenger* to the World Festival of Negro Arts in Dakar, Senegal, for prize consideration.[123] In 1970, Peter Hinzmann, an editor for an Italian publisher, expressed interest in acquiring subsidiary rights: "Another book has come to my attention that we will want very much to license, since this book has come to gain well-deserved recognition ten years after its original publication. The book is entitled *The Messenger*."[124] As late as 1974, Akira Takasawa, a Japanese literary agent, was writing to Farrar, Straus about the novel: "I found it intensely touch my own heart. At the same time, I feel it is a book to learn from, and consequently I am impulsively moved to make it and his literature known to modern Japanese readers. I also believe that it will be sure to arouse their literary interests."[125] That same year, Manor Books brought out another paperback edition, paying $2,000 for the reprint rights.

Despite this international attention, Wright received very few royalties from foreign sales. His advances averaged between $250 to $500, certainly not enough money to live off. But he did receive, starting on July 1, 1963, $300 per month for twelve months, for a total of $3,600, "over and above the advance against royalties" he had already received.[126] But Wright was not someone who was financially savvy, someone who saved and invested his money. He spent it quickly and lavishly, and one of the first things he did was go to Paris, inviting Vursell to join him in August.[127]

CHAPTER THREE

An Existential Reading of
The Messenger

In *The Messenger*, Charles Wright took events and traumatic experiences from his own life and transformed them into art. He tore personal objects from their assigned places and created new subjects and heterogeneous objects into the field of perception. He used the writing process to act out and work through his history of trauma, taking a writerly approach to trauma recovery, using the persona Charles Stevenson to work through his personal trauma. In addition, he reconfigured the existential genre to reconcile his conflicting feelings about writing, race, class, and sexuality. The real Charles Wright was a bisexual, working-class intellectual, and his novels were "in a certain sense" based on himself.[1] I argue in this chapter that Wright used his art "to create possibilities for interiority in the face . . . [of] social constraint and limitation" by turning "to mental and philosophical roaming as a mode of freedom."[2]

The main character of *The Messenger* is named Charles Stevenson, and in an insightful interview with John O'Brien, Wright described the things that happened to Stevenson as "quite typical. He goes through life, sensitive and aware, but really quite ordinary. The things that happen around him do not have a cancer. . . . He may be going through a bad time but eventually he will be all right."[3] Stevenson stays afloat when he can keep himself separate from events. "At times [life] does get next to him, and it takes a terrible toll, both mentally and physically. But he doesn't let it get him down. It's a survival technique."[4]

The concepts of Sartrean existentialism are central to the novel, though few critics mentioned it in their reviews. An existentialist believes that the human condition is absurd and that a person's only hope is to take responsibility for existence and to not allow social pressures to interfere.[5] Wright was steeped in the traditions, values, and existential definitions of modern western literature, and he created Stevenson as an existential hero who is thrust into a world without identifiable meaning. He comes to live in this world but is fully aware that he is not of it. Although initially he desires meaning and wholeness as protections from the absurdity of the world, his journey teaches him to not only accept pain and suffering and confusion in the world but also to take responsibility for himself.

When we first encounter Stevenson, he is living in the chaotic, absurd, godless world of New York City. We learn that he is a light-skinned African American, that he was born in a small Missouri town, that he had been traumatized at the age of four by his mother's death and his father's absence, that he was raised by religious grandparents. As a teenager, he begins wandering around the country; he reads modern western literature and discovers that he is comfortable in artsy white circles. After a stint in the army during the Korean War, he migrates to New York to become a writer. To support himself, he works as a messenger at the Rockefeller Center, a job that takes him all over the city and brings him into contact with all manner of people, giving the reader a sense of the sights, sounds, and smell of his environs.

> [He moves] with great speed between different locales and types, between New York's contrasting zones and regions and between people of different as the Rockefellers . . . and dead winos and abused children. He finds himself reporting on a whole gallery of ethnic and street life, especially the worlds of drag queens, pick-ups, partygoers and bar-flies—a spoiling, multi-sexual constellation of New Yorkers who pass across, and in and out, his times like actors on a revolving reel.[6]

But Stevenson is lost and confused in this strange world, and his inability to feel connected makes him anxious. He is twenty-nine years old, an outsider, drifting through a place that seems devoid of meaning—he "who [has] always been alone" and has "developed what others" define as "arrogance for [his] protection."[7] He has not figured out who is Charles Stevenson. Despair exists when life has no purpose, and Stevenson despairs when he realizes that the world, in all of its clutter and busyness, does not care about him. The sheer thereness of things wounds him deeply:

> The objects, chairs, tables, sofas are not specifically American. They, this room, have no recognizable country. I have always like to believe that I am not too far removed from the heart of America. . . .

Yet I'm drowning in this green cornfield. . . . The country has split open my head with a golden eagle's beak. Regardless of how I try, the parts won't come together.[8]

Stevenson is confused and alienated because he recognizes but does not accept the existence of the absurd world. The enlightenment logic of language and metaphysics clashes with the absurdity of his life in New York. Objects in a room seem to negate his own reality, causing him to become nauseous. Stevenson cannot use reason or human-built structures and myths to clarify the world. As Albert Camus wrote, "This world in itself is not reasonable . . . . But what is absurd is the confrontation of this irrational and the wild longing for clarity whose call echoes in the human heart. The absurd depends as much on man as on the world."[9]

Stevenson lives in an about-to-be-condemned fifth-story walkup apartment, where he is visited by a parade of memorable characters—sex workers, homosexuals, drag queens, con men, who are as lost and lonely as he is. He records their voices as fellow travelers, not as a critic. Stevenson is compassionate to Mrs. Lee, an aging, ageless coquette, who dances with an army of Puerto Rican gigolos. When she visits, he tells her what she has "come to hear." He tries to show interest in the abstract drawings that seven-year-old Maxine brings him, this child who loves him because she knows he is "for real." He plays father to Lena, a prostitute and a thief; and when she gets busted, he attends her trial.

At the colony, Wright had learned not to sentimentalize or judge the outcasts who would appear in his writing. With compassion and empathy, he dealt with them on their own, giving them full lives, complex subjectivity, and an interiority that stretched beyond good and evil, reterritorializing the normative society's stereotyped image of outcast subaltern African Americans. Yet in *The Messenger*, his character Charles Stevenson in being sensitive and aware recognizes that most people define themselves by social mores and that he and the other outcasts are marginal to those conventions. Rejecting the "square world," they have turned to different paradigms.

In his search for meaning, Stevenson has many sexual experiences, but they leave him unsatisfied. He keeps reading, searching for answers, but to no avail. For a while New York City was a powerful draw. It had a sense of adventure: "There was something [about the city] that held me powerless. The pace, the variety, the anonymity, the sense of walking on glittering glass eggs, walking in a city like a big-time prostitute with her legs cocked open. A challenge, wondrous city, fit for a wide-eyed country boy." But after five years he wonders what he is "doing in this city."[10] He still has not found meaning; he still cannot connect the fragments of his "rummaging memory." Therefore, in the hope of giving "anxiety an identifiable object—the lost object—and generat[ing] the hope that anxiety may be eliminated or overcome," he pushes himself "back through the bowels of his memory," looking for "a lost origin."[11] He recounts the death of his mother and the absence of his father. He recalls the "fun of living" with his grandfather and grandmother: "Cookies and cakes, licking the big cooking spoons. Fishing with Grandpa. Walking through the courthouse square with him, listening to his old cronies and their tales of the muddy Missouri River." This travel through memory helps him recognize that his younger self had not addressed the existential question, the "Great Why of Everything." Yet even then he had "beg[u]n to be aware of something . . . , something perhaps [he] had been born with, and which was never to leave [him]. Loneliness." In New York "this consciousness is here and with him now."[12]

A dream about his grandmother haunts him for days, and his grandmother's letters have not been cheerful. Therefore, Stevenson, suffering through the "hot days and nights" of a New York August, decides to hitchhike back to Missouri. He recalls his grandfather's lament, "This world is not my home," and realizes that he has "nothing to look forward to but [his] own death, which [he does] not fear. But this, this doomed air of the present; what will happen to me before I die? What could possibly happen after all that *has* happened?"[13]

When Stevenson arrives in Missouri, he is disappointed. He understands that in coming home he "was on the run, and fatigued, played out. And now [he] want[s] to turn around and flee the town." He knows that he "had loved it in another time when this town had been [his] world." But he has outgrown the place; it is no longer his world. He realizes that he "ha[s] lost whatever [he] had had in those days, a shy lonely boy, veteran of a small war at twenty-one, who had made the bohemian pilgrimage, without finding a roosting place."[14] The past fails to provide Stevenson with meaning, truth, or recovery, a roosting place.

After his grandmother dies, Stevenson, with "nothing to keep [him] in Missouri," returns to New York and finds himself in a "cluttered, yellowing room on West Forty-Ninth Street, in the heart of Manhattan. Here, there, again, and always, the Why of my life, the meanings. Terrible depression as I sit here watching darkness settle in the corners of this room." He is "aware of the loss of something" and feels the "suffocation of this small room." He is still plagued with the existential question of "Where did it all begin"?[15] As Camus has written, "that nostalgia for unity, that appetite for the absolute illustrates the essential impulse of the human drama. But the fact of that nostalgia's existence does not imply that it is to be immediately satisfied."[16]

Stevenson does not want to become one of the living dead. To be alive is to be aware and on the search; to be dead is to be sunk into the routine of everydayness. Death was his father, lost-looking and apart. He recalls Alfonzo, a New Jersey man who had given him a ride: "I thought of the expression on the man's face. It was like something terrible had happened to him once long ago that had destroyed his sense of being a man, but it didn't matter much anymore. Whatever it was, resignation has settled in the creases of the pale, puffy face and under the tear-filled, forlorn eyes."[17]

Walking through New York City one early Sunday morning, Stevenson notices that the streets are saddled with a numb, self-centered despair. He witnesses the "lonely people everywhere. . . . The shameful, envious, eyes-lowered glances at passing couples. You recognize other solitary fellow travelers. Both of you go separate ways, moving with the knowledge of Sunday papers, endless cigarettes . . . and the feeling of having missed out on Saturday night's jackpot prize" or the answer to the ultimate question of existence. Of course, bearing witness allows Stevenson to personally work over and through his own trauma. He watches Alice and Maxine, who take life as it is; despite their troubles, they "get such a bang out of just living." He observes the messengers he works with, who "are still very alive despite their various ailments."[18] He recalls people in his Missouri hometown who would accept their problems as they accepted the weather.

Wright portrayed Stevenson as an ordinary, working-class, Black intellectual in exile, but he was aware that few mainstream readers in United States would see such a person as ordinary. *The Messenger* makes this contradiction clear. In one scene, as Stevenson walks through the concourse of the RCA building, sneezing and completely absorbed in a book by Laurence Durrell, he suddenly looks up and encounters the long, startled face of Steven Rockefeller. "Doesn't he think poor people read?" Stevenson wonders.[19] But as Edward W. Said has written, "exile for the intellectual . . .

is restlessness, movement, constantly being unsettled, and unsettling others. You cannot go back to some earlier and perhaps more stable condition of being at home; and, alas, you can never fully arrive, be at one with your new home or situation."[20] Stevenson's exile, as Camus explains, "is without remedy since he is deprived of the memory of a lost home or the hope of a promised land. This divorce between the man and his life . . . is properly the feeling of absurdity."[21]

The exilic Stevenson has lost his country without acquiring another; he lives in double exteriority. He has existed inside both American and African American cultures but is not conventionally Black, Native, or white. He is the result of generations of bastard Anglo-Saxon, African, Black Creek, and Choctaw blood. Likewise, his bisexuality allows him to bend and challenge sexual categories without identifying as gay or straight: "I'm rather free sexually." He does not have "to lift weights, wear heels with clicks, to assert [his] maleness."[22] He does not have to dominate others.

He defies many categories. He is a working-class intellectual who does not embrace possessions or a work ethic but lives among outcasts. He listens to the blues and jazz and reads the novels of Hemingway and Durrell. When he needs money, he occasionally scores as a hustler. It seems that Stevenson wants equality without feeling compelled to accept identity; he wants difference without degenerating into superiority versus inferiority. In the words of Barbara Hernstein Smith, he "is a member of many shifting communities, each of which establishes, for each of its members, multiple social identities, multiple principles of identification with other people."[23] He is a dynamic, multifaceted subject who is made and remade through the ethical interaction with what or who is not him.

Yet Said emphasizes the "pleasures of exile, those different arrangements of living and eccentric angles of vision that he can sometimes afford, which enliven the intellectual's vocation, without perhaps alleviating every last anxiety or feeling of bitter solitude."[24] Although he lives in poverty and works a menial job, Stevenson "feels strengthened by the distance that detaches him from the others as it does from himself and gives him the lofty sense not so much of holding the truth but of making it and himself relative while others fall victim to the ruts of monovalency. For they are perhaps owners of things," but he "tends to think he is the only one to have biography, that is, life made up of ordeals—neither catastrophes nor adventures . . . , but simply a life in which acts constitute events because they imply choice, surprises, breaks, adaptations, or cunning, but neither routine nor rest." In his eyes, those who are not exilers/sufferers/ fellow travelers "have no life at all: barely do they exist, haughtily or mediocre, but out of the running and thus almost already cadaverized."[25]

Stevenson's exile puts him outside the social and political conventions that regulate the behavior of "civilized" humans. He has long been beyond the litigating absolution of the church. When his mother died, his grandmother told him the Christian story of death: that it was "a long, long sleep and you did not wake until you got to heaven." But already the child "did not believe that that was true." Later, when he was preparing to go to Korea, his grandmother prayed and then told him to pray. He "turned [his] head and stared out at the dark night. There was nothing out there. Darkness." Again, she reminded him to pray, but when he "bowed [his] head again and opened [his] mouth . . . the words would not come. [He] looked up at the porch ceiling. It seemed as if the ceiling was between [him] and God." Stevenson believes that his grandmother, along with her religion, is an agent of false solace. She thinks that "if you *believe*, it will be all right." But he knows that "the sin is believing, hoping," and he is "too tired, too afraid . . . to commit this sin."[26]

The working-class and exilic Stevenson also stands outside the middle-class narrative of work. He sees May Day and other "loyalty and Communist Front celebrations" as "just another day for this worker." When the "other messengers, especially the elderly men . . . who take their messenger jobs seriously, talk labor," he is "silent." During a stock-market crash, he sees that everyone else is in a panic and "tensely excited." Brokers are "picking their noses." An elevator operator loses $400. A nervous vice president overplays his role in managing the workplace. But all Stevenson wants to do is "deliver the stuff and go home. The sudden change of fortune has no effect on [him]." He would not give a "Goddam dollar" to help bring "this historic day to a close."[27]

Stevenson's working-class, sexual, and nonreligious awareness and exile also put him beyond/outside other sanctioned social rituals and conventions, as he lives in the world without a home. He is outside the "sophisticated scum of New York." He feels strangled by those millions of "feet making it toward Mr. Greenbacks and what it takes to be a 'smaht' New Yorker." Yet he also feels marginal among young, middle-class, African American intellectuals. At "liberal white parties and chick Black parties," they "[turn] out in Ivy League garb, usually with a pipe and mustache. Perfect gentlemen: sophisticated Uncle Toms. I certainly don't go for most Negro girls who have gone to a good college. They are usually phony intellectuals."[28] In both cases, he remains outside the narrative of American middle-class respectability.

Stevenson considers how he differs from the people around him. As he looks out at the Tiepolo-like sky above the towering buildings, he muses about the office workers: "They have found their niche in this world, and they are going to make damned sure that you know it and that you will not attempt anything foolish that threatens to destroy their world." In his view, they are "bourgeois right down to their underwear," "mummified Americans waiting for their cars to take them back to suburbia." Though he sees Black people also partaking of this middle-class dream, he understands that he does "not belong down there."[29]

In another instance, Stevenson looks out over a group of young people, healthy, laughing, contented as hens: "Their faces [are] indistinguishable as blades of grass. Look how happy they are! They are united and one." Like them, he is "as American as apple pie." But although he fantasizes about becoming one of them, he concludes that he "cannot, simply cannot, don a mask and suck the c——of that sweet, secure bitch, middle-class American life."[30] The existential Stevenson recognizes that the absurdity of these constructs and their ceremonies would diminish him as a person, as an agent of free will. They will not allow him to accept the mysteries in the world, to ask "the Great Why of everything."[31] He stubbornly resists any metanarrative based on a wish to infuse a random universe with meaning.

Near the end of *The Messenger*, Stevenson takes stock of himself. At twenty-nine years of age, he sees "a fairly young man with a tired boyish face, saddled with the knowledge of years and nothing gained, lacking a bird dog's sense of direction most of the time, without point or goal."

"I am the future," I once wrote in a passionate schoolboy essay. Now . . . I am not expecting much from this world. Fitzgerald and his green light! I remember his rich, mad dream: "Tomorrow we will run faster, stretch out our arms farther." But where will this Black boy run? To whom shall he stretch out his arms? . . . I need not think of tomorrow. I've come to a decision. I am getting my possession in order. Tonight, there will be an auction in my pad. Everything will be sold, got rid of. And then I'll go away.[32]

Although Fitzgerald's hopeful outlook on life has appealed to him, Stevenson does not view his future as optimistic.

Finally, at the end of *The Messenger*, Stevenson has arrived at an incredible existential revelation and breakthrough. Throughout the novel, drinking—along with jazz, sex, and reading—has helped him cope with existence, suffering, despair, and frustration. "Alcohol is merely a brace for my spine, the fine oil for my reflex." He calls it "a wonderful tranquilizer. Problems do not get less, but I can see them more clearly." Now, as his friends come to his apartment to bid him farewell, Stevenson acknowledges that he has been drinking all day. It has "done absolutely nothing for [his] head," but he is seeing himself more clearly: "There was horror in the knowledge that nothing was going to happen to me, that I was stoned on that frightening, cold level where everything is crystal clear. It was like looking at yourself too closely in a magnifying mirror."[33] He recognizes and becomes existentially aware.

He recognizes that the party in his apartment has turned into a microcosm of the world. His drunken friends, like people in conventional society, are searching fruitlessly for the "crazy kick," the metanarrative that will still their fear, frustration, pain, and confusion of being alive on this early August morning. But Stevenson has come to accept them as a part of life, including his traumatic past. He now knows that there is "no such thing as peace of mind and goodness." This knowledge becomes a prerequisite for establishing the self. It is the way out of the nothingness of existence and allows him to analyze his own culture and the world. And he acknowledges that all of his friends have acquiesced to unexamined or naturalized codes that are also deceptions: Shirley to middle-class respectability, Bruce to the Episcopalian church, Mitch to morality, Claudia to the notion of "a fabulous Negro drag queen," Jim to a desire to "save the world," Mrs. Lee to a "succession of lovers." "Self-deception," according to Jean-Paul Sartre, "seeks by means of 'not-being-what-one-is' to escape from the in-itself which I am not in the mode of being what one is not."[34] In the end, all of these systems seem absurd to Stevenson. And because he has decided that no meta-narratives can allay life's obstacles, he has no need to "find a roosting place."

Throughout most of *The Messenger*, Stevenson does not understand the nature of his search, his exile, his loneliness, in the absurdity that is his life, his actions. The societal results of his action do not equate. "I was searching for something I would tell Ruby. What? She would ask. I don't know, I would say. But I'll know when I find it."[35] Only at the end of the book does he synthesize and reconcile—by his own standards—his actions with his motives. He attains freedom by "scorning the absurd world": by seeing that his existence is valid although absurd, that the world is wrought with suffering and pain, that humans are nothing but what they make of themselves.[36] He knows that he cannot explain his "actions by reference to a given specific and human nature," that he is free, that he has neither behind him nor before him, "in a luminous realm of values, any means of justification or excuse." He is "left alone, without excuse." Thus, when Stevenson recognizes that existence precedes essence, that he simply exists, that he is his "own problem," he is "condemned to be free. Condemned, because he did not create himself, yet is nevertheless at liberty, and from the moment that he is thrown into this world he is responsible for everything he does."[37] It is this realization, this existential awareness, this freedom that allows him to assert his human independence and accept the fear, confusion, and the traumatic pain of being alive.

Wright once told Clarence Major that, though "I learned a great deal about writing and literary politics" from Lowney Handy, "most of what I've learned from writing I've learned on my own."[38] That is made clear in this novel. The power of *The Messenger* lies primarily within its existential philosophical countertradition. As he reconfigured and altered the existential genre and dealt forthrightly with racial oppression and sex, he broke away from the advice of Handy and others at the colony who wanted him to avoid issues of social harm and injustice. In so doing, he challenged the normative American definition of modern literature.[39] This is Charles Wright being daring and courageous.

While racial oppression and sexual objectification exist in the world of the text, Stevenson does not define himself as a victim of racial oppression—an expected convention of mainstream American literature. In his encounters with men in the Midwest and New York City—with the soldier Peter, who watches him at a bar and invites him into bizarre racial sex; with a New Jersey husband who offers his wife to him; with Mr. Bennett, who uses a "large collection of books" to lure him—Charles is represented as a sexual, racial other. For these men he is an object of arousal and fantasy, but he does not allow this objectification to define him.

In both Missouri and New York City, Stevenson experiences racism and injustice. A small-town cop stops him because he is a Black man walking in a white neighborhood. The son of a New York friend calls him a "nigger." A six-year-old playmate never comes to his birthday party, though he goes to hers. At the local movie theater, he has to sit in the segregated balcony on hard wooden seats, whereas the downstairs seats are upholstered with maroon leatherette. When Stevenson is fourteen years old, he spends a weekend exclusively with white people. After he arrives late for dinner, he hears a state senator say, "Maybe he won't come down because we ain't got no watermelon." At age sixteen, he takes a job as a pin boy at a bowling alley and listens to a white friend of his boss say, "Hey, Harry, see you have a coon back there." But these "wounds of my Missouri childhood were no worse than a sudden, sharp pain."[40] Stevenson chooses to overcome his obstacles rather than be defined as a victim by one of them: racial oppression.

The Messenger suggests that the blues and jazz have a similar philosophical supposition to existentialism, and in this way Wright further altered the genre and challenged the dominant society's limited representation of African American music. Like existentialism, the blues and jazz tell us that life is wrought with pain and suffering and that our objective is to confront and acknowledge this. Wright uses the blues and jazz as philosophical roamings, as modes of freedom. Throughout *The Messenger*, Wright uses this music to reaffirm a life that is condemned to be free, a life that is outside of dreams, expectations, and self-deception.

His character Ruby Stonewall embodies the blues. She accepts that suffering and pain are facts of life, and her world has been difficult. "She had bags under her gunpowder eyes that never seemed to give off any warmth." She is described as "one mean woman. She didn't give or take nothing from nobody." Her "red mouth always seemed to be on the verge of a smile that never appeared." Her "baby had the flu and died. Some bitching husband left [her], and [she] got into a mess with a white man in Kansas City." She has been forced to work low-paying jobs. "She couldn't make twenty-five [dollars] a week in a ginmill unless she hustled on the side."[41]

Suffering allows Ruby to establish the self, to find a way out of the nothingness of existence. Although she experiences racism, she refuses to pity herself, to allow racism to define who she is. She passes this blues attitude on to Stevenson. When he does not get a busboy job because of blatant racism, he feels sorry for himself, until Ruby lectures him:

> You make me sick. You go to that department store and ask to be interviewed and they tell you to wait outside. So you wait and wait and then some white boy comes along and gets the job. And you get hurt and mad as hell. Starting hating the white people again. If you had gotten the job, the white folks would be just fine. Now you're feeling sorry for yourself because you're Black. . . . Nobody has the tough luck that us colored people have. And you're too Goddamn miserable feeling sorry for yourself to get up out of the gutter.

When he asks, "Since when did you hit the big time?" Ruby snaps, "Since I stopped feeling sorry for myself. Since I learned that there ain't nothing really bad. There ain't nothing that can really hurt you." Then she gives him the ultimate blues advice: "I've spent thirty-five years discovering how rotten life is if you waste it on nothing. Never bitter, Sonny. Only people who can't face life and hate themselves are bitter. Maybe I was born Black and lost my voice to teach me a lesson."[42] In the words of Albert Murray, Ruby is "confronting, acknowledging, and contending with the infernal absurdities and ever-impending frustrations inherent in the nature of all existence."[43] She is teaching Charles Stevenson the meaning of the blues.

Likewise, good jazz, which is based on improvisation and spontaneity and does not exist as essence, tells no lies about a better tomorrow. It does not deceive us about progress; it does not promise salvation or resolution. Rather, as Murray explains,

> it . . . represents . . . an attitude toward the nature of [the] human experience . . . . that is both elemental and comprehensive. It is a statement about confronting the complexities inherent in the human situation and about improvising or experimenting or riffing or otherwise playing with . . . such possibilities as are also inherent in the obstacles, the disjunctions, and the jeopardy. It is also a statement about the maintenance of equilibrium despite precarious circumstances and about achieving elegance in the very process of coping with the rudiments of subsistence.[44]

Jazz, like the blues, generates, resignifies, and reaffirms existential life in *The Messenger*. When Stevenson lies "under the boardwalk at Coney Island" with Shirley, he listens as the "Black radio plays muted jazz." After a sexual encounter for money, he stops at San Remo's for a quick bourbon and listens to *The Billie Holiday Story*, a lovely, sad, bitter album. When he visits Barry's apartment, he hears the bedside radio playing jazz in the early morning. In the Step Down Bar, he plays a couple of Lady Day sides—"Yesterday" and "Ain't Nobody's Business If I Do." Visiting Jim and Laura, he turns on the old Zenith radio just in time to catch her singing "Fine and Mellow." Listening to his own radio, he hears "cool jazz."[45]

Jazz, which is spontaneous and open to mystery, helps Stevenson accept and, in Murray's terms, "confront . . . the complexities inherent in the human situation." It also helps him persevere, stay resilient, and maintain equilibrium, despite his precarious circumstances. Billie Holiday is a blues/jazz singer who confronts, acknowledges, and contends "with the infernal absurdities and ever-impending frustrations inherent in the nature of all existence." Her "timeless song" is not lamentation, protest, or exaggeration. Rather, it accepts pain and suffering and the "obvious fact that human existence is almost always a matter of endeavor . . . a matter of heroic action."[46]

Although the blues generates and reaffirms existentialism in *The Messenger*, the novel does not claim that it possesses the same power and universality. Whereas existentialism has an intellectual, rational dimension, the blues deals with concrete experiences. As James H. Cone writes:

> Freedom in the blues is not simply the "existential freedom" defined by modern [western] philosophy. Philosophical existentialism speaks of freedom in the context of absurdity and about the inability to reconcile the "strangeness of the world" with one's perception of human existence. But absurdity in the blues is factual, not conceptual. The blues, while not denying that the world was strange, described its strangeness in more concrete and vivid terms.[47]

Stevenson, the existentialist, is an intellectual who reads; Ruby, the blues woman, sings. He is concerned with abstract questions of existence and being, and she derives her knowledge from lived experience. The text clearly suggests that Ruby's blues are most effective in African American communities, whereas Stevenson has the world for his terrain. Yet the blues and jazz, like existentialism, offer a freedom that is beyond the absurdities of systems designed to oppress and suppress man's free will. They also challenge the mainstream's representation of the outsider/outcast African American.

Though *The Messenger* is an existential blues novel, its early reviewers, as I have said, never fully examined that aspect. Instead, many mainstream reviewers and critics repeatedly criticized its failure to deal more predictably with racial oppression. African American reviewers were particularly focused on its racial and social commentary, where the text's existential elements got short shrift, if they were mentioned at all. Even today the project has yet to be redeemed from such circumscribed criticism. Yet if we examine the novel's links to existentialist thought, we see that Wlad Godzich's conception of otherness closely applies to Stevenson. In his foreword to Michel de Certeau's *Heterologies: Discourse on the Other*, he writes:

> The disciplinary outlook permits each discipline to function as if the problem of fragmentation did not arise since the concepts that it mobilizes [and] the operations it performs are adequate . . . to its objects. . . . This may well account for the blindness of the disciplinary perspective to the problem of fragmentation: it is constitutive of that perspective.

Certainly, Stevenson embodies Godzich's "conception of the subject as the organizer of sense-maker of lived experience" and the "sense of fragmentation" so "widespread in our culture."[48]

For reviewers who focus on a racial-sociological interpretation, *The Messenger*'s New York scenes have no meaning because they say nothing about racism or racial progress. But this focus becomes irrelevant once we understand that Stevenson's problem is not one of race but of being—that his morality is outside, other than, a programmatic morality of racial victimization. Once we recognize that Wright's depiction of the absurdity of existence is grounded in reality and is artistically a metaphorical model of a person's cosmological environment ("alone in a godless universe . . . suffering anguish and despair in his loneliness"), we can most fully understand Stevenson and the absurd scenes.[49]

Some reviewers leveled criticism at the novel's episodic-journal structure. But if we define it as an existential blues text, we begin to identify patterns that Henry Miller's *Tropic of Cancer* and Jean-Paul Sartre's *Nausea* also share. For instance, like them, *The Messenger* is composed of a series of scenes presented as journal entries, as if Stevenson is recording the incidents as they happen. Each entry builds until the protagonist reaches a revelation. And, again, like Sartre in *Nausea*, Wright's main purpose is not to weave about Stevenson a realistic narrative but to explore the absolute revulsion he experiences as he confronts the world's absurdity.

Furthermore, if we consider the existential variants of free will and moral validation, we come to see that Wright's critique and exposure of all metanarratives, including racial ones, is his way of rendering them as false trials. Stevenson finds his redemption when he realizes that crazy kicks do not "still the fears, confusion and the pain of being alive."[50] His realization may be misguided or repulsive; it may harm the cause of African American liberation, survival, or unity; it may interrupt white or Black readers' need to define him as a victim or a devalued other. But these issues are irrelevant to an existential reading of *The Messenger*. Like Sartre and Camus, Wright knew that the authentic existential hero, or antihero, must be presented in a state of unconditional sin, one with no socially, culturally, or politically mitigating circumstances. It is to Charles Wright's credit as artist and thinker that he chooses to ground Stevenson in circumstances that would lead him so convincingly to a state of otherness.

But mainstream white and Black critics and reviewers—reinforcers of the ideological state apparatus—failed to understand or chose to ignore the existential aspects of *The Messenger*. They were not able to point to the text's contribution to their respective definitions of literary "knowledge." Therefore, despite positive critical successes from the literary community, *The Messenger* became marginal to both mainstream Black and white critics and reviewers. It certainly did not become a best seller. But later, it did become a classic.

Why was Wright's novel treated differently from other western existential novels? It certainly had forbears: Sartre and Miller but also Walker Percy and Fyodor Dostoevsky. What made his fiction different was its subject matter, style, and content, yet mainstream critics were unable to approach the text with a focus on what was written rather than what they thought was written. Nor did many of them recognize the problem of fragmentation in the modern, otherized, African American self. Within African America and African American literature, there is a "limited population" under some "limited set of conditions" that understands and identifies experientially and cognitively with existentialism. But until critics acknowledge this, *The Messenger* will never have contingent value.[51] It will never have cultural capital and therefore will remain marginal or out of print.

With *The Messenger* finished, Charles Wright became restless again. In May 1963, just before the publication of *The Messenger*, Wright wrote to Handy, expressing his "trying of other people." After the book was published, with some money in hand, he decided to "go far away," to a place where he did not know a "lying soul" so that he could "live a little."[52] In a birthday note to himself, he wrote, "If we don't live desperately and gamble, what is the use of tomorrow?"[53] In July 1963, at Vursell's suggestion, he returned to Veracruz to continue working on his next novel, *Toward Morning*. Veracruz was warm, socially open, and inexpensive. He felt good there; he was relaxed and was writing, with "[a] lot of good ideas . . . going through [his] mind."

On September 15, when four Black girls were bombed in a Baptist church in Birmingham, Alabama, Wright was in Mexico City. He recalled "walk[ing] through the streets, feeling as if [his] head and heart were trying to escape from his body. A friend from Morelia insisted that [they] go to the Cathedral of Our Lady of Guad[e]loupe. It [was] still dark and the distant mountains were lit by thousands of candles." When he asked, "What are those candles for?," he was told, "They are for the slain little girls in Birmingham."[54] Although he was in Mexico to rest and relax and write, he could not escape the (racial) tragedies in the United States.

Wright stayed in Veracruz until early December and then relocated to the YMCA in San Juan, Puerto Rico. He liked San Juan. Although he was supposed to be working full time on his next novel, he had not showed anything to Vursell. Instead, he was wandering around San Juan, taking an interest in the "mucho big noise . . . about statehood or independence." He was thinking about "trying to interview a couple of the guys" there. While in San Juan he was happy to read what Baldwin had said about *The Messenger* in the *New York Herald*: that "it was the best book he [had] read in 1963."[55]

Vursell sensed that Wright was not working on the novel, and he pleaded with him to "will discipline" and not allow himself to be "distracted or too easily discouraged, [because] you have it in you to become a fine writer."[56] Yet even though restlessness, lack of discipline, money problems, and alcohol were trademarks of his trauma and his distraction, they also seemed to be the engine behind his writing.

By the summer of 1964, Wright was back in New York City and living at the Hotel Park Savoy at 158 West 58th Street. He was excited about a new novel he was working on, *The Wig*. Writing to Handy in June, he promised to send her the first chapter under separate cover. He described the novel as a "mother grabber," as one of the "greatest satire[s] you've ever read." He did not think there was "another book like it written in this country." But he was still restless. He felt he was "going nuts in this city and ha[d] to leave. Would like to go [back to] Mexico? It's cheap and I don't know people there or at least no one will bother me." He asked Handy for $300 to help him travel to Mexico, promising to dedicate *The Wig* to her if she did not object.[57] She did not respond, however, and this was the last extant communication between the two.

In the meantime, the colony was in decline. After Handy fell out with James Jones, after he married and left the colony, it lost his generous subsidy and Handy now had to depend on her own resources, mostly drawn from a slice of royalties on books written at the colony (though many of the published authors neglected to honor their agreement to contribute), and on $400 a month from her husband.[58] Then Harry Handy died and Lowney herself became ill. She would die during the summer of 1964.

Regardless of how we assess its influence on him, the Handy Writers' Colony marked Charles Wright's beginning as a writer, and he was deeply saddened by the death of Lowney Handy. Three years later, in a retrospective column in the *Village Voice*, he wrote:

> And you dear, dead friend Lowney Turner Handy who discovered James Jones. We fought off and on for 14 years. The last year of your life—the death of Harry, the loss of Jim, living in a world that was becoming more difficult for you and the desire, need for pills increasing. Your dirty feet and all that broken glass, picking you up and putting you in bed, holding your hand and talking to you until you fell asleep. My love for you, respect, loyalty, and your magnificent generosity and love through the years—years, 14 years. "By God you treat me like I'm white."[59]

The honest, gut-felt homage to Handy signaled the end of a particular chapter, but not the influence, in Wright's writing career. After Handy's death, Wright's restlessness increased, and he decided to move to Tangier, Morocco, declaring "there is no place in greater New York where I can be le[ft] alone to do my work." Vursell was dismayed: "It's a rationalization on your part," he wrote. Then Vursell, who could display a sharp wit at times, snapped, "I wish to hell you did not think that this is what you have to do. However, it's time you were a big boy, and you will have to make your own decisions and live by them." Vursell would increasingly use this patronizing tone, especially as it became clear that Wright was not working productively. Reluctantly he paid Wright $1,200, giving him the means to travel to Tangier.[60] He thought Wright was taking an awful chance with his career, but Wright continued to live "desperately and gamble," as if tomorrow had no use.

CHAPTER FOUR

The Years in Tangier and the Finding of a Home

Because of his restlessness in New York, Charles Wright moved to Tangier, Morocco, hoping to find peace and a home. In 1912, the Treaty of Fez had established Morocco as a protectorate of France; and in 1956, with pressure from the Moroccan National Front, the French-Morocco Agreement granted the country full independence. Between 1923 to 1956, however, a coalition of Spanish, French, and British powers governed the Moroccan city of Tangier. Known as the International Zone of Tangier, the port had a population equally divided between Europeans and Moroccans. Tangier, according to the Harlem Renaissance writer Claude McKay, who lived intermittently in Tangier and elsewhere in Morocco between 1928 and 1933, "was a rare African-Mediterranean town of Moors and progressive Sephardic Jews and Europeans, mostly Spanish."[1] It was a place where "the Spaniards ha[d] created a modern town which stands up like a happy extension of the antique Moroccan. . . . The Spanish Morisco buildings gave more than lightness to the native Moroccan, and the architectural effect of the whole is a miracle of perfect miscegenation."[2]

The Treaty of Fez had created a weak administration incapable of enforcing laws efficiently, so illegal activities flourished, including the buying and selling of sex and narcotics. According to the English novelist and playwright Rupert Croft-Cooke, Tangier "had a reputation for cosmopolitanism and vice."[3] William Burroughs called it an "interzone," apart from the world, suspended among nations, cultures, and languages.[4] Tangier was a place of immediacy and ambiguity, one that remained outside standard narratives of nationhood and identity. Encounters between people from different nations, cultures, and religions were often transacted through sex and drugs, which served to break down other social and psychic barriers.[5]

Thus, Tangier appealed to a particular type of expatriate—among them writers, painters, and artists who were outcasts in the industrial West. As Croft-Cooke recalled, the city was "sunlit almost continuously, full of entertainment of the richest kind, piquant with many pleasures, [a place] in which fleshy delights [were] for the taking and much beauty, personal, scenic and of character, [was] evident. [It was a place of friendship and] of conversation uninterrupted by the annoyances of television or radio." He saw Tangier as being outside consumer culture, rationalism, rigid racial identity, racism, and American puritanism. Instead, there was "gaiety, the mixed European and Moorish characteristics, the absurdity, the wayward freedom and festivity."[6] Tangier, wrote Michelle Green,

[was] an enigmatic, exotic and deliciously depraved version of Eden. A sun-bleached, sybaritic outpost set against the verdant hills of North Africa, it offered a free money market and a moral climate in which only murder and rape were forbidden. Fleeing an angst-ridden Western culture, European [and American] émigrés found a haven where homosexuality [and sexual fluidity and bisexuality] was accepted, drugs were readily available, and eccentricity was a social asset.[7]

In addition, one could live frugally in Tangier, another reason why it attracted struggling artists. "American dollars," wrote Greg Mullins, "could purchase a comfortable standard of living at a bargain price in Tangier in the 1950s and early 1960s." Therefore, for writers and intellectuals such as Paul Bowles, Jane Bowles, Noel Coward, Williams Burroughs, Alfred Chester, Brion Gysin, Jean Genet, Allen Ginsberg, Jack Kerouac, Tennessee Williams, and others who wanted a place to live with no focal point, Tangier became the "site for a productive confusion of binary logics and preconceptions."[8]

Tangier's geography, cultural heterogeneity, diffuse political system, and illicit economy contributed to its aura of looseness and freedom. Its various interzones were established in dense and often contradictory relation to sex and sexuality, identity and desire. This ambiguity made it a haven for sexual rebels, and the availability of Moroccan boys and young men drew a thriving sexual subculture during the postwar years. Bowles, Burroughs, and Chester were open about their sexual fluidity. All "disliked the tendency in modern, urban societies to think about sexuality in terms of identity. They did not believe that the biological sex of one's partner prove[d] anything about one's identity."[9] For them, sex was something one did, not who one was, and they avoided identity terms such as *gay* or *bisexual*.

This was also how Charles Wright defined and dealt with his sexuality, though it was not always how others saw him. Acquaintances such as the novelist Steven Cannon and the poet Abba Elethea described him as a closeted homosexual who shied away from the subject and the label.[10] Another friend, Mary Jacobs, said that he was an out homosexual man among his accepting friends. Certainly, Wright had a strong attraction to young boys whom he could dominate.[11] But he also had relationships with women. Like McKay, Baldwin and the Tangier expatriates, he did not think about sexuality (or race) in terms of identity, and he felt at home among others like himself.

American and European expatriates came together in the Medina area of Tangier, often at Dean's Bar and Parade Bar, "which . . . served as meeting-places, gossip-shops and information exchanges."[12] Dean's Bar was located on a little street just below the Minzah, and Parade Bar was on the rue de Fez, and both "attracted the most prominent British and American exiles as well as a coterie of wealthy visitors."[13] In these sorts of places, within this complex and multiform subculture of Tangier, Wright—a dynamic, multifaceted subject who was constantly becoming—found "home," a place where he could imagine himself otherwise. He could live amid the "absurdity" and the "wayward freedom," and he could also be a sexual rebel. More importantly, he could be an American individual, something he did not think was possible in the United States.

Wright arrived in Tangier in July 1964 and found lodging at the Wagon Lits—Cook's.[14] Though he returned to the United States in January 1965, he came back to Tangier three months later, in March. By this the point, the city had ceased to be an international zone and had come under the control of the independent Moroccan government. But Tangier retained remnants of its international vibrancy. Many expatriate writers still lived or visited there and continued to "build social networks supportive of their own cultural formations while also coming into daily contact with Moroccan culture."[15] Their social fluidity and sexual subcultures remained central.

Wright had long found Tangier inviting. Before going there, he had read and talked about it with other New York City intellectuals. McKay published *A Long Way from Home*, in 1937, with a chapter describing his stay in Tangier. Jacobs, who met Wright in Tangier, said that he had come to escape the oppressive racism and sexual restrictions in the United States and to write. He also knew the city was "famous for homosexual writers."[16] McKay had come for similar reasons. Wright himself wrote of admiring Tangier's "cosmopolitan," "sophisticated flavor"; he saw it as "a place where Blacks didn't feel discriminated against like they did in the States."[17] In his view, "foreigners . . . felt very much at home in Morocco" because "the veil of Western frustration was lifted."[18]

Most importantly, in Tangier, Charles Wright was not invisible. He was accepted as an American individual with a complex subjectivity. "In Tangier I was Charles Stevenson Wright. Most of the time I could never stop marveling at the fact that people called me an American."[19] He had always believed that, "whether we want[ed] to accept that fact or not—we [were] Black Americans, and we live[d] in this country, and we ha[d] to operate under those methods, but being Black, we ha[d] to approach it from another manner."[20] In America, he thought, the problem was that Black Americans were not accepted as Americans. Therefore, coming to Tangier was a way of coming home. He did not want to go back to a predominantly "white environment ever," even "after making it to New York and feeling comfortable in the city."[21]

Still, Wright did have mixed feelings about Tangier. He acknowledged its magnificent setting but called it a "no action city." Nor was he "much impressed" by "the social and lit people of the city."[22] While its summers were breezy and dry, winters were grim; all it did was rain. Nonetheless, he quickly came to love and appreciate "the good Moroccans, my brothers, my loved ones, [who] touched us with their magic, made us live."[23] It was impossible not to be "aware of the poverty" in Tangier. "Many of [his] friends [were] poor" because there was "almost no industry in Tangier, as opposed to Rabat and Casablanca."[24] He listened to complaints about unsolved national problems and corruption in high places. People even voiced mild displeasure about the European-educated king, Hassan, who, unlike his father, the beloved Mohammed V, did not don the robes of the common people and visit the markets.[25] As Wright, poor and struggling, waited on the avenue España facing the sea, he watched the king arrive in Tangier for a visit. He was fully aware of the contradiction.

Wright arrived in Tangier intending to "spend the winter" there. Because it was "very cheap," he thought the city could be the right "scene for writing his new book."[26] He was making friends, including a female friend, Melinka. Soon he met John Mitchell, who ran the Fat Black Pussy Cat, a bar and restaurant. Mitchell also ran another café by that name in New York City. Wright came to the Pussy Cat because he liked jazz, and because he had heard that Mitchell also liked jazz and was friendly with Blacks.[27] On one of his early visits, Mitchell introduced Wright to Mary Jacobs, a graduate of Barnard College, who had sailed to Morocco for a summer's "adventure." Known as the "Tangier landlady" (a nickname bestowed by the Canadian novelist Brion Bysin), she managed a boarding house in the city and came regularly to the bar with her friend Martha Street, who was a friend of one of the bartenders.[28]

When Mitchell decided to travel to Spain and began looking for American cash, he sublet his small three-story villa on rue Grotious to Jacobs for $600.[29] The villa was about a block away from the Pussy Cat, and Wright was one of the first people Mitchell invited to be Mary's tenant.[30] In Tangier, Wright was seen as witty, handsome, intelligent, and opinionated. He was a presence in a room, and Jacobs was taken in by his charm. "My first Tangier resting place was the Mary Lou-Mustapha pad. It was a storied, swinging house, a head house, a sanctuary for dehydrated American and European souls." Eventually, Wright came to understand that he had not completely escaped racism and invisibility. In the foyer of the villa, he encountered an American who spoke French to him. When Wright replied that he spoke English, "this young man of peace never said another word in French or English [to him], as long as [he] stayed in the house."[31] Alfred Chester, too, would occasionally use the word "nigger" in Wright's company. But these encounters with racism were the exception rather than the rule.

Wright and Jacobs became life-long friends, staying close even after both returned to New York City and then when she moved to Bangor, Maine. Charles lived on the top floor of the villa, and he would sit on the roof deck, drinking beer and sending Moroccan boys on errands for him and giving them advice about life. He ruled his flock like a king but also enjoyed their companionship.[32] Mustapha Broeazio, a good friend of Mitchell's, also lived in the villa and became a comrade of Wright's. Mustapha was forty years old and from a well-to do Moroccan family.[33] He was a regular at the Black Pussy Cat and also liked jazz, particularly the music of Ray Charles.[34] Also, because Mustapha's English was very good,

Mitchell used him to translate from Arabic to English when he bought things in the Medina.

Through Mitchell and Mustapha, Wright met Florence Ward Roess, who lived across the street from the villa. Roess had arrived in Tangier in 1964 after a bad divorce in Florida had left her with very little money. She was a serious drinker, though Wright thought she "must have been lovely once and a very good wife, mother. But things happen to people."[35] In Tangier, she had an African boyfriend named Nate; and when that "love affair end[ed], she want[ed] to end her life." She made advances toward Wright, but he "only offer[ed] friendship."[36] Roess was not a writer herself, but she liked poetry and she encouraged Wright.[37] The two remained friends in later years, after their return to New York. Wright was also friendly with Jay, the bartender at Parade Bar, and Hajmi, a local Moroccan hustler and friend of Alfred Chester's partner, Dris.[38] In the meantime, Wright was learning that many of the local writers had read or had heard of *The Messenger*. He was, according to Jacobs, "the wonder boy over there on his first flush of writing money."[39]

At this time, the writer Alfred Chester was also in Tangier. In New York, Bowles had spoken of "the advantage of life in Morocco for a writer, and urge[d] Alfred to come and see for himself." After a detour to Paris, Chester arrived in Tangier in June 1963, where Bowles and his wife Jane were eagerly awaiting him. Chester easily adapted to the country's bohemian life, going so far as to learn to "speak Moghrebi, the language of Morocco compounded of Arabic and local dialects, a rare feat in the foreign colony."[40]

Chester and Wright had known some of the same people in New York, and the two emerging writers would meet face to face in Tangier. Chester was already familiar with Wright and told others that *The Messenger* had sold a lot of copies. But their relationship in Morocco was cantankerous and at times difficult, and a literary rivalry developed between the two. The poet Edward Field thought Chester was "nasty" to everybody, but others thought that he was particularly jealous of Wright because they shared the same literary agent (Candida Donadio) and because Wright had been published while Chester had not. Michelle Green recalled Chester as moody, and he was certainly insecure around Wright. As he told Field, "[he] throws me into the idea of Big Time and I feel like a failure."[41]

Knowing that they had the same agent, Wright initially sought out Chester at his apartment, hoping to spark an acquaintance. What he did not know was that Chester had recently fired Donadio. Wright intended to tell Chester that Donadio "sends [you] much love."[42] But when he arrived at the apartment, Chester told his friend Norman Glass to "send him away." The two intersected again at the Fat Black Pussy Cat, where, according to Chester, "blondes and niggers [were] all over the place." Chester claimed that he instantly fell "in love with" Wright: he "was so pure, innocent the way Americans are—not sitting there like everyone else in this country thinking what you are thinking and trying to destroy." Later, he would blame this initial admiration on being drunk. After taking Wright home, Chester became "a bit bored with him" but was not entirely sure about his feelings.[43] For the moment the two remained social, visiting and talking throughout Wright's first stay in the city. During an encounter with Paul Bowles, he even invited "Charles to act as a buffer."[44] Chester traveled with Wright to Arcila, Morocco, where they went to the market and the beach. In Tangier, they drank and dined together, but Chester resented how Wright would lecture him about his career or how to decorate his apartment.

The relationship continued to have its ups and downs. Both artists clearly struggled with neuroses and insecurities, and their uneasy connection revealed not only a desire to achieve power but also an urge to suppress pain. Several months later, for instance, Chester invited Wright to dinner. Wright arrived with a "horrible American economist friend" and drank but did not eat, though he dominated the conversation. Chester was "very annoyed" and found "Wright's friend boring."[45] Still, he continued to invite him for drinks and dinners.

Though Wright was busy socializing and drinking, he was also working on several writing projects. For the most part they were advancing well, at least when he had money for rent and food. Among them was the novel that would later become *The Wig*. Initially, before leaving New York, he had begun an action novel about a group of Black men in black leather jackets, very much like the Black Panthers, who wanted to overthrow the government of the United States. When he sent twenty pages to Donadio, she said, "We can't publish this."[46] Therefore, instead he began writing *The Wig*, a Nathanael West–like excursion into black humor and the absurd. Unlike *The Messenger*, it would be "pure fiction."[47] When he pitched the idea to Donadio, she said, "This is a novel. Write It."[48] Vursell was also aware that Wright was working on a novel titled *The Wig*.

In Tangier, he usually worked under the influence of alcohol and speed.[49] But he was confident and enthusiastic, convinced that *The Wig* was "going to be a motherfucker and get good reviews and make as much money as *The Messenger*." He was making progress, occasionally sending fifteen or twenty pages to Vursell, as he had done when he was writing *The Messenger*. But Vursell was wary. In a letter dated July 24, 1964, he said,

> Tangier sounds fascinating in a rather horrid way, but you are not to let it seduce you away from what is probably the most important thing you have so far done in your life: namely try to make *The Wig* the best book that you can possibly write at this particular time in your career. Critics are mean about second books. The kindness of discovery is gone; they lie in the weeds, with long sharp knives, waiting. So pull your socks up, man. We have a long way to go.[50]

But as his financial situation deteriorated, so did his ability to write.[51] Hoping for a contract and an advance, Wright sent Vursell eighty-two pages of *The Wig*. The editor was not impressed, as he discussed in a letter to Donadio:

> There is nothing much here that I hadn't seen before he went away or shortly thereafter, and some pretty good stuff seems to have disappeared. . . . It seems to me that the Tangier thing hasn't worked out at all. This is a lazy man's manuscript, the work of an undisciplined person, and I cannot offer a contract for it. . . . I think he should come home, get a job, and be forced to do the job properly. It would seem that he can't stand relative freedom and still work. He has to have the incentive to escape. When he does escape, he doesn't work, or so I read the situation.[52]

Vursell's assessment was accurate. Like Handy, he saw the conundrum inherent in Wright's writing life: he had the potential to become a great writer, but did he have the necessary discipline? Handy and Vursell were identifying an unconscious, contradictory conflict within Charles, a conflict that had underlying tendencies that were repressed or not dealt with. Throughout his life, as Wright struggled with this pattern, the conflict "produce[d] states of anxiety, depression, indecision, inertia, detachment."[53] Left unresolved, the pattern would affect his writing career. And it did.

Despite his money and writing problems, Wright stayed on in Tangier. By now he was mentally frayed and completely out of funds. On December 29, 1964, he went to the American consul in Tangier and sent a telegram to Vursell, informing him that he was destitute and needed $300 to return to the United States.[54] On December 30, Farrar, Straus sent that amount to the American consul, telling Wright that this transfer had emptied his account with the publisher.[55] At the same time, Chester told Norman Glass that Wright was "getting really flippy. . . . On New Year's Day he disappeared all together and [friends] Jay, Mustapha, Hajmi and I (his creditors) ran around like the mafia all over town looking for him."[56] One friend, Hajmi, who had been in Wright's apartment since 4 a.m., was worried that Wright might be dead and that the police would blame him. I am not sure where Wright was, but he did eventually return to his apartment. Finally, the four woke Wright up, and Chester surmised that his real problem was he owed everybody money and did not know how to face them. When Wright left for the United States on January 2, he said, "Charles is gone. I can't tell you how relieved I am."[57]

Back in New York, Wright spent the next month living between the Bowery and the Hotel Albert, revising and finishing *The Wig*, "thinking, working, like seven and, yes, sometimes fourteen hours a day [on *The Wig*]. It took me less than three hours to make the final changes before the publishers accepted."[58] Discussing Wright's approach to writing, Phelonise Willie recalled,

> Charles did not dabble in too much rewriting. . . . He was very proud of the speed with which he finished his books. His writing was always spontaneous and urgent. That was his excitement. But because it stripped him naked, exposed every fibre of his present condition of body and mind, it force[d] the reader to think about the writer as much as his tale.[59]

Willie thought *The Wig* benefitted from this approach, and it also addressed Wright's need for money. He was hoping this novel would bring him more fame and financial security, two powerful motives with "anxiety lurking behind them." As Karen Horney has written, "they aim primarily not at satisfaction but at safety."[60]

In Tangier, Chester had read "a draft" of *The Wig* and had "said that it was damn ambitious for [him] to try this [on his] second time out."[61] Wright thought Alfred liked *The Wig* "more than he admit[t]ed," and he himself believed that the book was far better than *The Messenger*.[62] More importantly, he was determined that it would be different, even though the novels were both dealing with the African American subaltern and the existential absurd. In a letter to Norman Mailer, Wright said, "At least the critics can't say I'm repeating myself."[63] He clarified this in a later interview with John O'Brien:

> As you know *The Messenger* was a first novel with almost nothing going for it and almost no advertising campaign. Yet, it took off on its own, found its own audience, and was well received by the critics. I realized that they were waiting for me to write a sequel to *The Messenger* or another novel like that. I said that I'll be damned if I'll do what was expected of me.[64]

Wright realized that a second novel like *The Messenger* could make him very successful, but he was a risk taker, and he was not going to play literary "games": "I have to remain true to myself, . . . though it's costly mentally, physically, . . . but I will still continue to do this."[65] Because *The Wig* is different from *The Messenger*, it produced a different audience.

Farrar, Straus accepted *The Wig*; and in March 1965, as it went into production, Wright took his advance with him back to Tangier, remaining there until mid-October. He found an attractive flat in a good location and decorated it himself. He painted the walls of the living room black, which the Moroccans thought was crazy, but he thought was chic. In May, he learned that the proofs would not arrive until August, which meant the novel would not be published until March 1966. Now he regretted the money he had spent rushing back to New York.[66] Frustrated by this news from Vursell, he complained in a series of letters to Donadio, but she did not respond.[67] Therefore, he decided to put together a collection of short stories and shop it to Grove Press. He began smoking marijuana while writing: "I have been experimenting with Kif [and] wrote whatever came into my head . . . when I was stoned. . . . I called it Kif collage, which has caused a lot of talk in Tangier." He also asked Charles Robb to send the long manuscript he had left in his care, telling Robb he planned to use it to "fill out this collection."[68]

With his second novel in the hands of the press, Wright relaxed. He, again, felt at home. Though he was one of the few Blacks in the Moroccan Medina crowd, people were familiar with *The Messenger*. He met a young Algerian who had encountered the novel in Paris. He met Alec Waugh, a British novelist and the elder brother of the better-known Evelyn. He met Susan Sontag, also published by Farrar, Straus.[69] He visited with the American writer Stuart Gordon and looked forward to meeting Robin Maugham, Somerset Maugham's nephew and also a writer.[70] One morning he went "for a walk along the deserted beach and then came home and had tea on the terrace and watched T-town come to life." He realized he was "goddamn grateful for this."[71] He was at home in Tangier, and for the moment at peace.

Most of the writers and artists in Tangier lived in the Medina, so they encountered each other daily, even if they did not necessarily become close friends. Among them were Patrick Dennis, the American author of the bestseller *Auntie Mame*, and his friend Guy Kent, whom Wright met "a couple of times," though they "never had a long or short conversation." He met Paul Bowles and William Burroughs and reestablished his friendship with the gregarious Jay Haselwood, owner of the Parade Bar, where Wright occasionally went for drinks. When he later learned about Haselwood's sudden death, he "felt very down" about it.[72]

During this second visit to Tangier, Wright also met Rupert Croft-Cooke, characterizing him as someone who "has written 50 books, nothing great, just a good old pro, who has a respectable name."[73] Croft-Cooke was an Englishman—a novelist, playwright, biographer, travel writer, and book critic; and Wright became friendly with him and his secretary and companion, Joseph Alexander, whom he had adopted as a boy in India. In 1953, Croft-Cooke had been imprisoned in England for nine months, charged with "gross indecency." When he was released, he and Joseph moved to Tangier, where they lived until 1968, when English laws regarding homosexuality began to change.

Croft-Cooke had read and liked *The Messenger* and had been trying to meet Wright for five months. When they finally did meet, they became fond of one another and got on nicely. They dined and drank together; they read and admired each other's manuscripts and offered support and advice. At one point, Croft-Cooke suggested that the two "should cross-dedicate novels to one another."[74] The pair also enjoyed visiting the "lower part of the town," outside the Medina, where Wright befriended the local whores and thieves, as he had done in the Bowery, and gave them advice. He told the gigolos what to put into the letters they wrote to their middle-class tourist lovers. "No, no," he would say, "if you want that expensive watch, you can't say it that way."[75] They repaid him with streetwise affection.

Mary Jacobs recalled that Charles Wright liked young men, usually ones who were "a little younger than him. But Wright was young for his age, he was lively."[76] Away from oppressive American racism, he moved confidently in this sexually fluid social space. He was the only foreigner who could wander drunkenly through the deserted waterfront alleys at three o'clock in the morning with total impunity. No one touched or bothered him.[77]

Although Wright and Croft-Cooke got on well socially and intellectually, they periodically had clashes. For a period Croft-Cooke would not speak to Wright, who attributed the discord to his own need to be himself.[78] From childhood, Wright had not been able to form long-term, stable relationships without occasional friction. While he could be patient with others, he could also have a temper when he was drinking, and perhaps this was behind their disagreement.[79]

Wright continued to be friendly with Florence Ward Roess, who was also close to Croft-Cooke and lived nearby. He thought she was "a very likable, intelligent woman"; and after she had an affair with a Black man who scammed her for $2,500, he encouraged her to write about her interracial relationship.[80] In his view, the white woman/Black male relationship had not been completely explored in fiction, certainly not from the white woman's point of view. As he did with all of his friends, Wright borrowed money from Roess, but he also asked Vursell to read one of her short stories, "The Firefly."

Eventually, however, Wright became bored with the café literary crowd in Tangier, calling them "dull and phony like old Eugenia Bankhead."[81] He reverted to his loner habits, staying at home because he had gotten the reputation of being a snob, of being elusive. He stopped going to popular venues such as the Parade, which he took to calling the Stork Club. By May 16, he had been in Tangier for about eight months but to the Parade only three times. Ideally, he wanted to "stay in [his] apartment and write, read, listen to [his] records, have a drink, drinks on the terrace with cigarettes and look out at [his] view. I don't want to be bothered with people at all."[82] Although he was a loner, he also had this gusto for life.

For a while, he did continue his cantankerous relationship with Alfred Chester. When Chester received a wire from Wright saying he was "coming back [to Tangier] tomorrow," his response was "Ugh."[83] Among other things, he was angry because Wright "did not bring the carbon paper [from New York] that I wanted. He is really a bastard."[84] But what finally ended the friendship was the party Chester gave for his partner Dris's twenty-third birthday: "Charles ruined the party. . . . He sat not eating or smoking or saying a single word. I had a chat with him a couple of days later and gave him to understand I didn't want him around."[85] Though they occasionally saw each other in town, they did not talk. Then, after running into each other at Dale's Bar, Chester received a letter from Wright asking for money.[86] He did not respond. In a letter to Glass, he wrote, "I've seen Charles and Jay a couple of times. They are unchanged."[87] Before returning to the United States, Chester mentioned that Wright had read his novel *The Exquisite Corpse* and had said he liked it. But, Chester insisted, "I could tell he was lying."[88] Yet something had vibrated between the two, for several years later Wright dedicated *Absolutely Nothing to Get Alarmed About* to Chester, along with Langston Hughes and Conrad Knickerbocker.

During this time, Wright began working on a short story titled "The Fruity Afternoons," a reworking of a long one-act play. He also continued putting together a collection of short stories, with Farrar, Straus now in the know. He sent the collection to Vursell, but the press did not buy it. As explanation, Vursell told Wright that he had a lot of natural talent but had not learned his trade. In his opinion, Wright's lack of discipline showed disrespect to both publisher and reader; and he reminded Wright that had the press published *The Wig* in the form in which it had been submitted, both he and Farrar, Straus would have been laughed out of the business.[89]

Again, Wright's financial situation became problematic. Earlier, he had refused Farrar, Straus's monthly stipend of $300, instead taking the advance for *The Wig* in a lump sum, and now he was broke.[90] As he borrowed money from his friends, he was telling everyone that he had not received royalties from the sale of *The Messenger* in England. Roess tried to help. In a letter to Vursell, she pointed out Wright's pride, keen intelligence, and great potential. But this was "being smothered under a withering sense of defeat because he had to accept loans from me to pay his rent and eat."[91] Vursell wrote back, informing her that Wright had already received his English royalties and that he and Donadio had begged him to let them break his advance into monthly payments. Wright, however, had "categorically refused," saying "he was a big boy" who could "manage his [own] money."[92]

Wright was even more depressed because Donadio was not responding to his letters. By May, he did not have any money and was about to lose his apartment. He did find some comfort from friends such as Mustapha, who when he saw Wright smoking a cheap cigarette bought him a better pack. "He's one of the best people I have ever met. And a character too. Got stoned one night, went outside to get sick, lost his lower false teeth plate. Doesn't want to sleep with me."[93] To survive financially, Charles thought about becoming Roess's lover, but he did not.[94]

Charles managed to remain in Tangier until the fall of 1965. When he returned to New York in October, he was still hoping to come back to Morocco when he received "the contract money [for *The Wig*] or they sell [the] paperback right." Life there may not have ultimately helped his writing, but in his letters to Croft-Cooke he averred that "Tangier [was] where I have always felt at home."[95]

After Wright returned to New York, he and Croft-Cooke continued a friendly correspondence. After Roess, who was still in Tangier, sent Wright Croft-Cooke's address, Wright wrote that he was now working his way through a "realistic" novel, which he wanted to finish so he could return "home" to Tangier. "When I left, I wasn't sure whether I'd return to Tangier. Confused in T-town—it was worse here. But things have settled down. After I finish this book . . . I will try to get a short story collection together, which moneywise, will see me through a couple of years. . . . I am going to try and get back by Christmas or at least by New Year's Eve."[96] In a letter dated December 10, 1965, Croft-Cooke was "trying to gather from [Wright's letter] when you will be coming back—which is what I want to know most. It seems that it may be for the New Year. I hope so—I miss you a great deal."[97] He reminded Wright of a reference to *The Messenger* in the *Times Literary Supplement*—that the character Stevenson exemplified "homelessness in America"—and repeatedly encouraged him to "recognize [his own] homelessness in America and come back to Tangier."[98] Wright responded, "I want to return to Tang[i]er where I have always felt at home. Can[n]ot though until I get the contract money or they sell paperback rights. . . . I hope you are well and working. Miss you, miss you."[99] Croft-Cooke answered with "I miss you very much here in Tangier and haven't been to the lower part of the town since you left. When am I to expect you back"?[100]

In one of his last letters to Croft-Cooke, Wright told of trying to finish "a childhood fictional memoir. My editor likes the first 25 pages. Hope to return home in July."[101] Repeatedly, Wright referred to Tangier as home. Not feeling safe, secure, and respected in the United States, he, like many Black expats, sought home elsewhere. In his final letter to Croft-Cooke he expressed concern for Roess and mourned the death of Jay Haselwood, continuing to insist, "I want to come back home and have a ball for a couple of weeks."[102]

As the 1960s advanced, Wright's views about America took a decidedly leftward political shift, as he continued to become, to reinvent himself. He believed that very little progress was made by Blacks in the United States in the 1960s. In 1967, as he wrote about the Newark riots and the fear of being Black in America, he also described his fear of the future:

> While everything seems to be very quiet and peaceful, there are things going on behind the scenes, so suddenly when the 80's appear and while we are very quiet and going our little separate ways and being happy and fairly successful with material things, suddenly something could happen . . . and you could be totally unprepared for it though you have gone through experiences from the 60's. . . . But I would suggest very strongly that every Black person should get all of their machinery together and be prepared for what might happen—in the 80's or next year or next month because I do not trust this country and especially since it is going so far to the right. And even in such a liberal city as New York, it is to the right.[103]

Given Ronald Reagan's election to the presidency in 1980, the backlash against civil rights gains, and the country's lean to the right, this feels like a prophecy. Yet in the late 1960s, Wright was still thinking of home and Tangier:

> I want to die under a Moroccan blue sky. One wants to die where one can get a drink of water. . . . Just book me on a jet for home—T-town. Tangier. I will be packed within the hour, give it all up, painful as it would be. I would give it up like a terrible illness I had contacted in a country that was home and was never truly home. I do not believe that it [the United States] will ever be home for me or my Black brothers or our children or their children.[104]

By the 1970s, Wright and Croft-Cooke had lost touch. In his book *The Caves of Hercules*, a book about his experiences and encounters with writers and artists in Tangier, Croft-Cooke lamented, "Charles has become as remote as one disappearing into the American continent a century ago, and unless he chances to see this, that taut, critical, generous character will remain lost to me."[105] The book describes Wright as his "young [handsome] friend . . . , a coloured American of immense charm and talent":

> We wandered round Tangier for whole nights, not looking for anything in particular but unwilling to leave one another and go home. From backgrounds so immeasurably different, with thirty years between us, with scarcely anything in common but the love of literature and gusto for life, we felt [for] one another a measure of what I can only call love.

Empathizing with him, Croft-Cooke saw Wright as someone alone, "without a family, without even a city or a country that he wanted to claim as his own," and for such a person "the possibilities are endless and grim."[106] Croft-Cooke recognized that the world was not Wright's home. The two never met again. Croft-Cooke lived in Tangier until 1968, afterward moving to Tunisia, Cyprus, West Germany, and Ireland. He returned to England in the 1970s and died there in 1979.

CHAPTER FIVE

The Publication of *The Wig*

When Charles Wright returned to New York City from Tangier in mid-October 1965, he fell back into his precarious, freewheeling, bohemian lifestyle, with a gusto for living. He later saw this period as "the happiest . . . of [his] life."[1] From late 1965 to 1966, he lived at the Hotel Albert on 23 East 10th Street, working at odd jobs. In 1967, Roess also returned to New York, and Wright lived with her part time. He finally met James Baldwin, years after Baldwin had written a blurb for *The Messenger*. Wright had returned for the production and release of *The Wig*. With this novel he thought he had created his best work, tapping into "the deepest and truest—indeed, the most prophetic—sources of his being."[2] Rupert Croft-Cooke, who had read an early draft in Tangier, thought it was more "esoteric and macabre [than *The Messenger*] but ha[d] the same power of unrestricted invention."[3] However, the reception of the novel proved to be disappointing, sending Wright into depression.

While *The Wig* was in production, Farrar, Straus sent galley proofs to Kay Boyle, Truman Capote, Robert Gover, Tennessee Williams, Dick Gregory, Joseph Heller, Ralph Ellison, Vivian Gornick, Paul Bowles, James Baldwin, Bruce J. Friedman, Terry Southern, Lucy Freeman, John Barth, Warren Miller, and others, asking for reactions and blurbs. In November, Wright contacted Norman Mailer directly, asking him to provide a "quote" for the book.[4] Shortly afterward, Roger Straus ran into Mailer at a restaurant and pressed the case. Mailer agreed to read and comment on *The Wig*.[5] But as with *The Messenger*, he became hard to pin down. Responding to a follow-up letter from Straus, Mailer said, "I'll try to read *The Wig*, but don't know about promising, because it's a bad time for me—I'm getting a book together."[6] In the end, he never got around to reading and commenting on the galleys. This meant that Norman Mailer, an acknowledged mentor, had refused to write a blurb for Wright's first two novels. Nor did any of the other writers submit commentary. Ultimately, the first hardback edition of *The Wig*, published in March 1966 and priced at $3.95, was released without a single blurb.

Wright later told John O'Brien that *The Wig* was one of the "greatest satires you've ever read. . . . I think that [the protagonist] Lester . . . is tragic."[7] Yet something about the book did not attract the prominent writers who had been asked to endorse it. That may have been because its influences were quite different from *The Messenger*'s, which still echoed the fiction of Hemingway, Sartre and Jones. *The Wig*, in contrast owed a debt to Nathanael West. It was satirical, not heavily plotted, and immersed in black humor and the absurd. Altering and expanding West's type of satire, the novel incorporated jazz and black hip; it dealt with internalized Black self-hatred and was filled with the cadence of Black vernacular speech. Wright's prefatory note stated, "The story itself is set in an America of tomorrow."[8]

In *Fables of Subversion*, Steven Weisenburger argues that *The Wig* is neither "degeneratively satirical nor even mildly grotesque." Rather, he sees it as "a conventionally mimetic satire, quite clear in its selection of targets: white standards of beauty, racial stereotypes, Uncle Toms and Inchers Along, [self-hatred and] the emasculation of Blacks under institutional racism." Deconstructively, it "subvert[s] hierarchies of values and . . . reflect[s] suspiciously on all ways of making meaning, including its own."[9] Wright's objective was to destabilize and expose selected American targets, ones through which society legitimated knowledge, without offering an alternative narrative or solution.

Wright set *The Wig* in Harlem because he saw it as "the place." In contrast, *The Messenger* was set less specifically, "in the metropolitan area of New York."[10] Wright emphasized to O'Brien that the books were very different, "even if they deal with the same subject." Yet as Max F. Schulz has noted, "both posit an absurd world devoid of intrinsic values, with a resultant tension between individual and universe."[11] To use Martin Esslin's words, both strive to "express its sense of senselessness of the human condition and the inadequacy of the rational approach by the open abandonment of rational devices and discursive thought."[12] But unlike the absurdist and tragic Lester Jefferson, the main protagonist of *The Wig*, the blues/existentialist Stevenson of *The Messenger* "retains implicitly a respect for the self." As Max F. Schulz writes, "although existence precedes being, to exist is to act . . . and to act is to assert the self." Thus, Stevenson draws some sympathy in his existential search for meaning in modern capitalist America, for he accepts and takes responsibility for his existence in an absurd, chaotic world. In existentialism, the blues, and jazz he finds "a rejection of supra personal law, dogma, and social order" and is able to retain "confidence in the dignity and ordering capacity of the individual."[13]

In contrast, Lester Jefferson's black humor "poses the primary difficulty" of *The Wig*. Schulz explains, "This is the consequence of a shift in perspective from the self and its ability to create a moral ambience through an act to emphasis on all the moving forces of life which converse collectively upon the individual." Lester exists outside the values of traditional families and communities. To survive, he eschews the self and moves postmodernly "toward role playing and identity achievement." His inner world is "equivalent to his external appearance, which in turn is the sum of the interchangeable products he uses."[14] Yet he hopefully, humorously, and tragically pursues the American Dream. His journey through Lyndon Johnson's notion of the Great Society is, according to A. Robert Lee, a "grotesque *rite-de-passage*, . . . through a world of fraudulent 'success' and myths of endless American opportunity which ends, as it must if Lester is to understand anything at all."[15] Unlike Stevenson in *The Messenger*, Lester makes, in Schulz's terms, "efforts to realize [him]self in relation to the outer world, with the focus less on the individual than on the world of experiences, less on the agony of struggle to realize self than on the bewildering trackless choices that face the individual," and this leads to his tragic downfall.[16] In other words, the major difference between the two texts is the sense of the self.

Like Stevenson, Lester Jefferson is a downtrodden outsider who exists alone in the chaotic, absurd world of New York City, where "everyone seem[s] to jet toward the goal of The Great Society" while he remains "in the outhouse, penniless, without 'connections.'"[17] But Lester's world is a surreal and menacing place, where children die in the streets and buildings collapse. Like much of America (though unlike the exilic Stevenson), he dreams of pretty girls and material things. As the satirist George S. Schuyler has written, "Lester only wants what most people want: a little love and a little recognition, and he works with a will to get them."[18] But these things are not available to him because he is Black. Both Stevenson and Lester are lost and confused; Lester lives among memorable but comic and sad outcast characters such as drag queens, sex workers, and fake society ladies. Yet unlike many of the middle-class reviewers, critics, and blurb writers who reacted to his books, Wright never used the word *seedy* to refer to these characters or their communities. They are humans first.

Lester and his neighbors all have "*something* working for them."[19] Unlike the characters in *The Messenger*, they define themselves through mainstream American narratives, rejecting who they are—their history and social reality of being Black in America—and impersonating someone else, mostly white people and white images. Yet *The Wig* does not sentimentalize or otherize them. Rather, it presents them complexly and sympathetically, even as it makes fun of their hopeless aspirations and romantic delusions, as they play roles or try to become something they can never be.

Using satire, Charles Wright showed, perhaps for the first time in African American fiction, how American media, particularly Hollywood and popular romantic fiction, had intervened into and shaped African American subjectivity. Looking "silly as hell and freakish," Miss Sandra Hanover, a Black transvestite in need of a shave, masquerades as a "White woman from Georgia." "Drunk with dreams of glory," she impersonates movie stars such as Gloria Swanson, Ava Gardner, Greta Garbo, Barbara Stanwyck, and Lena Horne.[20] She only sees the blood of suffering, taking on actions and behaviors these actresses perform in movies. For example, performing gender, she strikes grandly bitchy Bette Davis poses.

Other characters such as Lester's godfather Tom and his neighbor Nonnie Swift also take part in outrageous, inventive, and sad impersonations. They, too, are complex individuals. Tom, for instance, does a brilliant, over-the-top spoof of Harriet Beecher Stowe's character Uncle Tom. Yet "beneath a placid mask," notes the critic Frances S. Foster, he "has the face of a natural killer."[21] He is fully aware that he is wearing a mask and is deceptive. Tom has spent a fortune on newspapers, keeping demographic charts on white mortality and anticipating the day, centuries hence, when whites will be a minority. "Lord," he says, "I can hardly wait to act like a natural man. I've had to Tom so much that it's hard for one to knock it off."[22] Through characters such as Tom, *The Wig* destabilizes and reterritorializes the prevailing society's image of the Black man as simple and docile.

For her part, Nonnie Swift impersonates a high-yellow Creole woman of the sort described in popular paperback novels. She fantasizes about being pregnant and owning a mansion in the Garden District of New Orleans. She claims to be in Harlem only because she wants to see how the underprivileged live. Like others in her community, she depends on images from Hollywood and popular novels. Yet in her self-hatred, she defines herself as different and better than other Black people, whom she refers to as "you people."[23] The novel also presents Mrs. Turner, a bourgeois, want-to-be white lady from an aristocratic Carolina plantation. Mimicking a southern white lady, she leaves a dying request to have her remains sprinkled on the plantation bluegrass of her home state. As Wright makes clear, people such as Nonnie and Mrs. Turner "have to have a little make-believe" in order to escape selves that mainstream society treats as ugly, valueless, and degraded.[24]

Wright satirically deconstructed the societal white standards of beauty propagated by Hollywood and popular culture to expose Black inferiority, but he did not replace it with a different standard of beauty. Instead, writes Conrad Knickerbocker, he "join[ed] James Baldwin to testify that the worst burden the Negro must bear is not racial discrimination, but self-loathing."[25] As Ishmael Reed notes, "tricks define the lives of these characters. They spen[d] a lot of time tricking themselves, imagining that they [are] their favorite movie stars."[26] For Wright, the sin was not giving a performance or playing a game but selling "out to yourself," not "retain[ing] your] Blackness."[27] Unable to achieve their own individuality and humanity, these characters deprecate their Black selves and live "vicariously in the lives of celebrities."[28]

One character in *The Wig*, the Deb, is a sex worker who fantasizes that she is a Junior Leaguer from the society pages.[29] She defines herself as an all-American girl but hates her Black self and hopes for a pill that will "turn everyone white over night." The Deb wants money to get her kinky hair "fixed" and to "be[come] as white as Americans." Eventually, she follows a rich woman to Europe where, just like in the movies, she role-plays as a personal maid. Her vision is to "ride the high seas in full regalia."[30] What really happens is that she is taken up by café society and is constantly high on drugs.

The outcast characters in *The Messenger* have full, large lives within their marginal urban Black culture. In contrast, the outcast characters in *The Wig* believe that being Black is a sin in America. Rejecting their race and their individuality, they repress and subordinate their historical experiences, their full lives, their complex subjectivity, their interiority. They succumb to and define themselves by external forces and images. This denial and self-hatred reinforces white supremacy and devalues Black subjectivity, but it also takes the excitement and drama out of being Black.

Lester, too, wants to join mainstream American society. He traffics in the Horatio Alger myth of working his way up the ladder of success, insisting that he is an American. As Schulz notes, he does not feel like a "fully defined" person.[31] When the novel opens, Lester is twenty-one years old and wants desperately to join the Great Society. But "it was hard to maintain a smile," wanting "to make it."[32] His father, who had learned to read and write at thirty-six, had died when his son was ten years old, while trying to teach him those same skills. His mother had continued that work by candlelight, hoping to open a way for her son into mainstream society. But she, too, died, grieving for her husband. Lester then "vowed that I would learn to write and read, to become human in the name of my father."[33] He decides that his parents did not believe he had a future, but he, traumatized, is determined to prove them wrong.

In his desperate attempt to successfully make it in New York, Lester assumes and performs an "array of identities, all aimed at scoring, attaining the supreme American success of being a public celebrity, a media 'event.'"[34] He pathetically masquerades as a silent Arab waiter in an authentic North African coffeehouse in Greenwich Village. He is successful in tempting various dreamers of Gide, Ivy League derelicts, and hungry pseudo-virgins, until two old-maid sisters expose and unmask him. He tap-dances in front of the Empire State Building for a week but collects only $1.27. None of these jobs is a route to American success, but Lester keeps trying.

His main problem is his looks: like the Deb, he hates his kinky hair and his Negroid nose because he thinks they hold him back. As Albert Memmi points out in *The Colonizer and the Colonized*, "the rejection of self and love of another are common to all candidates for assimilation," which for African Americans began during slavery and has been passed down through generations.[35] So Lester thinks he has hit gold when he buys a bottle of Silky Smooth Hair Relaxer with Built-in Sweat-Proof Base: "with this," says the pharmacist, "you may become whatever you desire."[36] Lester believes the pharmacist, imagining that he could become a politician or a preacher. Therefore, he works to adapt to the standards of white society. He is already light-complected, and now he hopes his conked hair will allow him to pass, to assimilate; that it will confer upon him "the privileges of whiteness."[37] His new, fine, straight, reddish-brown hair will give him security, the sense that he is "reborn, purified, anointed, beautiful."[38] It will allow him to walk down the streets and shake his head triumphantly like any white boy.

"Charles Wright exploits the politics of hair in *The Wig*," writes Ishmael Reed.[39] But as Valeria Babb points out, this fantasy also "highlight[s] the stupidity of Lester's odyssey."[40] Along with changing his appearance, he hopes to make the "big Leap" into jobs, money, and gorgeous women. His ridiculous assumption is that "the Wig," his term for good hair as defined by white America, "will see him through these troubling times" and help him navigate "unorthodox channels, desperate situations, . . . and relationships."[41] In other words, he will succeed where his father failed because "the Wig wasn't just for kicks. It was rooted in something deeper, in the sorrow of the winter when [he] was ten."[42]

As he walks through the surreal streets of Harlem looking for work, Lester sings the hymn "Onward Christian Soldiers" and assures his neighbors, "My ship is just around the bend."[43] But the joke will be on him. Like many of the people around him, he gleans images, behavior, approval, and language from television and the movies. This is his source for how fathers should behave at breakfast, where he learns to imitate a Humphrey Bogart grin. He is a subject of media power.

At first Lester's acquisitional, satirical gimmick seems to work. The Wig's sneak preview is "magnificent," and Lester tells himself that he is no longer afraid: "At last, I have a dog's sense of security." Others reinforce this perception. The Deb, for instance, tells him he has pretty hair. Miss Sandra Hanover likes his beautiful curls. But Nonnie recognizes that his hair has been "konked," and this makes him angry. Lester's response is defensive: "How could a New Orleans tramp appreciate The Wig? That's the way people are. Always trying to block the road to progress. But let me tell you something: no one, absolutely no one—nothing—is gonna stop this boy. I've taken the first step. All the other steps will fall easily into place."[44]

Lester continues to believe that the Wig is his omen, his guide for entrance into the white world. Yet his employment ventures remain unsuccessful. Therefore, he joins forces with Little Jimmy Wishborn, a Hollywood has-been who once had a lot of money and made white people happy but is now broke and forgotten. Little Jimmy is America's "Dark Mickey Rooney." According to him, he was thrown out of Hollywood, sent into exile, just as he was about to receive an Academy Award. Now he basks in the "glow of the past," reminiscing about his twenty Cadillacs and his film career.

The two plan a big-time moneymaking deal as they walk comically together through the streets of Harlem. They feel a part of this world. Though Little Jimmy has some jitters, Lester asserts himself as a law-and-order American, cheering on the police, praising the system, and denying racial injustice. He declares, "The policemen were our protectors, knights of the Manhattan world. I wasn't afraid. I was goddam grateful."[45] He manages to keep himself totally ignorant of the historically troubled relationship between the Black community and the police.

Experiencing the power and glory of the Wig, Lester decides to apply for a porter's job in a bank and dreams of working his way up. But he is told he needs to fill out an application and take a six-week course in the "art of being human, in the art of being white." Instead, Lester and Jimmy visit the Duke, a frustrated musician and a drug pusher with a collection of expensive antiques. He shares marijuana and music, and Lester surmises, "Getting high is gonna see me through this world." In this bebop moment he realizes you "got to have something freakish about your personality or else the kids won't dig you. We gotta provide fantasy for their wet dreams."[46] With this visit to the Duke, Lester thinks he is now equipped.

During a cab ride, Lester and Jimmy dream of a smash career in soul music, and their white cabby encourages them, claiming that Blacks are the best singers and dancers. The two hope to be reborn as a successful singing duo. En route to a tryout at Paradise Records, Lester imagines a future where the Deb, the "all-American girl," is "spoon-feeding Lester Jefferson II—Little Les, while twenty floors below, [he] polishe[s] the Mercedes with Mr. Clean."[47] But at the record company, they bomb. "A white record producer flips over their bewigged image, [and] neither one can carry a tune," thus debunking the racist stereotype that all Blacks can sing.[48] They are thrown out of the studio, a disgrace to America and their Black brethren.

Lester does not give up. "One is not defeated until one is defeated," he says, remembering the druggist's comment about becoming whatever you desire. Regardless, he slides lower, taking a series of increasingly menial jobs, as "a porter, a bus boy, a shoeshine boy, a swing on [his] father's old Pullman run."[49] But these failures do not deter "Walter Mitty's target-colored stepson" in his pursuit of the American Dream. After the singing debacle, a farcical new image crystallizes in his mind, "an aristocratic image. . . . The image was based on The Wig, and was to be implemented by the forethought of Mr. Fishback," who is a prime mover of people, a Black magician.[50]

Lester steals Mr. Fishback's forged credit card and goes on a wild spending spree. Smoking marijuana and feeling powerful, he believes he is now "truly together," able to live like a rich American. He thinks of the Deb, who makes him feel warm, alive, and ambitious, and decides he wants to see her again. The two spend the night together, but the next morning, after she angrily walks out, Lester begins to have doubts. "I had such a celestial picture of being someone else, and part of the picture was that my luck would change. But had [it]? No, life still seemed to have me by the balls, stuffing poison enemas up my ass."[51] But he counters this brief revelation with "Oh, well, tomorrow's Monday" and does not return to reality. He still feels "the glow of The Wig."[52]

His glow is immediately undermined in the next scene. After the Deb tells Lester she is "cutting" him because he does not have any money, Lester hears Nonnie, like the first trumpet of morning, screaming from next door. She is calling him to kill a rat. The text exaggeratingly and humorously prepares Lester for combat: "Bare-chested, barefooted, I was sort of an urban Tarzan, a knight without charger. . . . I followed, hot with excitement, clutching my spear gun, ready for the kill. One hundred rat skins would make a fine fur coat for The Deb." It is a "magnificent rat, premium blue-gray, and at least twenty-five inches long," and Nonnie encourages him to call it Rasputin, the name of a Russian mystic and self-proclaimed holy man. Giving the V-for-victory sign, "I smiled sweetly and clamped my hands so hard around Rasputin's throat that his yellow-green eyes popped out and rolled across the parquet like dice."[53]

After Lester kills the rat, Wright presents an exchange between Lester and Nonnie that further underscores the thrust of his satire about Lester's ignorance about race and racism. "You killed the white bastard with your hands," Nonnie exclaims, making the rat a symbol for white America. Lester, who does not understand Nonnie's symbolic language, responds,

"Yeah. He's a dead *gray* son of bitch." But Nonnie insists, "He's a dead *white* son of a bitch. . . . White folks call you people coons, but never rats, 'cause that's *them*."[54] Lester, who is blind to the racism that will prevent him from succeeding, responds, "I didn't know that." As Robert P. Sedlack writes, in ridiculing "Lester's encounter with the rat and his pursuit of The Deb by overstatement," Wright achieves his "ultimate purpose—to reveal the futility of a Black man's attempt to succeed in the white world, a world that is defined as exclusively materialistic and personified by The Deb, who, though Black, reflects the white American world's standards [with] her motto, 'No finance, no romance.'"[55]

Yet Lester knows that he is in love with the Deb, even though she has rejected him. He has the blues; he is frustrated and confused, an average young man living in a terrible age, cuffed by ambition. On Monday morning, he begins desperately looking for a job, imagining that he and the Deb could have a ball together. After studying the available options in the *New York Times Directory of Employment Agencies*, he decides to become a chicken man. Now he crawls "through the streets of Harlem on [his] hands and knees, wearing a snow-white, full-feathered chicken costume," calling out "Cock-a-doodle-doo. Cock-a-doodle-do! Eat me. Eat me. All over town. Eat me at the King of Southern Fried Chicken." [56] The scene is an illuminating demonstration of the absurdity of subscribing to the narrative of the American Dream.

When Lester learns that the Deb is going to Europe, he is devastated. The news feels like a bullet, the death of a bright dream, and he puts the blame on his impersonations. To survive and move forward, he decides to visit Madam X to learn how to kick the love habit. Madam X is another of Wright's imaginative, fantastical inventions. Steeped in magical Black culture, she is a dark woman of undefinable age with a gentle "clown's mask of a face." When Lester tells her that love is driving him crazy, she informs him that love is a ridiculous, bourgeois sin, something the devil "invented to make mankind *nervous*." She tells him that "the only passion that's worth suffering for is a passion for hard, cold cash." Madam X advises Lester to get rid of the Wig and become more authentic, for his hair is a form of vanity, putting him on "the road to self destruction." She encourages him that "all is not lost. . . . You may find the way, despite The Wig."[57] But Lester "rejects her offer of ritual, marijuana, and money as the realities" that will "replace the American Dream."[58]

Even though he is now a celebrity as a chicken, Lester acknowledges that no one knows who he is. The job does not bring him fame and fortune or make him happy or successful. "Impersonating a chicken, cackling, I was alone. I'd go on living by myself in my small airless room. I'd continue to be a trapped person, and if I ever got to heaven, I'd ask God one question: 'why?'" He wallows in self-pity and self-awareness—"All I wanted was to be happy. I didn't know to want to be happy was a crime, a *sin*." Then he receives a letter from Mr. Fishback, who tells him that the Deb is dead, killed by a school bus.[59] Lester goes numb; now he realizes that his pursuit of the Deb and the American dream has been futile. What was once eye-catching and outrageously funny has become desperately sad.

Again, Lester walks the chaotic and absurd streets of Harlem, where he encounters a group of Black Muslims standing in front of the Theresa Hotel. They offer to take him to Georgia in their armored tank, but he would prefer to go to Biarritz or Cuernavaca. He meets a young man with a French poodle and realizes that he does not need poodle curls; he has been his own Samson, with Silky Smooth hair. In a bizarre encounter, he watches a mother kill her son because the child does not want to go to a segregated school. Frantic, he tries to get into the Black Disaster Diner, but the white owner throws him out. Near Central Park, he encounters four Puerto Ricans pretending to be Brazilians. They are the inheritors of the social place vacated by Blacks.

Calmer now, Lester continues to walk the strange streets of Harlem. He is lonely; he wants human connection; he wants to talk to someone. A middle-aged woman, who is not accustomed to beauty, catches sight of his hair and shuts her eyes tight. He meets an elderly white couple who are befuddled by the changes around them. He encounters a fat Negro with a shopping bag of Silky Smooth. But Lester keeps going. Nothing can stop him. He is a celebrated chicken; and though he has been targeted, he feels he is taking a step in some direction and that the Wig has been his guide. Lester has progressed to the front door of hell, though all he has been striving for is a quiet purgatory. "[He] did not find it strange that hell had a soft blue sky, a springlike air, music, dust, laughter, curses."[60] But what he really wants is a friendly face. As Steven Weisenburger writes, "his transition from aspirant to dupe is nearly completed."[61]

In the final scene, Mr. Fishback, who has the authority to decide whether Lester's pursuit of happiness is an unalienable right or a crime and a sin, takes full control of Lester's life. Like Madam X, he teaches Lester "the capitalist gospel while combining business with pleasure."[62] The ending for these impersonators—Nonnie, the Deb, Mrs. Turner, and Lester—is tragic. As Eberhard Kreutzer explains, Lester "will not admit the contradictions of his behavior, and finally give[s] up in utter resignation to the dehumanizing forces around him."[63] Unlike Stevenson in *The Messenger*, who knows that the sin is in believing and who is therefore able to find hope in taking responsibility for himself outside society's laws and institutions, Lester doggedly remains in sin, believing in the Great Society and the American Dream. He has failed to learn that the American white norm is produced around the positioning of the Black as devalued other. He can never be assimilated into normative, white American society. Albert Memmi reminds us, "It is the colonized who is the first to desire assimilation, and it is the colonizer who refuses it to him."[64] After the death of the Deb, the one person he had hoped to be with in the Great Society, Lester allows Mr. Fishback to castrate him and thus prevent him from bringing children into this absurd world.

All of Lester's dreams and schemes to achieve the American Dream turn out to be parables of frustration. Despite his desires to join the Great Society, Lester encounters failure after failure. As Schulz writes, "by limiting himself to their bureaucratic order, he hopes to impose a rationale upon his existence. Instead, he finds himself paralyzingly isolated, bereft of individuality, a faceless integer who counts simply as a population statistic." His identity has become a composite of his impersonations, yet for most of the novel he never loses hope or gullibility. Its poignancy lies in this dogged optimism, and its tragedy is his final disgust at his own failure. His story, according to Schulz, is "a comic rendering of the Black American's disenfranchisement from the human race."[65]

Though Lester encounters Black music and Black magical culture, they do not offer him an alternative to the bureaucratic order of the Great Society. For example, on his way to visit the Deb, he recognizes the sound of the blues coming out of a bar and grill. But he does not engage with it. In another scene he stops briefly to listen to a jukebox grinding out Jimmy Witherspoon's "C. C. Rider" and then moves on. In still another he encounters a group of young people playing a song by the jazz musician Charlie Mingus but does not stop because the sound of Mingus always saps his energy. Even when he walks down the streets of Harlem whistling

Billie Holiday's "Them Their Eyes," the song does not seem to touch him. At some level he knows the blues are the real thing:

> Folks, these are the blues. From way down home. In the southland of Brooklyn. They tell a story of sweat falling from people sitting on stoops on hot summer nights. Too hot for them in bed. They ain't got no money. Got nothing but the pain of fighting a lost cause. So what can they do? They sing, yes, they sing the blues.[66]

But he does not call on the blues to save and protect him, to help him make sense of absurdity.

Frances S. Foster argues that Wright "presents his characters as harmless humorous examples of modern man's loss of individuality in an attempt to fit into life as they have been conditioned to see it. . . . No one is trying to comprehend or to assert his own individuality."[67] As a consequence, they are crushed by society. The world of *The Wig* has no positive values, not because humans have thrown them away but because they have reached a time in history when they can no longer delude themselves. The novel shows the poststructural/postmodern tendency to deconstruct but lacks the modernist features of correction. None of Lester's dreams have ameliorated the pain, suffering, and misery of human existence; he and the other Black characters must accept reality as absurd and move forward. Yet they cannot endure this reality without dreams. They go on living because they dream or play roles, however short-lived. But this means none of them can grasp reality; none can live the myth and simultaneously deconstruct the myth.

Wright's biting satire reprimands the dominant American society for propagating a dream that Blacks cannot achieve, for spreading stereotypes of African Americans, for devaluing and excluding them. As Joe Weixlmann notes, "Buying the promises of America . . . is too expensive for the Black male. To do so, he must sacrifice his identity and, ultimately, his manhood—and both in vain."[68] Yet *The Wig* also castigates Blacks for wanting to reject themselves and become white. This was a truth that many upwardly mobile, middle-class Blacks did not want to hear in the 1960s and still do not want to hear today.

According to A. Robert Lee, "In lambasting America's entrepreneurial myths and their debasement of human life, Wright join[ed] older company, like Melville, Twain, and Nathanael West, in decrying a major betrayal in America's promise to its people."[69] In other words, he became one of a host of American writers who have written about America's betrayal. None-theless, most mainstream white and Black critics ignored *The Wig* on its publication. Perhaps they were unsettled by its dark, uncorrective ending. Perhaps they were disturbed because the text did not contribute to their idea of knowledge and therefore reproduce expected values, conventions, and perspectives. Certainly, in some cases the satire backfired. The ironic text—which was intended to allow the reader to laugh at absurdity and get through its pain—was misinterpreted as a blisteringly honest account worthy of cultural exaltation. This, too, alienated reviewers.

For example, the mainstream Black literary newspapers and journals were not kind to *The Wig*. "No one in the publishing industry," wrote an edi-tor at the African American *New York Amsterdam News*, "want[s] to repre-sent this type of book by a Black writer during the height of the Civil Rights Movement."[70] Likewise, the African American critic Loyle Hairston wrote, "*The Wig* does not in my opinion deserve a review at all, despite Charles Wright's undoubted talents. It is a flimsy exercise in literary masturbation, juvenile in concept and execution."[71] Even Black queer scholars and review-ers ignored *The Wig*, despite the prominent presence of queer characters.

Wright was in a quandary: he had wanted to tell the "story of his out-rage and bitterness toward white society," to share this tale of capitalism and racism, yet he also wanted his novel to reach people.[72] He was baffled as to why Blacks did not understand his purpose. In a conversation with Clarence Major, he recalled his confusion:

Can you imagine me being against Black people—now that just shows you [how] Black readers [are] being influenced by the white press and I'm not at odds against Black society—how could I possible *be*, being Black myself and having gone through these experiences? No, I'm not at odds against Black society except in one sense that I do hope that somehow that we would get some strong Black leaders who are not so easy to [be controlled by] the white man.

Wright was interested in Black leaders who were "not concerned with becoming public personality—because once you become a public person-ality, you become involved in all—with the media, with the money and all the sideshow business," and these entities defined and controlled you.[73] He was interested in Black leaders who were not invested in the mainstream ideological state apparatus and who would educate and speak truth to Black people. But somehow *The Wig* had not reached these people.

Mainstream literary reviewers, who represented a powerful form of gatekeeping for the literary field and who belonged to and advocated some of the values and definitions of the ideological state apparatus, also violently rejected the novel. In their view, Wright had failed to "write for [a] set of expectations and readers."[74] Referring to *The Wig* as "Wright's ugly second novel," Victor S. Navasky of the *New York Times Book Review* said, "Mr. Wright has lots of talent but little compassion. White folks won't find much to celebrate here."[75] In *Commonweal*, William James Smith wrote, "*The Wig* . . . very nearly goes overboard with its humor. . . . Unfortunately, the novel is not successful as a whole."[76] A *Kirkus* reviewer summarized the plot, concluding, "Very funny and tremendously effective once or twice, but the rest is chaos."[77] A number of influential periodicals, including *Publishers Weekly*, "refused to review the novel."[78] Most book clubs did not want to touch it. Editors at the Literary Guild of America read the galley proofs and decided that "this deliberately outrageous satire just isn't for book club use."[79] The Queensborough Public Library refused to order a copy, claiming that *The Wig* did not measure up to *The Messenger*.[80] In short, the novel did not reproduce a mainstream definition of Black literature, so critics rejected it. Later, Langston Hughes told Wright, "White folks don't want to know [what] any Black person feels and thinks intensely enough to write a book like *The Wig*."[81]

As a result of such pans, *The Wig* did not sell well. Farrar, Straus's big ad in the *New York Times* generated few American readers and moved no books.[82] But some members of the political and cultural left as well as some foreign reviewers were more open to the novel. A critic for the *Nation* wrote a complex review:

> *The Wig* is a book that needs to be deciphered before it can be read. On the surface it is an awkward little book: the imagery is piled, the comic dilemmas are rigged, the jokes are heavy; there is too much nervous kidding, there is no poetry in the slang. . . . But underneath, in the allegory, we find a complicated piece of orchestration: to be free you have to succeed, to succeed you need masquerade, but masquerade means the sellout, and the sellout means you can never be free.[83]

A review in the London-based *Books and Bookmen* was also positive: "Lester's career takes him through a series of picaresque episodes peopled with comic, strange and satirical characters. First person narration allows for a vigorous, slangy prose and many of these collisions are brilliantly funny. . . . Maybe *The Wig* is slight, a comic raspberry, but within its limits it works."[84] Conrad Knickerbocker, whom Wright had long respected, wrote in the *New York Times* that *The Wig* was "a brutal, exciting, and necessary book": "Mr. Wright's style [is] as . . . mean and vicious a weapon as a rusty hacksaw, [and] is the perfect vehicle for his zany pessimism. . . . His jibes confirm the wounds no Great Society will ever salve, and his laughter has no healing powers."[85] Importantly, James Baldwin praised the novel as "daring and honest."[86]

The overseas literary market responded positively to *The Wig*. In early 1966 Wright moved to a new literary agency, Russell and Volkening, which now controlled his translation rights and promoted *The Wig* internationally. The German publisher Schlack Verlag wanted to include translations of excerpts from *The Wig* in an anthology of love stories by African, West Indian, and African American writers. The British publisher André Deutsch expressed an interest in purchasing British rights, but in the end Farrar, Straus sold them to Souvenir Press. Herbert R. Lottman, who worked for Farrar, Straus in France, expressed an interest in the French rights, but the option went to Stock.[87] There was a huge discrepancy between mainstream Black and white reception of *The Wig* as well as between foreign and left-leaning reviews

Farrar, Straus reminded potential reprint publishers that Wright's first novel had been considered better than Baldwin's work, and its marketing materials for *The Wig* emphasized the novel's focus on "the Negro who wants to share in the American Dream. In Wright's hands this much discussed problem of the Negro's struggle to participate in the Great Society becomes a novel of black humor, disturbing in its brutality and bitter satire."[88] They sent this packet to publishers, book clubs, awarding agencies, and literary outlets such as Readers' Subscription, Fawcett World Library, and Book Week, inviting them to bid on the paperback rights. In December 1965 Fawcett responded, calling Wright a "marvelously talented writer" but declining to reprint *The Wig*. Eventually, however, it did bring out a paperback copy.

As Foster explains, "like other Black Humorists," Wright was "isolated from the American literary mainstream by his constant concern [for] . . . new perspectives on all aspects of reality." Because of his race and his subject matter, he was "isolated from even the Black Humor tributary of American literature, . . . [though his work] shares the same slightly-raised eyebrow

attitude . . . [of] the other authors included in that casually coined term."
Nonetheless, even by "being a Black Humorist, he represent[ed] a deviation
from what is considered the usual course of the Black writer."[89] Therefore,
because it was marginal to these two dominant American literary traditions
as well as to expected Black literary traditions, The Wig was rarely judged,
assessed, and critically evaluated according to its own unique merits.

Still, Wright thought The Wig was his best literary effort, and he and his
team at Farrar, Straus had "anticipated that the book would be greeted by
raves when it appeared in February of 1966." In a letter to Vursell, Wright
predicted that The Wig "will do twice as well as Messenger. I will become
a millionaire."[90] Sadly, they were mistaken. The hardcover edition did not
sell well.[91] Ballantine printed 7,500 paperback copies and sold only 5,085,
half the number that were sold of The Messenger.[92]

Vursell soon had to tell Wright, "The Wig [i]s not going to be a financial success."[93] He tried to be practical, suggesting that Wright should find
another job while working on his next book, but he also made it clear that
he understood how devastating this news would be:

> I know this has been a long, nasty period for you, and the end is not in
> sight. I am convinced that the only good life for a writer is a quiet life
> and a working life. Helling around gives you a great sense of jazz and
> excitement, but it doesn't truly translate onto paper as good writing.
> If you have learned by the last three years what *not* to do, what kind
> of people to *avoid*, your writing will benefit. If you go on knocking
> yourself about as you did do, you will never make it. I trouble to speak
> to you frankly because I have affection for you and because you have
> talent.[94]

Nonetheless, after having so much hope and expectation for The Wig,
Wright went into a deep depression, which included a prolonged binge
of drinking. His spirit was depleted by the experience. "I was destroyed
by The Wig," he later said. He felt he had to get away from New York City,
"either that or crack-up or else commit some violence. There were several disappointments for me there from which I still haven't recovered.
The Wig was one of them. That's my retarded child. I had to get away."[95]
He felt a "terrible rage within [himself]," thinking that the book had been
"deliberately not reviewed."[96]

For solace he turned to Langston Hughes, who had become something
of a mentor to him.[97] In a letter to Hughes, written more than eight months

after the publication of *The Wig*, Wright admitted, "This has been a very bad year for me—mentally and physically. Nothing happened to *The Wig*. It was not even reviewed." He told Hughes that he was "looking for a job":

> I don't really care but would like a job that pays fairly good. It seems to me that with my books, two very different books that I have displayed more than the average writer's talent, enough to get a fellowship. Is it true that one has to move in certain, fashionable literary circles to get one? I know a few famous writers slightly, although I don't move in their circles."[98]

He told Hughes he needed money and inquired about publishing his short story "A New Day," in Hughes's forthcoming anthology, *The Best Short Stories by Negro Writers*.

Hughes reminded Wright that "*The Wig* was *so* reviewed someplace, because I have the *New York Times* review of March 5 (which I thought quite good one)." He invited Wright up to Harlem for drinks around the holidays, said he wanted to hear about Morocco, and promised to write a letter of recommendation for a fellowship. He also enclosed a personal check for the right to reprint Wright's story in his anthology.[99] Later the two met at the Old Dover Tavern in the Bowery, and Hughes gave Wright some fatherly advice. "If what you want is for [readers and critics] to love you again, just write another nice little book like *The Messenger*."[100]

But that was not advice Wright wanted to hear. The critical response to *The Wig* sent him into a downward spiral. Since childhood, he had craved love and empowerment, and now he had again failed to receive them. To make matters worse, he had applied for several fellowships, which would have allowed him to write full time, but had not received any of them. A friend, Michael di Capua, had requested an application for Wright from the National Foundation on the Arts and Humanities, even sending them his two novels, but to no avail.[101]

Frustrated and angry, Wright vented and began to compare himself to other contemporary Black writers. He saw himself as the most talented and promising; what more would it take to win a fellowship? He considered William Melvin Kelley, "a good but ordinary writer" who was able to win fellowships, and decided that his "typing, spelling, [and] punctuation must be superb."[102] He wondered why John A. Williams had won an award from the "Academy of Arts for his first novel, *Night Song*. Was it because [Williams] was dull, and . . . *Night Song* was a respectable little book and they felt they should give an award to some Negro writer, and he was the only one around"?[103]

Fed up with New York, Wright went back on the road, traveling to Paris and Tangier and eventually moving back to Veracruz. He continued to drink heavily, but he also consciously decided that he would now write things people would like. Therefore, by July 1966, he was working on a new book, "a childhood fictional memoir." In a letter to Rupert Croft-Cooke, he said, "My childhood memoir is coming along fine but slow. I should get a reaction from my agent and publisher next week."[104] He sent a batch of the memoir to Vursell as well as a section of a new novel, asking for an advance, but Vursell again advised Wright to get a job. In a letter to Candida Donadio, Vursell fretted:

> His life at present is made up of worry, drink and god knows what else. He would write better if he has less time to dissipate and to think about himself. He would not be the only author who cannot live by his pen alone. . . . If he were to do something like that, I would be willing to supplement his income with option money, so much per page as he turned it in, as we did when *The Messenger* was being written. Then when we had, say, 250 pages of manuscript, we would know whether we had something we could make a book out of or not.[105]

But this novel-in-progress was never finished, and Wright returned to New York, where he took up his old job as a messenger at Rockefeller Center and stopped writing for a while.

In 1967, about a year after moving back to New York City, Mary Jacobs ran into Wright at Florence Roess's penthouse apartment: "I was delighted and surprised [to see him] and he looked terribly weathered. Maybe it was *The Wig*; he was having trouble at that point. . . . [H]e was burning his candle really heavily somehow with probably speed and booze. I don't know which was worst." It was also at Roess's apartment that Jacobs met Charles Robb for the first time. Robb would later follow her to Maine, for he was "enchanted" by the type of work Jacobs did[106]

Eventually, however, Wright began to write again. Partly this was because his spirits had lifted. When his story "A New Day," came out in Hughes's anthology, readers and the literary establishment were pleased and relieved. The story is a racial uplift tale about successfully achieving the American Dream. Yet though it lacks the satire, irony, and absurdity of *The Wig*, it still emphasizes the price a Black man must pay for denying the self and pursuing mainstream success. The protagonist, Lee Mosely, is a twenty-five-year-old Black man who wants to advance in America but is having problems finding the appropriate job. He has been working as a shipping clerk at French American Hats, but the once-promising job is not taking him anywhere. As the story opens, Lee is preparing for an interview for a new job. His family supports him; "It's honest work, ain't it?," says his mother.[107] This new job has been arranged by Lee's Aunt Ella, who lives in South Carolina; and Lee would be working in New York City for Maude T. Davies, a rich southern white woman who has employed members of the family for a long time.

Lee is told it will be an easy job. He will wear a uniform and "mouth a grave Yes mam and No mam" to Mrs. Davies. But, Lee thinks, to this point "he had never said one word to a Southern white woman in his life, had never expected to either."[108] Mrs. Davies has taken a suite in a hotel on Central Park South for the spring, and he will be responsible for driving her and her dog Muffie around Central Park and fetching her meals from room service. He will receive a salary of $150 a week, and on his days off he can borrow the custom-built Packard.

During a drive around Central Park, Lee attempts small talk with Mrs. Davies, but she curtly asserts her superiority and shuts him down, clearly erasing him and delineating their racial differences. When the two return to the hotel, Lee waits anxiously for room service. It will be his responsibility to receive the food, prepare it and serve it to Mrs. Davies, and then eat his own meal in the serving pantry.

Mrs. Davies wants to eat her lunch near the window in her living room. After Lee serves her, he retreats to the pantry and begins to eat his lunch. As he launches into his fried chicken, mashed potatoes, gravy, and tossed salad, he thanks God for the meal. Then he hears Mrs. Davies scream, "Nigger!" In disbelief, he continues to eat, suppressing his rage and frustration. But the history of that word and all it represents affect him. He feels "the pain of digesting, but the quicksand sense of rage and frustration, and something else, a nameless something that had always started ruefully at the top of his skull like a windmill."[109]

Before he can regain his composure, Mrs. Davies screams, "Nigger boy!" The words enter "the pantry door like a human being." Lee feels his blood "congeal, freeze, although his anger, hot and dry came bubbling to [the] surface." What should he do? Should he cry? When Mrs. Davies screams,

"Nigger!," again, Lee realizes "that some evil, white trick ha[s] come at last to castrate him." His stomach and bowels grumble in protest but he stays where he is, finishing his meal. Then, after drinking a beer and lighting a cigarette, he walks into the living room and calmly asks Mrs. Davies, "Did you call me?" She warmly smiles and says, "Lee, you and I are going to get along very well together. I like people who think before they answer."[110] Nothing seems to change: by recognizing and accepting his place in the racial order, Lee keeps his job and Mrs. Davies maintains her white supremacy.

As Wright was well aware, "A New Day," unlike The Wig, fit into the mainstream literary convention of Black victimization, social protest, and racial uplift. It was the kind of story that mainstream Black and white critics and reviewers expected and relished. But it also showed the violence and the degradation that the Black subject had to endure to get and keep a job. In many ways, Lee was like the characters in The Wig. He, too, had to deny his individuality and take on a dehumanizing role, denying his own history and his distinct subjectivity.

During this time, Ishmael Reed, Steve Cannon, and Cecil Brown of Umbra visited Wright at his studio apartment in the Albert Hotel. According to Reed, Knickerbocker's review of The Wig had pushed him to consider this move. In his view, Wright was doing crucial work, breaking "Black writers out of the aesthetic prison that critics had placed around them." There was something about his style—his satire and black humor— that Reed and his colleagues found attractive. In his introduction to the 2003 reissue of The Wig, Reed said that novel was "fresh, something that broke the model of the monotonous predictable conventional novel":

> [It is] comic in a sardonic manner, absurd, surrealist, campy, hip, Jazzy. . . . Charles Wright's novel marked a change in African American fiction; it had neither the lofty and Biblical heft of James Baldwin's works, nor the opaque elusiveness and obeisance to New York Intellectual fashion found in Ellison's Invisible Man. . . . It was Richard Pryor before there was a Richard Pryor. Richard Pryor on paper. All of us who wanted to "experiment," as we were seeing our painters and musician friends experiment, used it as a model.[111]

Upcoming writers such as Reed and later Clarence Major began to see themselves as younger brothers of Charles Wright, and Wright was elated and validated. According to Cannon, he was exuberant during Umbra's visit to the Albert Hotel, and he was excited to talk about his writing. At this period, he was spending time with other intellectuals in the Village who were also interested in existentialism and the absurd.[112] But though his New York social life was busier than it had been, Wright remained essentially aloof from Reed and others, though Reed was one of his major supporters. The one writer he was drawn to was James Baldwin, and Cannon recalls that he was enthusiastic about Baldwin's novel *Another Country* (1962).[113] Later, the two did become friends. When Baldwin would visit New York City, they would hang out at McCaul's Bar, where Baldwin's brother David worked as a bartender.[114]

In *The Wig* Wright experimented with style and form, incorporated Black language and music, relayed a marginal satirical American tradition, and spoke to a contemporary moment that most mainstream white and Black Americans did not fully understand. Yet though he was ahead of his time, Wright's work was in "keeping with novels reflecting the growing [Black] anger."[115] As Phelonise Willie wrote in *Vice Versa*, "eventually, the critics who destroyed *The Wig* begrudgingly conceded that, at the very least, Charles Wright had become the undisputed father of Black satire."[116] Wright himself told Vursell, "All your [Lyndon] Johnsons and [Martin Luther] Kings are trying (perhaps sincerely) to do something. But first they should read *The Wig*. I told it like it is. Things are not getting better. It is only after we realize this fact that we can attempt to do something about the problem."[117]

As the dominant American literary establishment expanded and the social, political, and literary movements of the 1960s constructed a more inclusive definition of literary taste, *The Wig* entered a different constellation, one in which it was reinterpreted and valued. Some American critics, both Black and white, began to acknowledge that within African American literature there was a "limited population" under some "limited set of conditions" who understood and identified with satire.[118] In 1971, Frances S. Foster's article "Charles Wright: Black Black Humorist" reassessed the literary and critical value of *The Wig*. Likewise, in 1973, the critic Jerome Klinkowitz admitted that "*The Wig* . . . in fictional form caught the truths of life in Lyndon Johnson's America which the historical record noticed only years later."[119] In *Black Humor Fiction of the Sixties*, Max F. Schulz devoted a chapter to the works of Jay Friedman and Charles Wright, discussing Wright as an innovative black humorist. In his introduction to the

2003 paperback reissue of *The Wig*, Ishmael Reed called it "one of the most underrated novels written by a Black person in this century" and credited the book with influencing his prose technique.

In 1966 Ballantine Books reprinted the novel, paying Farrar, Straus $3,500 and offering a 10 percent American royalty and a 6 percent Canadian royalty.[120] In 1973 Manor Books released paperback editions of *The Messenger* and *The Wig*.[121] It paid Farrar, Straus $2,000 for reprint rights to *The Wig* but ended the agreement in 1975. In 1977, Klinkowitz applied for a grant to the National Endowment for the Humanities, proposing to use awarded funds to include *The Wig* in a series reprint of Classics of Contemporary Fiction.[122] In 2003, Mercury House reprinted *The Wig* as part of its new National Endowment for the Arts Heritage and Preservation Series: "We hope to revive this electric novel these many years after its initial publication."[123] The novel remained in print until Mercury House went out of business. But by the time Wright received these accolades, "fate had changed its course."[124] The mental and physical damage had already been done.

In 1968, Wright published the short story "Sonny and the Sailor" in *Negro Digest*. Set in New Franklin, Missouri, it introduces a character named Stonewall Jackson Fourquet, who disrupts the close-knit, homogeneous community where young Sonny lives. Stonewall is a sailor, returning home from Hamburg, Germany, and bringing foreign music with him. Most of his family is now buried in Crown Hill Cemetery, but older people such as Sonny's grandparents remember him and the violin that had belonged to his father, who had played it at cakewalk dances. Since then, Stonewall has played this same violin in Paris, Marseille, and Spain. He has become a wanderer and a loner. "The sea is my wife and the violin my first born," he says.[125]

In New Franklin, Stonewall plays at the Hughes Chapel and around the county, sharing his "real foreign world with our foreign world of dreams." He boards at the widow Wilma Clark's house, and it is rumored that he is courting her, though she is seven years his senior. He becomes an integral part of the community, a sparkling change, as everybody takes a liking to him and his music: "Someone would say: 'Hey, Jackson, play us a little tune.' And he'd reply: 'What would you boys like to hear?'"[126] Sonny observes the sailor closely. He has discovered the works of Hemingway that summer, and now he, too, has "foreign world dreams."

Then his aunt Laura Jane Scudder returns to town with her naval bride-groom. Her husband Keith takes up company with Stonewall, and they meet every day in the "beer garden behind O'Connor's bar and restaurant," drinking "corn liquor until it [is] time for the young groom to stagger to his father-in-law's house." Laura Jane worries that her husband is becoming a drunk, and she asks Sonny to tell her father to talk to Stonewall. But by this time Stonewall is ready to move on. He explains that spending time with the navy man "made things stir in me again. All the love and money in the world couldn't make me stay in this town. The sea is my friend and what man would desert his best friend."[127] Sonny's imagination is fired by these words: he wants to pursue dreams, wander the world, seek adventure and freedom.

As Wright's works became more available in the press, a few college writing programs began inviting him to lecture or read. In October 1965, the Writers Workshop at Delaware State College in Dover, which had no budget, contacted Farrar, Straus about sponsoring an appearance with Wright, but he was still in Tangier.[128] The following fall, after he had returned to New York, the Literary Society of the State University of New York at Fredonia invited him to lecture, and he agreed. He wrote to Vursell, "Although I'm not college, I think I'm intelligent enough for an evening," and Vursell offered to look at his notes.[129] The author, editor, and teacher Charles Hoyt of Bennett College in New York invited Wright to present there several times. And there were different sorts of attention too: for instance, in 1970, the film directors Michael Mayer and Luis Arroyo flirted with purchasing the film rights of *The Messenger*.[130]

In 1969, Jay Martin and his colleagues at the University of California, Irvine, invited Wright to accept a faculty appointment in English and American studies "at the highest possible rank and step."[131] In a letter to James Jones, Martin requested information about Wright's "potential teaching ability, his personality, and his qualities as a writer of fiction and journalism."[132] Jones "heartily recommend[ed] Charles Wright . . . as a teacher of Modern American Literature and Creative Writing":

> I have not seen or corresponded with Mr. Wright for a long time, but I have read his novels and his journalism, and I am sure of his continuing devotion to writing. He has an understanding, sensitive and perceptive personality which should contribute greatly to his ability as a teacher. Despite what some might consider his lack of

formal education, I know that he made an intensive study of modern American literature at the Handy Colony while I was there, and that he did very well at it.[133]

Vursell, now a vice-president at Farrar, Straus also was contacted and wrote a letter of recommendation:

> These writings are the man himself. They come out of his direct experience, and they reveal both his strengths and his weaknesses. You know that his formal education has been minimal. You can tell from his writing that he is a gentle man, and one who looks at the world seeing not abstractions but people. He has less hatred for whites than any Black I know. This is not to say that he is not aware that he is Black, nor does it mean that he wishes he were white. . . . He is not a simple man, and he is capable of perceiving shades of gray. His life has not given him much security, and this fact has taken a certain toll on the organization of his personality.[134]

Despite these wonderful recommendations, the job did not materialize: either Wright did not accept the offer, or the appointment was never fully extended. Vursell followed up with an inquiry to Martin, asking for "a confidential word as to how, if at all, the matter of [Wright's] perhaps teaching on the West Coast is developing."[135] Martin did not respond, but Wright did eventually visit the Irvine campus, where he lectured and sat in on a writer's workshop.

Other institutions were also interested in Wright's work. In 1968 and again in 1971, Howard B. Gotlieb, chief of Special Collections at the Boston University Libraries, told Wright that the University very much wanted a Charles Stevenson Wright Collection in its research center: "Your work is admired here, and it is our feeling that the materials relating to your career, and to your life, should be carefully preserved."[136] Though Wright was ready to sell his papers to Boston University, Candida Donadio, who was his agent into the 1970s, blocked the transaction because she did not think he should sell them so soon. Wright also received a letter from James Vinson, the editor of *Contemporary Novelists of the English Language*, informing him that more than twenty eminent critics and novelists had suggested that Wright should be included in a list of the five hundred most important writers in English. Thus, throughout the late 1960s and early 1970s, he was known nationally and internationally as a prominent literary figure and was in demand.

During these years, Wright began a number of new writing projects. As was his practice, when he had written thirty or forty pages, he would send them to Vursell, not only hoping for an advance but also seeking some support for his writing. Still undisciplined and unconfident, he craved guidance and approval. At times this made Vursell angry. He would always tell Wright that he had talent, but he was frustrated that he would not put in the necessary time to develop his craft. In response to a question posed by Wright, asking if he had changed since May 1962, Harold Vursell wrote:

> You have not changed enough. In these four years you should have worked harder and learned your trade. You ought to be a first-rate professional by now. You ought to be a big boy, and I am not sure you are. Talent you've got, but you still need self-discipline and the ability to carry a piece of writing to publishable perfection without too great a reliance on the offices (good or bad) of an editor. Daddy won't be here always.[137]

In *Black Queer Freedom*, GerShun Avilez defines queer injury as the "multiple kinds of threat (microaggressions, intimidation, humiliation, displacements, detention, defamation, medical abuses and misgenderings) that racial and sexual minorities experience."[138] While most of the people around him simply defined Wright's actions and behavior as a part of his character, his situation was much more complicated. I am not sure Wright was fully aware of this contradictory conflict in his life. More importantly, no one was able to help him recognize, engage, and resolve the underlying tendencies. Perhaps he wanted to live out the conflicts in his life without resolution. By challenging logocentric thought, he revealed his many different selves.

CHAPTER SIX

Writing in the 1970s and the *Village Voice*

Since 1967, Charles Wright had been writing a column, "Wright's World," for the *Village Voice*. Therefore, by the early 1970s, when he had returned to New York from Veracruz without any prospect of publishing a new novel, he saw this work as "the only thing that has kept me going. Without it I don't know what would have happen to me."[1] He was disappointed by the 1960s. Neither the state apparatus nor the political and social systems had radically changed, and the plight of African Americans had changed only symbolically. In a 1978 interview with Clarence Major, he said:

> As we know now that there were very few gains made, and for all the organizations, Martin Luther King, Eldridge Cleaver and all those people—it was, I felt, the wrong approach because having lived in Mexico where if there's going to be a revolution, there's going to be a revolution—everything would be destroyed. Now that may not be a good thing, but it's going to change the system. . . . Look at the 70's now: what have we gained? Nothing really. Oh, sure there's a little, token bits and pieces.[2]

Wright was not alone in this opinion. "The civil rights movement achieved some major legal victories," argued the political theorist Nancy Fraser, "but what were won were *rights on paper*, which haven't translated into anything remotely close to social equality, . . . [including structural changes in] the criminal justice system, employment[, and] housing."[3] Neoliberalism delivered material gains to the rich and to the upper reaches of the professional-managerial classes but not to the masses of Americans and African Americans, and the assaults on labor rights and wretched working-class living conditions contributed to structural and institutional racism.

Still, Wright was not entirely disheartened:

I would certainly hope that with the younger generation of Blacks know that they could get something—power is what it is, and since we are Americans, and money—that is it. If we can get a good education and we are fairly savvy, and you get the money, you could control because that's what this country is based upon, and until blacks get that money and that power base, we are still going to be like the [1960s] and the 70's.

With education and power "there would be very interesting result[s], because you would begin to learn about power and what . . . Blacks could do in America. . . . [You] can do these things and still remain yourself. . . . You can retain all of your dignity, intelligence and your courage . . . [without] selling out or playing a game or giving a performance."[4] Wright had practiced this philosophy throughout his life, though it had cost him dearly.

One of the ways in which Wright, as a writer and an artist, chose to respond to racism and the unequal social and economic situation of American Blacks in the 1970s was to "observe" and "write," despite the fact that this made him "extremely depressed and sad and angry and bitter."[5] For "Wright's World," he produced journalistic pieces that were more overtly political and social than his fiction was. He addressed institutional racism and class oppression, the Newark riots, the Vietnam War, the death of Martin Luther King, Jr., poverty, welfare, police brutality, male homosexuality in the Bowery, the fugitive Angela Davis, sex workers in the Chinese Garden, and venereal disease. But he also wrote personal pieces about his grandparents and about the deaths of Lowney Handy and Langston Hughes. He had been the last friend to see Hughes alive, on the rainy night of May 21, 1967, before the poet checked into the hospital for a routine operation. After Hughes died the next day, Wright fell into depression.[6] He had lost yet another person who loved and supported him.

Between 1967 and 1971, Charles Wright wrote intermittently for the *Village Voice*, using his columns to help him understand what was happening to him and to America. He later told Major:

I was going through experiences that I never had gone through before that I knew existed, but that had never happened to me, . . . but they were happening, and I just decided to be very open about them, and in one sense, I suppose that when I was writing these columns for the *Voice*, it was to explain not only to the readers but to myself.[7]

He wrote as a witness to the collective trauma of the United States in the 1960s and 1970s, hoping that he and the reader could work through their experience of this trauma.

As early as 1967, Wright had begun to think of getting "an eventual book" out of these pieces.[8] Vursell encouraged him in this idea, recommending that he put together "a non-fiction book, a freewheeling, . . . honest, [and] completely frank treatment of whatever the hell comes to your mind. Roughly the kind of thing that you have been doing in the *Village Voice*."[9] The encounters in Mexico and at the *Village Voice* allowed Wright to continue to become and create and produce. Thus, both before and while he was in Veracruz he collected, amended, and revised some of the pieces from the *Voice* and imaginatively and creatively transformed them into a hybrid fiction/nonfiction book that he initially titled *Black Studies: A Journal*. The publicity department at Farrar, Straus strenuously objected to this title: "The salesman," Wright wryly stated, "thought that it would get put on the wrong bookshelves."[10] Therefore, he changed it first to *Black Rider* and then, at the suggestion of Vursell, to *Absolutely Nothing to Get Alarmed About*. Again, we have Wright taking objects and events from his personal life and creating new objects and new forms of perception.

Farrar, Straus signed a contract for the book, and on May 7, 1971, Wright received an advance of $400. During the production phase Lynn Goldberg, the press's director of publicity, wrote to Clarence Major, saying that "both Ishmael Reed and Joe Johnson have suggested that [she] send [him] a set of galleys of Charles Wright['s] new book." She hoped Major would share their enthusiasm and share something quotable about it. In any case, she "would very much like to know" what he thought of it.[11] Major read the galleys and wrote a glowing report:

> Charles Wright is one of the best. He has worked out a language and a landscape that is a kaleidoscope of mystery and simplicity, filled with miracles and puzzles. . . . *Absolutely Nothing to Get Alarmed About* is terrific! It is surreal, erotic, comic, satirical, alive! When I say he's a good writer I don't say that lightly; I always recommend him to my students.[12]

Reed, too, had praised the book: "Charles Wright is the aristocratic poet-in-residence of America's Seamy Side. The Bowery glistens from his

Royal Touch. He doesn't flay so much as haunts."[13] Kay Boyle, who had written a blurb for *The Messenger*, now wrote:

> Charles Wright has written a book that is unlike anyone else's, that no one but the most honest and fervent of men could have written. He has accomplished this by the simple act of thrusting the pen with which he writes courageously into his own heart. He has written with his own blood, in compassion, humor, and despair, a book about the human condition that takes its place among the most honest testimonials of our time.[14]

Farrar, Straus went to great lengths to promote *Absolutely*, and this included reaching out to other publishers. Thus, even before publication, Ian Dear of Angus and Robertson expressed an interest in reprint rights. Richard Huett, editor-in-chief of Dell Publishing, also inquired.[15] Roger Straus, who had become known as Europe's favorite American publisher, gave a copy of *Absolutely* to the English editor John Bright-Holmes: "[Wright is] an author for the long haul. . . . [He] is in his middle-ish thirties and is currently working on a new novel."[16] Review copies were sent to Yoshio Taketomi of Japan, Gunnar Dohl of Sweden, J. P. Cendros of Spain, Adelphi Edizioni in Italy, and Slovenska Literaras Agenture in Czechoslovakia. Advertisements for *Absolutely* ran in the *New York Times*, the *Village Voice*, the *Los Angeles Times*, the *Chicago Tribune*, and the *San Francisco Chronicle*. The book was even mentioned in the *New York Times*'s list of recommended summer reading.

In the fall of 1971, while *Absolutely* was in production, Wright suddenly decided to escape from New York and return to Veracruz, where he hoped to relax and write. He remained in Mexico through the early months of 1972 and continued to write for the *Village Voice*. During this visit, he also became involved with a woman named Ana Maria, whose father beat her and called the cops on Wright when he found the two together. The situation was messy because Wright was also involved with her younger sister.[17]

Why did this small tourist city on the Gulf of Mexico continue to attract Wright? Not even the locals tended to stay in Veracruz for long, yet he had returned three times. One of the reasons he gave was that the city, like Tangier, was cheap. It also had literary connections. Katherine Anne Porter, whom he greatly admired, had lived there. He liked Porter because he could relate to her offbeat style. Also, like Porter, he wanted glory. He had read and liked Graham Greene's novel *The Power and the*

Glory, which features a priest catching a boat to Veracruz. Wright was also a fan of Malcolm Lowry's novel *Under the Volcano*, which was set in Mexico. In a letter to Kay Boyle, he wrote of having recently reread Lowry: "[We] might not have been related, say—a year ago. But now, we are brothers."[18] Most importantly, however, Mexico, like Tangier, allowed Wright to live with fewer societal and sexual constraints.

Yet he remained connected to New York City, and it was still the subject of his writing. While Wright was in Veracruz, Andree Conrad of Farrar, Straus was shopping the first draft of his one-act play, *Something Black*, to Helen Murray Jones at the New York Shakespeare Festival, Robert MacBeth at New Lafayette Theatre, and Douglas Turner Ward at the Negro Ensemble Company. "It's a campy, sadistic play in high drag with low overtones," wrote Conrad, "and I think you could make it very ferocious on stage."[19] But the play was apparently never produced and, like many of his unpublished texts, has since disappeared from his oeuvre.

Absolutely was scheduled for publication on March 1, 1972, and a number of writers were willing to write favorable blurbs. In Mexico, Wright read responses from Kay Boyle, Anthony Burgess, Ishmael Reed, Clarence Major, John O. Killens, Steve Cannon, Al Young, and Ron Welburn. Though he was extremely grateful for this outpouring, he chose to use only Boyle, Burgess, Reed, Major, and Killens for marketing because he did not want the public to think he needed "all these people . . . to prop him up."[20] Farrar, Straus dispatched galleys to journals and book clubs such as *Ebony*, *Dues*, the *New York Post*, *Publishers Hall Syndicate*, and the *New York Times* and, at the suggestion of Reed, to major Black literary figures such as H. Pritchard, Larry Neal, Sarah Fabio, Hoyt Fuller, Wilmer Lucas, Mel Watkins, Carmen Moore, Claude Brown, and Quincy Troupe.[21] However, as with Wright's earlier books, mainstream journals and book clubs such as *Psychology Today*, Book-of-the-Month Club, and Quartet Books were not interested in *Absolutely* because of its subject matter.

Throughout 1972, Wright received installments adding up to another $200 advance against royalties. He was also earning $100 or $125 per piece from the *Village Voice*. The money was wired to the Banco Nacional de Mexico in Veracruz, where Wright could pick it up. Meanwhile, he was becoming a keen observer and an astute social critic of Mexican society. In a column for the *Voice*, he noted that in Mexico the "color of a man's skin is almost irrelevant," that the term "Black" was exclusively American. Puerto Ricans and Cubans, he observed, could also be as "dark as the midnight sky." It was the "laws of class," he wrote, that "separate[d] people" in Mexico. Even though the country was racially mixed, "only class remains and the small box with the automatic jack-in-the box lid where a nightmare clown resides, a cuckoo bird with a hyena's whine."[22] He worried about "materialistic desire," which had by now "caressed into the mainstream of life" and risked "turn[ing] Mexico into another second-rate America. Its rich and vital culture will be destroyed."[23]

By March 1, Wright was back in New York, waiting for the scheduled release of *Absolutely,* which was now delayed. He was not in good physical shape, and Vursell was worried that he was filling his "body and brain with all kinds of stimulants" in order to keep writing. Vursell begged Wright to "work for . . . conscious control of [his] writing talent." Instead, Wright returned to Veracruz in the fall of 1972, just as his short story "Act of Surrender" was appearing in volume 2 of Reed's *Yardbird Reader*. He wrote it, he told Straus, on "one rainy night in Veracruz when [he] was broke and had absolutely nothing else to do."[24] Notably, the characters are not portrayed racially but as complex human beings with everyday problems, and the woman is the active agent of change.

Set in Harlem on a rainy Saturday night, "The Act of Surrender" is a subtle, clever, and detailed narrative about a failed reunion between Sarah Green, a twenty-year-old nurse, and James De Moss II, the son of a doctor. The story unfolds as the music of Dinah Washington ("But That Was Long Ago") and Nancy Wilson ("Forget the Affair") plays in Sarah's head. Sarah and James had a high school romance in Birmingham, Alabama, and now they believe they will be reunited in Harlem. They are not, however, and the reasons for the separation and the failed reunion become clear as the night proceeds. James has spent the past two years in an emotional rut after his father's death by suicide and his mother's move to Chicago. Sarah, who has put her romantic life on hold for him, is visiting him for the first time in his one-room kitchenette in Harlem. They expect to rekindle their relationship, but over drinks Sarah becomes distracted. Instead of focusing on James, her mind is wandering off to her friends Ruth and Addie, who are waiting take her to Chinatown. Her mind is full of music, and in the middle of the conversation she bolts into the bathroom, where, in the mirror, she sees herself as a "Black female in limbo." She reflects on the men from her past. There was the West Indian lawyer in Birmingham with a "sense of humor, [who] was kind and worshipped her." There was the rich southern white guy who said he would marry her if that is what she wanted, although he told her he had already had all kinds of women. Yet she has not resolved her feelings for James. She has had difficulty letting go of him, this sad man who has "drifted to New York" and "apparently floundered. . . . The tragedy of a Black family splattered against the wall by the father's shotgun suicide."[25]

In the bathroom Sarah has an epiphany. She realizes that the relationship will not work and that the two of them will not "do the do" tonight. She knows she must leave the apartment. James tries to stop her, offering to buy her at whatever cost, but Sarah will not submit to another male power play; she will not commit the "act of surrender." Instead, she leaves the apartment and joins her friends. This was a story not only about a woman's choice but also about her desire. Sarah took control and managed her life.

By the early 1970s, Wright's Tangier friends Mary Jacobs and Florence Roess were back in New York City. When he returned from Veracruz, he had dinner with Roess every Friday. He also made new acquaintances. In 1973, he met Phelonise Willie at La MaMa, where Larl Becham was a dance instructor. Told that Wright was a writer, Phelonise "was intrigued and confessed [to him that] she wanted to write." She later recalled: "Charles said, rather imperiously, okay then, write 30 pages by such and such date. [I did and] that was how our relationship began."[26] Jacobs said that Wright liked Willie very much: "She was an American Black and she was beautiful and just cool. She was really cool." Yet, as with all of his friendships, their "strong" relationship ran "hot and cold."[27]

Absolutely's publication had been delayed because of a permissions disagreement. Because many of the pieces had originally appeared as columns, the *Village Voice* believed that it owned the rights to them. Straus, however, believed that the copyrights should have reverted to Wright. A war broke out between Farrar, Straus and the *Village Voice*. Straus at times could be "vulgar, classist, and sexist"; thus, instead of working with Diane Fisher, Wright's editor at the *Voice*, he went over her head to deal directly with Carter Burden, the owner.[28] "Please let me know," he wrote to Burden, "if we can unsnarl this from the top."[29] Angry at this move, Fisher stopped taking Straus's calls. But he was determined and eventually won the battle. In future, Straus said, Wright should send his pieces to him and he would decide, with Candida Donadio's help, where to send them. The plan was to hustle "big potential" pieces to magazines that paid well and send smaller ones to Fisher.[30]

Absolutely was finally released on January 1, 1973. Like *The Messenger* and many other existential novels, it has a loose, episodic, journal-like format with a first-person narrator. Its main character is named Charles Wright, a fictional self of the author Charles Wright who is telling a story of Charles Wright. The question becomes: is *Absolutely* Wright's attempt again to find and define Charles Wright? In a conversation with Clarence Major, Wright spoke of "that other private Charles Wright . . . [who] is not involved in [some of] the novels at all." The character in *Absolutely* was different: "all of those horror stories that were happening to me at that time, . . . these were things that I felt the readers of the *Voice* should know about."[31] It is the result of his becoming a witness to America.

In his journal entries, the narrator of *Absolutely* deals with multiple subjects. Some are personal, such as letters from his lover Maggie in Paris, while others are larger social and political issues. Each entry builds to a revelation or an insight. Like Wright's first two novels, *Absolutely* compassionately addresses the underside of New York City, the marginal people, the outcasts. But its geography is more expansive, extending into Union Square, Times Square, the Village, the East Village, the Bowery, "a cinema in hell where classic films play forever."[32]

Absolutely returns to the existential search of *The Messenger*, even as it incorporates issues of the Black subaltern, homosexuality, capitalism, and literary experimentalism, again altering and expanding the genre. Like Stevenson in *The Messenger*, Charles Wright the narrator is existentially aware, "a lifer in search of life."[33] But death is everywhere in the early 1970s; America is riddled with assassinations, riots, wars, so-called urban renewal, racism, drugs, poverty, decay, police brutality, and national malaise. The narrator is disoriented, confused, dread-filled in the absurd, chaotic, surreal, meaningless world of New York City. Nothing appears to have any preordained order or form; the world is characterized by the complete absence of necessity. According to A. Robert Lee:

> [*Absolutely*] exudes something of the flavours of a modern *Notes from Underground*, a subterranean chronicle of desperation, rapid surges of change, lives often marred and erased by New York's criminal and drug cultures. And always, for Wright, there exists New York sexual aura, the city's power to arouse instantaneous sexual heat and needs.[34]

Working-class, intellectual Charles Wright the narrator is described as an "Afroed, slender, Levi, bell-bottoms, striped mock turtleneck shirt [man, with] perhaps a couple of books under his arm."[35] He is searching for "the deeper truths of our lives."[36] But unlike Stevenson in *The Messenger*, he is also searching for historical loss. As Albert Camus noted, "the mind's deepest desire parallels man's unconscious feeling in the face of his universe: it is an insistence upon familiarity, an appetite for clarity. Understanding the world for a man is reducing it to the human, stamping it with his seal."[37] Charles Wright the narrator wants to reduce the world to the human; he wants meaning and clarity. But the absurd world will not be humanized, and this is the major conflict of the book.

When *Absolutely* opens, the narrator is living in the Salvation Army's Bowery Memorial Hotel, fighting "arrogant cockroaches" and the half-world of sleep as he drinks his way to consciousness and clarity: "With less than four hours' sleep, fourteen shots of vodka, six twelve-ounce bottles of beer, two speed pills, one marijuana cigarette—I chuckled in my pale, lemon-colored cubicle." Despite his haze, he remains a writer who is engaging deliberately with the world, "desperately trying to get a reassuring bird's eye view of America," In the opening journal entry, the narrator observes: "F. Scott Fitzgerald's sunny philosophy had always appealed to me. I believe in the future of this country. At fourteen, I had written: 'I am the future.' Twenty-six years later—all I want to do is exercise the past and share with you a few Black Studies."[38] The narrator intends to document and explore the landscape of New York City as it is being transformed and devastated by capitalism and drugs. He is training his eye on the deformed world that many readers would rather refuse to see.

According to A. Robert Lee, Charles Wright the narrator is "consummately street-wise," "yet always a fugitive presence. . . . He speaks as the city's Defoe-like eye, both compelled yet alienated."[39] As a writer and an artist, he perceives things differently. "Blending the narrator's deepening spiral into alcoholism and depression with compassionate and persuasively rendered set pieces about others in his social circle who experience similar travails along the precipice of urban squalor," to use Lee's words, the narrator becomes a witness to 1970s New York.[40] The character explains, "Like an addicted entomologist, I am drawn to people. Let them flutter, bask, rest, feed on my tree. Then fly, fly. Fly away. Goddamit."[41]

Charles Wright the narrator is more mature than *The Messenger*'s Stevenson and is also more politically and socially engaged, but the two characters are equally compassionate. The narrator of *Absolutely* participates in the life of the East Village, the Bowery, and the Chinese Garden, and his journal entries offer "testimony to a city, which is at once literal New York and supremely this 'unreal city.'"[42] Once again, a character became Wright's way of working through his own trauma. Like the author Charles Wright, this narrator, too, writes a column for the *Village Voice* and is the author of two novels. And to escape the grind of New York, he travels into the Catskills, where he lives in a children's dormitory and works as a hotel dishwasher and porter.

Like Stevenson and Lester Jefferson of *The Wig*, Charles Wright the narrator lives among outcasts of all races—children with inattentive mothers, sex workers, drug pushers, drag queens, drug addicts, winos, people with venereal disease, homosexuals, hippies, con artists, and the poor—and he strives to understand the meaning of their world. Enlightenment critics such as Miles A. Smith have reduced these subalterns to "degraded street people," portraying them as wallowing in "a world of pills, booze, sex, panhandling, and crime."[43] But Wright the narrator re-represents and gives them agency and humanity.

The narrator lives on the Lower East Side because he will not leave the city permanently and cannot afford to live anywhere else. He is still washing dishes to make ends meet. Yet he is a known writer, so he also moves among the Black middle class, a group he intensely dislikes. When he begins writing for the *Village Voice*, he becomes visible to these people, who seek him out. He receives letters and invitations to parties. He begins to see old acquaintances again. He observes the middle-class "Black breed" on the West Side "that was conceived in the idealistic Kennedy years, passed their youth in Johnson's Great Society, grew to maturity, prospered in the subtle South Africa of the United States of 1971." They are, in his view, as bourgeois as a Republican vice president might be. The narrator attends a party hosted by the lawyer T. C. Moore, where he mingles with socialites such as Mr. and Mrs. Roosevelt Robinson. The party embodies a "new mass department-store culture," which he finds smothering. There he meets an Afrocentric poet named A X, who is "Afroed, bearded, serious, [wearing] a rumpled suit and tie." The narrator wonders "why . . . the majority of Black poets sound alike"; he questions if such poetry is art and makes a sarcastic dig at rigid, homogeneous Black cultural nationalism.[44] In contrast, to such single-mindedness, the narrator is dynamic and multi-dimensional. In the words of Barbara Hernstein Smith, he has "multiple social identities, multiple principles of identification with other people."[45]

Sometimes the sensitive and aware Charles Wright the narrator simply observes scenes, but usually his observations lead to a revelation. He takes note of the rioting Black kids in the Village and realizes that "their parents had lost them just as this country had forgotten the parents." He mingles with victims of the welfare system, which he sees as their addiction. Many drink too much or are on drugs, using these avenues to blunt their impoverished social and economic existence. The narrator watches Jojo, an ex-garage mechanic and ex-con, who is "extremely bright, but frightened of touching his brain."[46] When Jojo receives his welfare check, he pays "off a $7 loan, then invites [the narrator] for beers, hard-boiled eggs. Later we switched to wine and watched the sports shoot pool. Life can be good for survivors."[47] But, the narrator asks,

> Have you ever thought of the reason why these Black guys might drink . . . cheap wine? . . . I think with the young people, you will grow up and you will marry, and you will have children and unless you are very strong, your children will end up just like [this] in some cases, those men on the Bowery or in all the boweries of America.[48]

The narrator witnesses this chronicle of desperation, lives marred by poverty and erased by New York's drug culture.

He also watches Nellie, the mother of seven illegitimate children. Apologetically, she tells him she wants to stay stoned every night as she waits for the next man to have sex with. The children are usually hungry, "thanks to their mother's careless life-style." They have also become "ferocious little warriors," always on the defense, only relaxing after they begin to trust you. Then they open and begin to play childish tricks and laugh, but still "you feel as if melancholia is smothering them."[49] The narrator gives the children candy, nickels, and dimes; he empathizes with their plight because he, too, was a child on welfare. It becomes clear to him that the government maintains and surveilles the poor but does nothing for their wellbeing: "[It] will give them enough so they'll be content and will cause us no trouble."[50]

Over the course of *Absolutely,* Charles Wright the narrator takes note of the Newark riots, the death of the writer and activist George Jackson, the death of Langston Hughes, and the assassinations of major American figures as well as considering war, decay, and national malaise more generally. He moves around the East Village, pondering racism and police brutality. Blacks and Puerto Ricans are "roughed up daily before they see a judge or jury. It happens everyday to the little people from the urban jungle. Seldom do we hear or read about it." Racism, he says, "has been with me for a very long time, even before I could read and write":

> The guys at Smitty's gas station in Boonville, Missouri, called me dago. Aged five, I knew dago was not nigger. But they [dago and nigger] have remained stepbrothers to this day, forming an uncomfortable army with kike, Polack, poor white trash. But I had nigger, Negro, coon, Black, colored, monkey, shit-colored bastard, yellow bastard. Perfect background music for nightmares.[51]

His name has been erased, denied visibility so many times that he wonders if he has ever been called Charles Stevenson Wright.

The narrator does not shy away from showing his anger and bitterness, calling out "whitey" for failing to understand Black anger. But he also remains sensitive and aware. He tells about Sally Reinaldo, who had been his lover years ago in Hell's Kitchen. She had wanted to marry him, but he could not change his social and sexual habits, his need for booze, pills, and pot. Meeting her later, now divorced and the mother of a four-year old, he sees the desperation in her eyes. After learning of her suicide, he walks down the street, aware that he has lost something. Sally was a person with American dreams; and to reach them, she had danced, sung, modeled, and whored. She had wanted to become a star or a housewife. She had wanted to become an American success, but she became a casualty of the American Dream.

In *The Ethics of Ambiguity*, Simone de Beauvoir writes that in order to achieve true freedom, one must battle against the choices and activities of those who suppress it.[52] This notion resonates in Charles Wright the narrator. As he walks through the Bowery, "stoned," "clutching a tumbler of despair," he understands that the world is not giving him answers. He sees the street people as tourists on a dead planet. Against their will, "they had detoured from the route of dreams. Frightening, oblique—loneliness became the fellow traveler."[53] Like Sally, these Americans had had dreams that failed or destroyed them. The narrator longs to do something to make the world better, but there is nothing he can change about their situation. Instead, he must "concentrate on exile" from society and on his own existential existence. "It is time to take leave of it. But for the moment, I am comforted with nothing but the prospect of another sunrise, buried in my own mortality."[54]

In one journal entry, the narrator begins by writing about Norwegian "tinned sardines," but he ends up discussing work, labor, and class exploitation. As he drinks vodka, he drifts off to talk about his sixteen-hour workday and alludes to Hemingway, the Norwegian novelist Knut Hamsun, and the playwright Henrik Ibsen. But eventually he returns to the sardines:

> The smoked sardines are a perfect complement for the vodka. But I'm thinking about the cost of labor, the men and women who fished the sardines out of the sea, the people who packed them, the profit of the Norwegian businessman and the American importer and the Chinese owners of the store where I bought them. . . . I believe in free enterprise, and hate indifference, cheap products, cheap people, and careless people.[55]

As the journal entries progress, we learn that the narrator is preparing to leave the Bowery because a rapid surge in gentrification is destroying his familiar community. People are being evicted from their apartments, small businesses are being forced to close or move, neighborhood bars are disappearing, neighborhood restaurants are folding, and hotels are being demolished to make room for elegant lofts. As Samuel R. Delany explained in his book about Times Square, this "highly diversified neighborhood with working-class residences and small human services . . . [would] soon be a ring of upper-middle-class luxury apartments around a ring of tourist hotels clustering about a series of theaters and restaurants."[56]

With gentrification, the young Blacks and Puerto Ricans are being forced out of the Bowery. Charles Wright the narrator notes that there are no longer any Black bars in the neighborhood. Yet the Bowery has always been racially diverse, home to weak drinking men from the South; home to immigrant Poles, Jews, Italians, Chinese, and Irish. They, too, have been misled by the American Dream, and now they also must move elsewhere. "With the rush to accommodate the new," writes Delany, "much that was beautiful along with much that was shoddy, much that was dilapidated with much that was pleasurable, much that was inefficient with much that was functional, is gone."[57]

They are being replaced by the affluent children of suburban white America, a group as "cold and capitalistic as the parents they fled." The newcomers label the street people *bums*, a nuisance; they want them gone. A recently arrived, upper-middle-class artist treats the narrator like everyone else: "Hell, I've told you about sitting on my stoop. I got an old lady and kids."[58]

The narrator wants to create a new design for living, new territories to justify his existence, but instead he moves to the Chinese Garden, an isolated Chinatown community, where he finds temporary solace. He becomes the senior citizen of the garden, the resident historian, and the wild-grass accountant. This neighborhood, too, is chaotic and absurd. Young Black, white, Puerto Rican, and Chinese artists paint graffiti on every surface except for dirt and grass. It houses invaders who want to blow up New York, but it also houses elite artists and Chinese immigrants.

The narrator encounters sad and surreal scenes in the Chinese Garden. A fat, laughing Chinese girl falls in dog excrement. A poodle tries to have sex with a four-year-old boy. The Cat Woman—delusional, neglected—is convinced that her buried cat has come back to life, and this gives her hope, something the narrator has not seen since the early days of the Great Society. There is no police presence in the garden. Cumulatively, such incidents overwhelm him, yet each time all he can do is to decide that there is "absolutely nothing to get alarmed about. . . . [This is] just another domestic scene in current American life."[59] Thus, he remains calm and humane amid the chaos and absurdity.

In his journal, the narrator records the sex practices of Chinatown. He observes that some Chinese men prefer encounters with foreign partners, which explains why there are many white female sex workers in the neighborhood. Because there are no whorehouse hotels here, sex takes place in cars, in door entrances, on dark, deserted streets, or in hotels near the Bowery. The narrator watches Miss Nell, a strawberry blonde from Dallas. A shrewd businesswoman, she appears with a male customer, finds a dark place to work, and begins performing oral sex. When the narrator tries to watch, she blocks his view.

In one entry, Charles Wright the narrator tells of a country-club divorcee without alimony who is forced to turn to prostitution to survive. He considers the title of an academic symposium, "Toward the Elimination of Prostitution," comparing its absurdity to the imagined presence of the Ku Klux Klan in Iceland. Though feminists such as Susan Brownmiller want to eliminate prostitution, he believes that such campaigns are "caught in the breeze that whispered [to] Joseph McCarthy."[60] The scholars Nancy Fraser and Rahell Jaeggi concur, arguing against "extreme prohibitionism in which social actors aim not only to establish a boundary but to make it virtually impenetrable. . . . We could also use the term for those feminists who seek to outlaw all commodification of sex, reproduction, and carework."[61]

"What passes for good now is often bad, and certainly vice versa," writes Jerome Klinkowitz in his study of Wright's work, which, in his view, "examines the reality of our culture and carefully sorts out the unreal."[62] The narrator of *Absolutely* is depressed by "hen-pecked solutions to the female-male misunderstanding." After defending prostitution as "easy work and fast money," he asks, "Why can't we redesign the lifeboats, take a good hard look at our male-and-female relationship? Perhaps redefine sin, morality, and corruption for our time on this earth."[63] He is critiquing the middle-class puritan narrative that fails to acknowledge or even recognize the reality of human life. "I'm for legalizing prostitution," concludes the narrator.[64] "

The narrator moves again, this time from the Chinese Garden to the East Village. Again, he witnesses chaos and absurdity. The lawless streets are monitored by junkies, thieves, pushers, and sex workers who sip iced Cokes and coffee in the heat of the afternoon. Garbage litters the pavement. Domesticated hippies walk their Dobermans, while Black and Puerto Rican teenagers, natives of the neighborhood, "motherfuck each other with words." The poor and uneducated are "powerless against the government's yearly rape."[65] The narrator makes it clear that he is familiar with the local junkies who try to sell him a pair of ice skates at the elevator. He is used to longhaired Jerry who wants to cry because kids attack him. He knows Miss Ohio, who occasionally gets high, talks about being hung up on some guy, and spends most of her time with the neighborhood children. She seems out of place in the East Village, and, in this way, she resembles the narrator, who is actively present but intellectually alienated.

To get away from it all, Charles Wright the narrator has a drink at the White Horse Bar with two of his more stable friends. Memories of parties at the Hotel Albert lead him across town to the Old Dover in the Bowery, where the regulars respect his privacy. He listens to the babbling voices around him and plays music on the jukebox to escape chaotic, absurd situations. Then Catholic Leather Jacket pulls up a chair, orders more drinks, and confesses that his old lady has thrown him out and that he has lost his job. The narrator thinks, "Apparently family and Church have failed these weak men. Unable to recognize their latent disturbances, they simply hustle them down the medieval road of morality and guilt. Any intelligent child questions that road, especially if it detours from the reality around him."[66] But these men do not question the road: they simply feel guilty about not being successful.

The next journal entry recounts the narrator's visit to southern California with a bird's-eye view of America. It begins in Orange County, where he has scented the presence of the political far right: "The only way I can describe the scent is to say: Inhale ether or imagine facing a double-barreled shotgun ten feet from where you are presently standing or sitting." Orange County makes him "slightly uncomfortable," as does Newport Beach, home of June Allyson and John Wayne, who once stated in a *Playboy* interview, "I believe in white supremacy."[67] Then, as in a film, the narrator shifts the scene to Brooklyn, where he now lives and is "waiting to fly or crack up."[68] In a later conversation with Major, the writer recalled:

> The library in my fashionable Brooklyn Heights chic neighborhood has six copies of John Wayne's *Why I Love America* and that tells me a hell of a lot about fashionable, liberal white America when a library can have six copies of that stuff, so you see—that great urban city of New York, the capital of the world, and in Brooklyn Heights, no one would think of John Wayne—it's too fashionable . . . and to me that tells a helluva lot about the zone that I live in.[69]

Here, the narrator connects conservative Orange County to fashionable Brooklyn, defining them as the same politically. Back in New York, Charles Wright narrator still feels like an outsider, invisible. He is not perceived as a thinking, intellectual, individual American who has written several books. He is not seen as a complicated human who loves his country but "always [as] the intruder, the rapist, the mugger." His ancestors have been here "for four hundred years," yet he is treated as "a stranger."[70] He writes of visiting the Forest Hills housing project for low-income residents and defines it as a monument to American racism.

Yet in the same entry, the narrator writes about moving between two different economic worlds in New York City and relating to both, acknowledging his many selves. He visits his old friend James Anthony Peoples on the Upper West Side, just below the frontier of Harlem on Central Park West. There he witnesses middle-class Blacks and whites leaving the Black Broadway musical production of *Ain't Supposed to Die a Natural Death*. And just beyond 110th Street, he witnesses the living dead—the world the middle class refuses to see or recognize. On his way to get a six pack on 115th Street, he discerns subway junkies on both sides of the street. Desperation in their eyes, "they resembled black ghosts. Dachau survivors. . . . Watching their desperate street bits, [his] heart broke. Life had ended for them. *But not for the people who had created them.*"[71] Here, the narrator offers a devastating critique of class and capitalism, showing how they crush and destroy the lowly. The entry ends with a discussion of the exploitation of dishwashers, of which he is one. At Le Mansion on Long Island, he surmises that he will take a leave of absence and try writing again.

Again, from California to Brooklyn to Long Island, the narrator gives us a chaotic, economically unequal, careless, racist, absurd America, showing us the chronicling of desperation among exploited workers. There is nothing in this world that appears to have any preordained order or form. The narrator is implicated in this absurd world, having a fugitive presence. Yet he is alienated, witnessing America, asking questions, and making observations, as he contends with the "horror stories that were happening" to America and the author. He wants the reader to know about these stories, even if they do not want to, for it will allow, he hopes, the reader to act as witness for something that will catalyze a change within her.

Next, in his journal, working-class Charles Wright the narrator offers a diary entry about poverty and corruption. Now living at the Valencia Hotel, the narrator drinks brandy and reads in the *New York Times* that millions of dollars of poverty funds have been lost to fraud and inefficiency. Meanwhile, his acquaintance Nina has an executive position at the city's anti-poverty agency, and she wants to expose corruption in the government's anti-poverty program. She knows the narrator is struggling financially and wants to hire him to investigate and write a report. But her boss, who has bought signed books from the narrator, thinks otherwise. "Bureaucrats don't like writers," Nina tells her friend. "The written word gets them uptight." Bidding him good-bye, she presses $25 into his hand and says, "Get stoned or laid, baby." She adds, "See that sports car on the opposite side of the street? It belongs to an office boy. He's stealing the place blind."[72] Here, Wright the narrator is bearing witness to and exposing the unreality and corruption of the poverty program as he works over and through trauma in his larger social and cultural setting. Also, the testimony of the chaotic trauma extends to the reader of the text, who then becomes a witness to the collective social trauma of New York City.

The scene shifts to Philadelphia, where Charles Wright the narrator finds himself covering bands such as Sly and the Family Stone, Creedence Clearwater Revival, and the Grateful Dead. With a mood like F. Scott Fitzgerald at Princeton, who felt out of place, the narrator leaves New York and becomes a writer lost in Philadelphia. As he pops pills, sips Cokes, and digs the crowd, he admits that he is "not a rock frontiersman," but he does latch onto Janis Joplin, an artist capable of making unreality real. Like a contemporary Cleopatra, she presses sincerity to her bosom. The narrator thinks Joplin is the real deal; and as the young people dance and rush onto the main floor, he acknowledges rock's power, but the acts leave him exhausted.

Back in New York City, the narrator reflectively recalls the dark days of the 1950s and 1960s, the cold, righteous McCarthy years, a contemporary Salem witch hunt. "Hysterical, stoned, bored, frightened, some of us shot holes in the roofs of our tents [and] tried to shoot bullets at the stars, shot heroin, sniffed cocaine and went to the whorehouses with the zeal of aspiring politicians." As time passes, the narrator remembers a moment of splendor and hope. But it is followed by the senseless assassinations of Malcolm X, Robert F. Kennedy, and Martin Luther King, Jr., and despair sets in again: people are unable to find purpose in life; the absurd world cannot be mastered or humanized. The narrator recalls the photographs in the *Village Voice* of intellectual heavyweights such as the critic Susan Sontag, the novelist Norman Mailer, the poet Robert Lowell, the activist Sidney Lens, and the critic Dwight MacDonald. He stares ironically at a photograph of Mailer in a glossy magazine and thinks, "The face of an urbane carpenter in a $200 suit." These intellectuals, who had once worked for civil rights, are now protesting the Vietnam War. The narrator concludes that the liberals have found a fresh new cause and wonders if these people will "marshal their forces and elect a President . . . who will guide them toward a peace-loving future. That is our only salvation. If they [can] mainline moral reality into the American way of life. If. If. If—."[73]

In the East Village, Charles Wright the narrator considers the unrelatable, the extreme, things that the normative world would rather refuse to acknowledge. In the course of writing about venereal disease among the young men of Manhattan, he visits the Chelsea Health Center, which he sees as both bureaucratic and faintly sinister. The center is located amid a public school, a warren of housing projects, and a devastated block that ends at 12th Avenue and the Hudson River. Though the small two-story building seems asexual, it is the site of salvation for sufferers of gonorrhea. He observes "fellow travelers. Tense young men who usually acknowledge each other with a sly/shy you-got-it too grin. The promiscuous earthlings are cool."[74] What intrigues him are the young men who arrive at the center with luggage, knapsacks, sleeping bags, and shopping bags. Lost and dislocated, they give false names and addresses. They do not want to be known; they are ashamed of their desires.

The narrator watches the young men take blood tests and receive penicillin shots. He listens to their interviews with the social worker. He hears them lie about whom they slept with, and he becomes depressed and begins to drift: "All I want to do is stay stoned; despair is the masochistic lover, chained to my feet as August spends itself slowly; time the miser with the eyedropper. Summer. Summer's end. Will the summer ever end? Will I escape this time?" Charles Wright the narrator experiences an existential vacuum of anxiety. He is overcome by despair. He buys a Sunday *New York Times* and reads the book reviews. His own writing makes the news today, but that fails to relieve his despair. His frustration, his peasant's labor at work are still fresh in his mind. "After showering, I feel less tense, prime myself with ice-cold beer. It's a mother of an afternoon. The sullen sky gives no promise of relief, rain. . . . But booze won't elude me. No."[75] Yet alcohol only temporarily banishes the despair. To escape the dread of existence— the negative feeling arising from the experience of human freedom and responsibility—and the summer's heat, the narrator cannot decide whether to hit the streets or visit friends with air conditioning. He realizes that these options can only accelerate the drift. "What am I frightened of?," he asks himself:

Death, aging, my fellow men, madness—frightened that one terrible morning or night I will no longer have the marvelous ability to drink, drink, knock it down, as they say: Yes! Mix it up, pop a variety of pills, smoke grass and hashish—frightened of what might be my inability to love, although I am loving, generous, understanding with friends, strangers.[76]

As he sits alone, drinking cheap white wine and listening to Little Richard on the radio, his neighbor, Birdie Greene, the Valencia Hotel maid, visits him. She asks if he has seen Joe and Helen, who live down the hall, and he replies, "No baby. I've been looking for Charles Wright."[77] Tired, annoyed by his neighbor's predictable questions, the narrator goes out to the corner store to buy ice and a half-gallon of wine. When he returns home, he listens to the Modern Jazz Quartet on the radio and suddenly realizes he is "frightened that something might happen, and I'd never be able to write the book I believed I was capable of writing."[78] He hopes to use writing to justify his existence, yet he cannot fully accept the absurd world. This is why he constantly seeks to escape.

The narrator returns to the Catskills and his dishwashing job, "here—where it's green and serene—these flat, informal, manicured acres. The eye looks upward and sees dense treed mountains, a pearl-blue sky. Tall poplar trees ring the lakes and golf courses."[79] But he cannot stay long, for his working and living conditions are terrible: "No unions or overtime, which is why hotels fail to secure stable employees. You work long enough to get wine money or 'talking back' money and move on."[80] Here, again, as a worker himself, he exposes capitalist greed and the dreadful exploited life of the non-union worker, allowing what was previously invisible to become visible. Therefore, he comes back to the city and checks into the Valencia Hotel. He likes the "pace, the anonymity." New York is a "challenging, wondrous city. But do I want to stay here? In fact, do I want to stay in the Unites States of America? I have never felt at home here." He thinks of his grandfather's saying, "This world ain't my home," and says, "Ah yes! I'm coming from the edge of despair. Booze and pills fail to ax despair."[81] Human existence is absurd, and the best way to view it is as ironic and pointless but somehow comic. Again, he wants to be alone, putting him outside the social, the herd. Seemingly, Wright the narrator cannot find a roosting place, a sense of home in the Catskills or in New York City. Therefore, he remains in exile, searching for meaning and connection and laughing in the face of life.

As the narrator waits for summer to end, he moves again, this time to the Kenton Hotel on the Bowery. The Bowery is a place where sex between masculine men is more common than sex between masculine men and girlie men, and the narrator decides he wants to write about these young and old men, who sit in the foyer of hell as they wait to be escorted into the ballroom of death. "But it is always cocktail hour for the 'girls' who are sometimes called garbage and ash-can queens. Their past lives and wine have pushed them beyond *The Boys in the Band*."[82]

He watches a straight-looking, bisexual man picking up tricks in the Chinese Garden, noting his midwestern-style crew cut. The scene provokes an epiphany: the narrator realizes that such closeted, masculine, bisexual men have been the backbone of the U.S. military. Many have families; many blame women for their sense of self-defeat, and they turn to alcohol and the company of other men. This scene exposes the stereotype of the homosexual and gives the reader a reality he or she prefers not to know. He is making the invisible visible. The narrator witnesses and empathizes but does not judge. He recognizes the America they live in, and he understands their situation.

The narrator desperately wants to write, but he has lost the passion. He is at an impasse. His last book was published four years earlier. Although he has financial difficulties, he refuses to take a job as writer-in-residence at a small Black college in the South. Drinking wine, he steps out on the fifth-floor fire escape of the Kenton Hotel. The view is glorious. A screen of pollution filters the burning afternoon sun. There is no breeze but "a sort of suspended quiet":

> I can see traffic moving down Chrystie Street; children playing ball in the park; drunks in twos and threes, supporting buddies like wounded soldiers after the battle of defeat. Toward the east, a row of decayed building has the decadent beauty of Roman ruins. . . . Taking another drink, I think: I wish I could fly, fly, far away. . . . Here, there, again, and always, the Why of the last seven years. Skulled depression as I sit and watch the sun disappear. Aware of the muted, miscellaneous noises that drift up from the street, I am also aware of the loss of something. Thinking of all I've done and not done. Thinking and feeling a terrible loss.[83]

He is aware of "the loss of something," and he is mourning the present, hoping to give his anxiety an identifiable object so that it may be eliminated or overcome. For the past seven years, he has been asking about the why of things as he continually fails to come up with a meaning or purpose, a reason to exist. When he becomes inundated with despair, he takes to drinking and popping pills, hoping to find an answer to the despair, hoping to fill the existential vacuum of anxiety. But he knows that the pills and booze are not effective; they do not erase the despair. Instead, they bring clarity to it. What is out there is mad, chaotic, "incapable of being understood."[84] The pills and the booze do not resolve his situation, but they allow him to cope, to suppress the despair, making the situation clearer to him.

Charles Wright the narrator's existential, heightened awareness will not let him find a roosting place, a home. It puts him outside of social laws, rituals, and institutions as he tries to assert his human independence against reason and determination. Because he is working class, he rejects the American middle class, both Black and white. Consumer culture smothers him. He feels exploited by capitalism. Youth culture and rock music tire him out, and the women's movement is politically narrow and rejects sex workers. He refuses to make the literary cocktail rounds; he will not get a grant by knowing or sleeping with someone. A nonbeliever, he stands near the statue of Jesus Christ at the Holy Name Mission and Church at Mott and Bleecker Streets, desperately searching for "a lift. Take me higher. Ground the motors of the stockcars racing in my brain." Instead, he ends up quoting from Hemingway's *The Sun Also Rises:* "God never worked very well with me."[85] He thinks about rereading Lowry's *Under the Volcano*, hoping that it might help him understand his despair and elevate hope. But he doesn't; he goes back to the Catskills and the cycle continues.

The conclusion of *Absolutely* is dismal and unfulfilling. In contrast with Stevenson in *The Messenger,* the protagonist is not able to come to terms with the historical trauma of American society. He is outside of social rituals and conventions. The absurdity of such narratives and rituals would diminish him as a person, as an agent of free will, yet he also refuses to foster his own freedom. The book ends with a letter to Nathanael West: "Now Absurdity and Truth pave the parquet of my mind. The pain is akin to raw alcohol on the testicles. But I'm not complaining."[86] Does this quote mean that, by not complaining, he accepts the pain and absurdity as part of the truth of existence?

Throughout *Absolutely*, the narrator processes—as in working over and through—trauma personally but also collectively. In this way, the author Charles Wright opened a door for readers, giving them the opportunity to understand—to know. Knowing is rooted in the basic human consideration for others—to empathize and know others, and to change as a result of this knowing. His book asks them to bear witness to the reality of New

York City, to its contradictions, devastations, desperations, chaos, and absurdity.

Absolutely had a first print run of 12,500 copies.[87] As it had done for *The Wig*, Farrar, Straus worked hard to promote *Absolutely*, running advertisements in the *New York Times*, the *Village Voice*, the *Los Angeles Times*, the *Chicago Tribune*, and the *San Francisco Chronicle*.[88] After learning about Tony Brown's radio program *Black Journal*, Straus wrote to Robert Kotlowitz at WET/13, offering *Absolutely* for a possible "dramatization."[89] Lynn C. Goldberg of Farrar, Straus wrote to Keith Darby of *Book Beat* on WTT-TV, forwarding two copies of *Absolutely* and asking if the show wanted to feature Wright.[90] Barbara Neilson, the press's director of subsidiary rights, pushed the book with Leona Nevler, the managing editor of Crest and Premier Books.[91] Neilson also snagged "an alternative selection in the Book Find Club" for *Absolutely*.[92] Peter Heinzmann of Farrar, Straus reached out to the Book-of-the Month Club, the New Critic Book Club, *Esquire*, the Playboy Book Club, the *Saturday Review* Book Club, the *Intellectual Digest* Book Club, the Reader's Subscription, Publishers Hall Syndicate, and the Literary Guild of America. He promoted *Absolutely* as

> this visceral description of poverty, drug addiction, prostitution and all the ills that beset the underprivileged in American society. Charles Wright's voice has a markedly distinct tone from other writers that have taken excursions into the so-called "underground," since the impact of harsh realities in this book is balanced by a compassion and an understanding that are found only too rarely.[93]

By this time Wright was a known writer with an international reputation, and *Absolutely* was favorably reviewed in a number of mainstream and elite journals. Here, unlike with *The Wig*, there seemed to "exist strong connections between publishers, editors, periodicals and reviewers," which constituted a "social and commercial circle in which opinions and preferences about books get amplified and reproduced."[94] In *The New York Times*, reviewer David Freeman noted:

> Wright continues to see his life as a novel, and one of the pleasures of this book, which is rich in pleasures, is that one is never certain what is fact and what is fiction. There is a slide show of vignettes, characters quickly etched, observations on the washing of other people's dirt and on the nature of welfare. This material in lesser hands and lesser

minds would come out [as] new journalism. Charles Wright brings it closer to the truth.[95]

Publishers Weekly also praised the book:

Wright brings verve and a stinging style to his almost cinema graphic pictures of his highs and lows as a young Black haunting the streets and scrubby parks of the city from 1967 to the present. He has a knack of bringing a reader into the heart of a scene, describing his wild fellowship with the homeless and the hopeless. He draws the city in a clear and moving light.[96]

In the *Atlantic*, Phoebe Adams wrote:

Mr. Wright has now published a sort of journal, sketches of the ghetto and gutter New York from which he collects the material of his fiction. In fact, being Black, he lives with his material, bang in the middle of it and in constant danger of being submerged. He describes his own troubles with grim humor and peripheral disasters with unsentimental sympathy, miraculously remaining intelligent and humane in a situation where there is everything to get alarmed about.[97]

A reviewer for the *New Yorker* said:

Charles Wright is a good novelist. . . . This raw-nerved, bitter journal, begun in 1967, explains why, and is also probably the clearest picture to have emerged of what it feels like nowadays to be poor, Black, and American . . . . These close ups of friends and strangers are sometimes cruel, sometimes wry, . . . but always intimate—and unquestionably, depressingly true to life.[98]

Praising Wright's first two novels as "brutally, lovingly unearth[ing] the underside of the city," Bernette Golden argued in the *National Observer* that *Absolutely* clearly had "larger implications . . . for Wright's New York. Here, he emerges above ground for a closer look at the whole urban tapestry."[99]

The novelist Anthony Burgess wrote to Andree Conrad at Farrar, Straus about *Absolutely*. Commenting first on the rich pleasures of *The Wig*, he, reviewing *Absolutely*, said:

Mr. Wright has a masterly prose-style, a highly individual melodic and rhythmic sense, and a humor that comes out of a long European rather than an American tradition. The comparison with *Candide* is not out of place. It would diminish him to call him merely an important Black writer. Such talents as his transcends race: his concern is with the entire human condition.[100]

The writer Al Young, submitting the following comments about *Absolutely*, told Lynn C. Goldberg at Farrar, Straus: "It's a powerful, haunting document . . . . Charles Wright is an original American writer with a genius for transforming everyday underdog reality into a vivid high-tension prose that sings."[101]

In its marketing materials for foreign publishers, Farrar, Straus declared:

> Charles Wright . . . has written a journal in which he describes the harsh life of a Black artist in New York, the poverty, drug addiction, prostitution, murder, bureaucratic indifference, race riots, rage and . . . all the ills of underprivileged society but incredibly balanced with a tone of compassion and understanding and even at times, humor in the best sense of the word.[102]

In the end, many European publishers decided the text would be too difficult to sell. But Harold D. Cohen of Metromedia Producers Corporation did contact the press about "the motion picture rights."[103]

Jerome Klinkowitz, a strong supporter of Wright's fiction, assured Andree Conrad that he would work to make it available to a more general contemporary market:

> Charles Wright is not going to be another Vonnegut, but I'm certain he could compete in the college market now buying books by Barthelme, Kosinski, Robert Coover, et al. . . . I am trying to get people reading Charles Wright, Ronald Sukenick, Steve Katz, Gilbert Sorrentino. . . . The books must be got out of New York, out of reviewers' hands and into examining-for-adoption professors' hands, before much will happen.[104]

In a subsequent note to Straus, Conrad explained, "Jerome Klinkowitz is one of three college professors, along with John O'Brien at Northern Illinois University and Charles Hoyt at Bennett College in Millbrook, New York, . . . who have told me that we are insane not to have Charles Wright's *The Messenger* and *The Wig* in Noonday editions." She emphasized that the market was not black studies but contemporary literature, "which in the long run seems more promising as far as sales are concerned."[105]

Nevertheless, despite these promising promotions and reviews, Charles Wright's profile and sales remained low. He was a published writer without a visible, mainstream audience. What literary community would imbue his fiction with values? His fiction was not defined within a situational literary context. Although he was an American modernist, he was, as Klinkowitz had made clear, not included among his peers because his race and subject matter set him apart. The middle-class, American reading public, in sync with the ideological state apparatus, had never taken a strong liking to American literature that dealt with poverty, prostitution, racism, and "all the ills of underprivileged society." They did not see themselves—their middle-class message and upward mobility—as the subject of the discourse of non-white subaltern or proletarian texts. Therefore, modern American texts about the underclass never became bestsellers. This was a long-standing pattern in American publishing.

Theodore Dreiser and other proletarian writers of the 1930s, who wrote about poverty and the capitalist exploitation of workers, were not bestsellers because they were not "interested in postwar affluence and class mobility."[106] For the same reason, most middle-class white readers and critics were not interested in the fiction of Charles Wright, which dealt with racism, capitalism, and subaltern African Americans. Except for a hand full of literary white critics such as Conrad Knickerbocker, Jerome Klinkowitz, Max F. Schulz, A. Robert Lee, and others, Wright was ignored or marginalized by mainstream white literary critics. Therefore, his fiction attracted a small amount of serious critical reception but did not generate mainstream literary capital and sales.

Furthermore, most mainstream white critics and reviewers did not know how to deal with a modern text, with a subaltern or Black subject with a homosexual undertone, during the modern postwar era. For most of them, western, modern literature was about the alienation and fragmentation of the white middle or upper middle class. Here, we are talking about the fiction of John Updike, Saul Bellow, and John Cheever. In the 1960s, most mainstream white critics equated Black literature with social protest. In his essay "Black Boys and Native Sons," Irving Howe questioned, "How could a Negro put pen to paper, how could he so much as think or breathe, without some impulsion to protest, be it harsh or mild, political or private, released or buried?"[107] Darryl Dickson-Carr agreed:

> The [white] Western literary canon tends to deem African and African American literature and culture a primarily social protest literature, a restrictive designation not normally given to traditional, European literature and culture. Judged by the standards established by Western scholars, they have been declared patently inferior, decried as hopelessly derivative, deracinated from their cultural contexts, or unduly romanticized.[108]

But Wright's existential and absurdist satirical fiction did not fit into this sanctioned protest tradition nor into other accepted African American modes. Therefore, he did not generate a Black readership, major attention, or sales. Describing two of these major sanctioned traditions, Frances Foster explains:

> Ralph Ellison represent[ed] the guardians-of-Western-literary tradition who feel the writer's basic responsibility is to "the maintenance of a certain level of precision in language, a maximum correspondence between words and ideas and the things and processes of this world." [Amiri Baraka represented] the artists-as-social-conscious-of-society when he said, "The Black Artist must teach the White Eyes their death, and teach the Black man how to bring these deaths about."[109]

In addition, the magnum opus *Norton Anthology of African American Literature* erased Charles Wright. Nor was his work mentioned in *Brother to Brother: New Writings by Black Gay Men, In the Life: A Black Gay Anthology,* or the groundbreaking Black queer critical texts of Samuel R. Delany, Robert F. Reid-Pharr, Darieck Scott, and GerShun Avilez. As the managing editor of the influential *Negro Digest* wrote in 1968, "Charles Wright . . . is unknown as individual and as author to most Black readers and, indeed, to other Black writers, although his two novels received favorable notices."[110] Middle-class Black readers—who preferred to see themselves in racial uplift or protest narratives—were not particularly interested in the African American subaltern or the existential Black character.

These silences, erasures, and neglects excluded a great deal of satirical African American literature, including Paul Beatty's *The White Boy Shuffle,* Darius James's *Negrophobia,* George Schuyler's *Black No More,* Rudolph Fisher's *The Walls of Jericho,* Hal Bennet's *Lord of Dark Places,* and William Melvin Kelley's *Dem* and *Dunsfords Travels Everywheres.* Likewise, the experimental/postmodern texts of Percival Everett, Clarence Major, Ishmael Reed, Xam Cartier Wilson, Charles Johnson, and John Edgar Wideman were erased, marginalized, or ignored. "For all of its innovation," writes Kinohi Nishikawa, "Black postmodern satire (and Black postmodern texts) is still a neglected corner of the African American literary tradition." In the 1960s and 1970s, "with no discernible movement supporting their work, . . . [Black] satirists soon fell into obscurity. Over the next couple of decades, the institutionalization of African American literary studies then legitimated that absence."[111] Although marginalized or ignored, many of these satirical and experimental/postmodern Black writers, in contrast to Charles Wright, continued to publish fiction, as I will explain later.

Yet Wright was a twentieth-century western writer whose diverse living experiences and lifelong reading and studying of modern literature had enriched his fiction. In other words, his work had been fed by close familiarity with West, Porter, Fitzgerald, Duras, Beckett, and Camus. Nonetheless, many mainstream critics did not know where to critically situate him. Discussing the difficult reception of *The Wig*, Joe Weixlmann wrote, "There is no denying that it is atypical of the American fiction of the mid-sixties and *most* atypical of the Afro-American fiction of that era."[112]

Wright did have a forebear. A. Robert Lee argues, "If Charles Wright's novels [particularly *The Wig*] . . . could be said to claim a spiritual forebear, it could be Nathanael West. . . . For like West, through a style always distinctively his own, Wright depicts a city world which borders on phantasmagoria. . . . His world is thus as utterly New York as West's Hollywood in *The Day of the Locust*."[113] But West, along with the satirical American literary tradition, was not wholly critically received and therefore was marginalized by the mainstream canon of American literature.

Writing of maverick Black writers, the novelist and essayist Darryl Pinckney described them as "go[ing] against the grain" in their "obsessive's solitary journey." Wright, too, stood alone. In his life and fiction, he chose to go his own way. He found his "liberation from European culture in the pluralist reality of the United States," though it mostly ignored him, "rather than in pursuing a sense of belonging to Africa."[114] The price he paid for this choice was to die without a home or much honor, hurtling himself toward obscurity in the process.

Sadly, the maverick Wright never fully understood—or maybe he did and simply did not care—was that his choice of genres (existential and satire), even when he played with them, and his choice of subject (the outcast, mostly the African American underclass), regardless of how brilliant the fiction, would never bring him riches and fame during the modern postwar era. He could never be a best-selling author in the United States because he did not focus on the discourse of the white middle class (or the Black racial uplift narrative) and its desire for upward mobility—the hallmarks of bestsellers. He could only be a cult or marginal great writer.

But Wright did not accept kindly the price he paid for being a maverick. His exclusion from mainstream and marginal American and African American literary traditions devastated him; as a result, he was not able to find a personal and literary home in the United States. The chronic traumas, the contradictory conflicts, and the exclusions did not make it possible for him to live off his writing, and this refusal to hear his literary song ultimately caused him to become depressed and sent him to alcohol and drugs for self-medication. Trips to Tangier, Mexico, Puerto Rico, and Paris released Wright from racial and sexual oppression and the hectic terror of New York. He took advantage of their lack of restrictions on sexual activities and allowed himself to believe that he could live more freely and write full time again. Finally, these trips also allowed him to "transgress the heterocentric norm and dominant narratives about identity and place" and experience a sense of home and freedom, if only temporarily.[115] But they did not sustain him as a writer or provide a long-term home for him.

CHAPTER SEVEN

Life after *Absolutely* and the Hodenfields

After *Absolutely* was released in 1973, Charles Wright became known in literary and journalism circles throughout the United States and the world. He was sought out for lectures, and magazines solicited his work. Yet despite attention and good reviews, his book's sales were still disappointing, and he continued to work at menial jobs to survive. What were the obstacles? The novelist Toni Morrison has suggested that market saturation might have been one factor. Discussing her own case, she said, "The market can only receive one or two Black women writers. Dealing with five Toni Morrisons would be problematic."[1] This might have also been true for Wright.

Ishmael Reed thought the problem was linked to literary racism: "Charles Wright refused to audition as a hatchet man contestant in the Manhattan token wars in which only one Black writer is left standing during a given era. . . . Tokenism deprive[d] readers of access to a variety of Black writers."[2] Wright himself had come to a similar conclusion. He observed that Langston Hughes "did not sell out to whitey with his simple tales. He did not sell out to himself. . . . He created something that was real. . . . He had to eat and buy shoes. And none of it was easy. And it seems to me, Langston, that you knew something your literary Black sons haven't learned; it's a closed game played on a one-way street."[3] This echoes Wright's earlier comments about maintaining your dignity and not selling out. But Wright's situation was complicated by his status as a working-class bisexual who refused to be a token. He did not fit the collective image or practice the values of a gay individual who was "at home in the positive, confident, upwardly mobile world of assimilationist politics and culture."[4] Therefore, Wright did not get the sales and the awards given to token Blacks and assimilationist gays.

The real problem, however, was inequality in the publishing industry. Of the 620 bestselling novels published between 1950 and 2000, the modern postwar era, only three were written by African Americans. White male authors accounted for 74 percent of bestsellers, white women for 24 percent. As Richard Jean So has written, "Bestselling [white] authors [during this era] tended to write about what they knew best—themselves— and the struggles and joy of achieving the best version of what they were born to do: strive for upward economic mobility."[5]

Black writers, even those with good reviews and prizes, rarely produced bestsellers. Rather, literary prizes were a "mechanism to promote multiculturalism." Prize givers, explains So, were "interested in rewarding forms of identity diversity," whereas "the bestseller appear[ed] to value . . . a marked commitment to whiteness." Middle- and upper-middle-class white reviewers and readers were always looking for themselves as the "subject of the discourse."[6] When they found their identities, values, and struggles in the content, they bought books. Wright, however, may not have been aware of this publishing dynamic, for throughout his career he clung to his subject matter—outcast, subaltern African Americans—while believing that one day he would make real money as a writer.

Yet he was facing another major issue: the long-standing discrepancy in advances for Black versus non-Black writers. This problem continues today in the mostly white publishing industry, and one can assume that Farrar, Straus also followed that pattern, giving Wright advances that were much smaller than the advances white writers on its roster, despite his international reputation.

In addition to promulgating these inequities, the commercial publishing industry was brutally capitalist during the modern era. By the 1960s, most houses had hitched themselves to large corporations, and literary books "were now judged by their profitability, their status as commercial products, rather than, as it once was, as social goods that bore a responsibility to enlighten the public."[7] Writers were badgered to sell books because publishing houses wanted to make a profit. Thus, when Charles asked for advances on work he had not completed or rushed to submit work in order to get cash, he was responding to the market. This created trouble for himself at Farrar, Straus. This was the case with the story collection he had been working on in Tangier. Vursell was infuriated by the situation: "You speak of a volume of short stories on which I should give you a contract by July 10. Are you being sensible? I doubt it. I do not want to see any more hastily written, ill-spelled, ill-typed manuscripts. And anything I do see should come through Candida."[8] But Vursell did not take into consideration Wright's drive to sell his book to make a profit. Though Vursell thought four of the stories—"A Sermon for Life Everlasting," "Cassie," "Moments to Forget," and "Mr. Beckett and Mr. Alsop"— were good, he believed the manuscript as a whole was not up to standards, and he told Wright to get a job in Tangier "to tide you over until you have got your gifts as a writer sufficiently in hand to produce something that Candida can sell, or I can publish without sweating my guts out rewriting."[9] Wright was trapped in a catch 22. He needed money to write, but he could not write publishable fiction without time and money. And in Morocco jobs were difficult to obtain for non-Moroccan citizens. This was the way of life for Wright. But he had a way of dealing with these hardships and obstacles. In the middle of financial crises, he chose to live with gusto, pursue adventure, and exist inside the whirlwind. He always had laughter and humor to protect him. During this time, when everything seemed to be working against him, he wrote to Roger Straus, "I'm fine, still got the crazy sense of humor and can laugh death in the face."[10]

There were other obstacles confronting Charles Wright the writer. His relationship with his literary agent, Candida Donadio, was also problematic. Often, she would not respond to his letters or answer his requests, nor did she make any attempt to nurture him. It was clear to the staff at Farrar, Straus and even to other agents in her firm that she was treating him with disrespect. Her associate Hy Cohen told Andree Conrad at Farrar, Straus, "It seems to me that the author would do better with an agent who is more sympathetic to the tonalities of his work, and understands them better."[11] Donadio also did not seem to understand the depth of his financial woes. When Boston University invited Wright to donate his papers to their new library, she told him to say no. "Later, they will have monetary value," she said.[12] Wright took her advice and thus lost that revenue stream. As years passed, the relationship between the two became distant and strained, and Wright took to referring to her as "a lady whose name I refuse to use" and eventually as the "great literary Mafia queen who was my agent."[13]

While exterior factors certainly contributed to Wright's struggles, his own history and self-destructive behaviors continued to hold him back. His childhood traumas—the death of his mother and the rejection of his father—and the later loss of mentors such as Lowney Handy and Langston Hughes triggered anxiety, depression, indecision, conflict, and detachment. In addition, these personal factors, along with the guilt and shame around his homosexuality/psychic injury caused Wright to unconsciously hold onto and constantly repeat certain choices and behaviors, which were destructive and counterproductive to the maturation and longevity of his writing career.

Finally, to paraphrase Virginia Woolf, Wright never had a "room of his own." He continued to hustle jobs, many of them low-paying and menial, for he could never make enough money to write full time. His writing habits were hectic, irregular, and undisciplined: "I may screw around all night until midnight. Then when I start to work, I worked. I'll build and design houses for maybe two days. And then for ten days I'll do nothing but write."[14] This schedule was not conducive to being a comfortable, full-time writer. With these obstacles, he increasingly escaped into booze and pills, and they, in turn, affected his ability to hone his craft and manage his money. Though he used his existential writings to ferret out solutions to his pain, he was, in the end, unable to "chang[e] those conditions within his personality that [had] brought them into being."[15] Therefore, both aware and unaware of other forces in his life, Charles Wright continued to exist and write under constant stress. He continued to live with gusto, to desperately gamble with life and to laugh in its face—even when people thought he was wrong.

Still, 1974 was a relatively tranquil period in Wright's life. He spent four weeks living in his friend Sam Floyd's apartment on Horatio Street in the West Village. This gave him access to music, books, air conditioning, and plenty of quiet. For the moment he still had some money in his account, the remains of an advance. His short story "Act of Surrender" had just appeared in *Yardbird*, and he was excited that Manor Books would be reprinting *The Messenger* and *The Wig*. Moreover, James Baldwin thought that Wright should interview him and had suggested that he ask *Vogue* to pay him to travel to the south of France for the opportunity. Wright began to envision a future in which he could write full time without worrying about money or washing dishes.

Yet Wright continued to have trouble getting published. That year he submitted a semi-completed, three-part manuscript, *The Orgy of Hesitation*, to Farrar, Straus. Wright told the press that Baldwin had already read the third section and had agreed to write an introduction.[16] But an editor at Farrar, Straus was perplexed by the manuscript. Unclear if it was a novel or a collection of "occasional pieces," this person decided to pass on it, despite being "nagged by a still small voice saying that that might be a mistake."[17]

The Orgy of Hesitation was never completed, but Wright did publish part of the third section as a short story, titled "The Orgy of Hesitation." The piece begins as pornography but soon transcends that label, moving beyond social and sexual categories into a focus on freeing desire. In this way, it is much more daring than his previously published stories. The story is set in the Village just after the end of the summer fiesta on Fire Island. A group of young, diverse, artsy New Yorkers find themselves in a fourth-floor apartment on a Friday night with nothing to do. "Not content to sit around a Franklin stove," they are self-consciously bohemian. They see themselves as the heartbeat of hip New York: "This is where things happen," the narrator ironically explains. "Trends are set here. We are the avantgarde capital of the Western World. Aristocrats, we try to drain the splendor from our world in the off hours."[18]

The narrator describes the setting as "a tenement building [which] has taken on the status of an upper East Side apartment building, peopled by people who have made it or soon will be making it. Citizens of Manhattan's swinging map, or so they like to believe. People who at one time or another might have read the novels of Paul Bowles and dream." In search of excitement, they call Eddie, a legendary drag queen and a source for pills, pot, and poppers. Out of drag, Eddie looks like "Central Casting's idea of a Black longshoreman, returning from the dock."[19] But in drag, he can always be counted on for a grand Bette Davis pose.

Like him, many of the people in the story are performers, and most also enact images from Hollywood movies. In this way they recall some of the characters in *The Wig*. There is Lulu, a Latin American actress who will always be twenty-eight years old, who has had many lovers but thinks that potential husbands are lousy lays. She will never be a star and is known in her circle as an honest woman. There is Mrs. Barnes, a portrait painter and a divorced mother of three, who resembles Geraldine Page in a Tennessee Williams drama. There is Joan, posing like a wistful Lauren Bacall. And there is Ned, a young reporter who has just returned from Vietnam. His writing is going badly, and he is looking for action, something to spark his imagination, to distract him. "Like the others, he has nothing to do and wants to get high, hoping that perhaps by that time, something will turn up."[20]

The young people in the apartment follow Eddie to a party at a Chelsea brownstone, where they gather at the kitchen table with Alfred and Joan, the hosts. Another couple, Peggy and Ron, joins them. The time is shortly after midnight, and they sit at the table like actors, "waiting for the director to say 'lights. camera, action.'" The group drinks brandy and coffee, and gradually they shed their Hollywood images and begin to act on the free flow of desires. Lulu makes a pass at Joan and takes her into the bedroom. Eddie follows them, later dashing back into the kitchen to say, "Miss Lulu is tonguing Joanie's tits." After a while Lulu returns to the kitchen and says she wants to dance. "She knows Eddie will join her and that they will add the smell of funk to the dead hope of a Friday night scene." Alfred asks the group what they want to listen to, soon "the sweet Texas voice of Janis Joplin explodes from a kitchen speaker, bringing with it the cry of the raunchy gutter."[21]

The music is the overture, and now everyone begins to pay attention and relax, snapping their fingers and humming. As Eddie sings, Peggy stands up and dances toward him. Mrs. Barnes touches Ned's leg under the table. Slowly they all move toward the bedroom, toward "Friday night's performance of the orgy of hesitation."[22] There they struggle, sometimes violently, to escape their accustomed sexual categories, their social façades, so that their fantasies and desires emerge. But Eddie laughs, for he knows that for a few hours these strangers and friends will become one—sharing, giving, and taking. When Lulu comes through the door, he reaches for her and she goes to him, like friends who have been separated for years. From within them "desire blossoms and grows on the people in the beautiful bedroom, which becomes a stage for a group play, written, performed, directed by all of them, and who now know a little more about each other. Certainly, they are no longer strangers and can never be the same again whether they meet in a bar, or at a party or on the street."[23] The social "hesitation" melts away and the people genuinely connect and get to know each other. The guests freely engage in open and unrestrained sexual activity or group sex. The story was a shift in Wright's short fiction, focusing not on difference and tolerance, as we get in his previous stories, but on free-flowing desires that challenge social and sexual mores and categories.

At some point in the early 1970s, Wright met the *New Yorker* journalist Jan Hodenfield. Familiar with Wright's pieces in the *Village Voice*, Hodenfield asked him to write a piece about Motown for *GQ Scene*, a magazine aimed at teenage boys. Wright agreed but missed the deadline. Hodenfield recalled, "He was a very strange man, and after we met, I thought, 'Well, this is not going to work.' Then he turned in the most perfect manuscript I'd ever received."[24] The two developed a "mutual respect for each other's talent," and they soon became close friends. Hodenfield's wife, Lynn, and their children, Hallie and Tor, also became attached to Wright.[25] He was invited to spend as much time as he liked in their apartment.[26] Eventually, in 1976, when Hodenfield saw that Wright was spiraling into oblivion, he offered him a room in his home: "He came to stay for a few weeks in 1976," at the age of forty-four. "And he stayed until just before he turned 64. He was a second father to both my children."[27]

Hodenfield did not earn much money as a journalist, nor was he naturally good at being a father or a husband. Therefore, Lynn shouldered most of the bills, and Wright helped her tend Hallie and Tor, overseeing their days, taking them to school, and becoming Lynn's consoling friend.[28] For twenty years, he lived intermittently in the household, which was often in turmoil. When things got too tense, he moved in with other people, among them Charles Robb and Florence Roess. In the late 1970s, on a mission to track down the novelist Jean Rhys, he spent more than three months in Paris, a month in Scotland, as well as time in rural England. In the early 1980s, he lived with Mary Jacobs and Al Upton for more than a year and also with his lover Juan.[29] And I am getting ahead of myself again.

In the mid-seventies, Wright was feeling restless about his writing. He had not published any fiction since 1974 and had grown tired of working with Dianne Fisher at the *Village Voice*.[30] In 1976, he sent Roger Straus a list of book ideas dealing with liberated women, homosexuals, Black women, mixed-race Blacks, and militants. He recognized that some of these topics were racy and assured Straus they had been "conceived with only paperback in mind," asking for advice on "dealing with the paper houses without getting ripped off."[31] Straus replied that "none of the book ideas . . . make sense for FSG, but when you are full of ideas like this, you ought to get an agent and let him/her peddle [them], if not to us, elsewhere including paperback originals."[32] He forwarded a list of agents, but Wright continued to approach publishers directly.

In about 1977, Wright wrote to David Godine of the Quality Paperback Book Club, inquiring if it were possible to reprint a pair of his previously published novels in one volume. Farrar, Straus also discussed this idea with Godine: "[Would it be] possible to do that with two of these not-overly-large Wright books—say, *The Wig* and *Absolutely Nothing to Get Alarmed About?*"[33] Godine ultimately decided against the offer.

In 1978, Clarence Major invited Wright to the University of Colorado at Boulder "to give a reading from [his] work."[34] Wright agreed, provided Major could schedule a date before Wright left for Europe: "I'll stay a few days [in London], then in an English country house (I want to be the Black that does that novel like Hemingway and Fitzgerald, discussing the rich.) Then, off to Paris for the winter."[35] In Boulder, Wright stayed in Major's apartment, and the two became friends, discovering a shared interest in literature, painting, and travel. Yet the faculty noted that he was very thin and that he was chain smoking and drinking heavily. Although congenial, he was a "bit shy and withdrawn." At dinner, he ate next to nothing, which had become a habit. But he consumed "cocktail glass after cocktail glass of whiskey on the rocks."[36] Still, his drinking did not interfere with his presentation, which focused on his own and Baldwin's work in the context of the "Black urban experience."[37] He believed that he and Baldwin "presented the Black urban experience more authentically in their work."[38]

In the meantime, Wright had submitted another book proposal, *The Black People's Book*, to Farrar, Straus. "Unfortunately," the editor Pat Strachan told him, "sober thought brought us to the conclusion that it wouldn't be the kind of book—monograph—that we do best with, and that we'd best step aside for both your sake and ours. I really hope you're able to place it elsewhere."[39] In the margins of an internal memorandum, the editor wrote, "Excellent concept, but clumsily, amateurishly executed by Wright."[40]

In 1979, after returning from Colorado, Wright traveled to Paris. He spent three months there and was moved by the "legendary city," though he had not "expected to be."[41] He visited the haunts in the Moulin Rouge area, where Black expats had lived during the first half of the twentieth

FIGURE 3. Charles Wright and Clarence Major, Boulder, Colorado, 1978. Courtesy of Clarence Major.

century, and sensed an abandoned freedom, something he always felt outside the United States. While in Paris, he learned that Manor Books would publish a paperback edition of *The Wig,* and he wondered if the West German publisher Schlack Verlag would be interested in bringing out translations of *The Wig* and *Absolutely*. He also heard from Gary Stuart of the *Gramercy,* a review journal with a rapidly growing reputation, who had written to ask if Wright would contribute to a special edition: "[We] would be proud to be able to have your work represented in the publication."[42] There is no evidence, however, that he ever submitted anything.

By the fall Wright was in Hertfordshire, England, after spending a month in Scotland. He was staying at Nicki Freud's place while she was away. Freud was a friend of Peggy Guggenheim, and Wright called her "a crazy duck. I like her. She's in Marbella for three weeks."[43] Though he quickly became bored and restless, he was here for a purpose: he was hoping to meet and interview the novelist Jean Rhys. Barney Han, a member of the board of directors at *Vogue*, knew Rhys and planned to introduce the pair. In the meantime, Wright was attending "uptight dinner parties" and had learned that he was also about to become "an honorary uncle" to the Hodenfields' new daughter, Hallie.[44] In the end, his visit to England was busy and adventurous but not very productive, as Rhys died before he had a chance to meet her.[45]

CHAPTER EIGHT

Stalled in the 1980s

In the fall of 1980, Charles Wright returned to New York City from Europe. He lived with Mary Jacobs and occasionally with Charles Robb, though the Hodenfields in Brooklyn were still his fallback. When Albert Upton who was from Berkeley, California, and had moved to New York City in the early 1970s, came to live with Jacobs, Wright was still there, though "he couldn't afford to pay for rent or his share of the rent." At some point, Jacobs recalled, she "just sort of shrugged and said, 'Oh, well, it's Charlie and he's got no income.' So we kind of let it ride. And he was such a gracious spirit. He was always up; . . . he was always energetic; he was never lying in bed and looking for people to wait on him."¹ Wright stayed with Jacobs and Upton for about a year, and the two men became good friends because they respected one another's minds. Upton was a poet, and he shared Wright's love for literature. Jacobs recalled Wright as charming, talented, intellectual, opinionated, witty; he was good company and a great conversationalist. The three made plans to buy a building together, but Wright could not come up with his share of the money, and the deal fell through.

Eventually Jacobs moved to a smaller place, and Wright began living with his young lover, Joey, who was of Polish descent. Joey had faked a car-accident injury; and with the insurance money he received, the two rented an apartment together. Their relationship lasted on and off for about three years, and it fit into an ongoing pattern in Wright's life.² He liked younger men, and he liked to sexually dominate them.³

In the early 1980s Jacobs gave birth to a daughter, Sarah, with Wright serving as the child's godfather. Then, in 1983, mother and daughter moved to Maine. Robb, who was in love with her, soon followed. Though the two never married, they did have an affair, against Wright's wishes. The two broke up when Robb failed to take care of her house. He allowed her "mortars [to] get neglected and soaked, and . . . [her] two dogs [to] get into porcupines." Jacobs would remain in Maine, where she built cabins

143

on lakes and in the woods and rented them out.[4] She would continue to see Wright on her occasional visits to New York City.

But just before Jacobs, Upton, and Wright separated in New York City, Jacobs recorded nine hours of conversation among them in which she served as the moderator and questioner. When I visited New York in 2017, Jacobs permitted me to listen to them. I heard Wright's voice for the first time and acquired a sense of him. At the time he was a controlled drinker, and on the tape he sounds intellectual, witty, and charming. He talked about everything, from literature to movies to police brutality to Jackie Onassis. Well read and knowledgeable, he used literature as the framework for many of his discussions. There was a moving moment when he talked about Hallie, who at the time was three years old, and said that he wanted her to travel the world, meet all kinds of people, and in the process become a better human being. He also joked about his refusal to sleep with James Baldwin.

By the fall of 1980, Wright's connection with Farrar, Straus had changed. Although "precariously low," *Absolutely* was still in stock. Farrar, Straus sent Wright fifteen copies, with its "compliments."[5] After Harold Vursell died in 1977, he was turned over to a new editor, Pat Strachan, though he continued to interact with Roger Straus. Vursell had been "a jack-of-all trades who could move fluidly from production to copyediting to acquisition." He was "worldly and well traveled," fluent in French, "cosmopolitan [and] intellectually sophisticated," and he supported Wright's work, even when he was frustrated by it.[6] Strachan dealt with Wright differently, not seeing him as one of the family. She did not share Vursell's belief in Wright's talent and was not committed to nurturing his writing.

Meanwhile, this was not a productive period for Wright. He sent stories to the *Village Voice* and *Penthouse*. *Savvy* considered a 1,000-word piece. He contacted Jan Hodenfield about several possible *GQ* profiles. He also found a new agent, Ron Bernstein, whom Strachan described as "effectively aggressive."[7] He learned of Wright through Donadio. Wright told Strachan he was "planning to put together a book with the working title *The World of H and H* (hetero-homo). Some of it would be old material, updated from two . . . [unpublished] books, plus new material. Of course, FSG would get first refusal."[8] He made it clear that he was writing this book strictly for financial reasons; his primary intellectual interest at the time was his research on Jean Rhys, though he ultimately never completed it. Strachan considered the proposal for *The World of H and H,* and she told Bernstein that she was amused by Wright's "absolutely unique point view": "there are few writers who can exploit the seemingly seamy side of life with his combination of real interest and ironic detachment." But she was "nervous about finding readers" for such subject matter so decided to reject it.[9]

Although homosexuality and sexual fluidity had been in the margins of Wright's earlier fiction, they moved to the forefront of his later unpublished works. The reasons for this shift are unclear. Perhaps he wanted to embrace a gay identity more publicly, as the issue had clearly been on his mind for decades. In a letter to Handy in the early 1960s, he wrote:

> I am pleased to report that I am not as queer as I thought I was. I went to a party, mixed party, mostly queer though. I saw this lovely girl looking so out of place and lovely and damn [I] just couldn't resist going over and talking to her. And I am really shy too. But I make my pitch. We hit it off great. And Lowney she is good looking. Very nice small-town New Jersey girl, colored. There are good girls around who are not thinking of a bankroll. I'm not seeing her now. Mainly because, all of my free time is taken up with my writing and she is a little too young (20) a young 20. And though I still look like a kid, I feel so old, I've been through so much shit.[10]

In 1961, he told Norman Mailer about "a girl I was a little in love with once," who "came back on her own to bug the hell out of me."[11] In a 1965 letter to Rupert Croft-Cooke, Wright mentioned dreaming about a woman named Anna: "Is she well and still in Tangier"?[12] In a recollection of Veracruz, he mentioned that he might have gotten a girl pregnant. In a conversation with Phelonise Willie, he discussed being involved with a woman in New Mexico. Clearly, he had had relationships with both women and men, and Ishmael Reed referred to him as bisexual.[13] Still, many of his closest acquaintances thought he was a closeted homosexual. Perhaps he defined homosexuality not as a dominating factor in his life but as one among many in the formation of his existence. Certainly, that appears to be the way in which homosexuality manifests in his fiction. As the film director Marlon Riggs has noted, "the way to break loose of the schizophrenia in trying to define identity is to realize that you are many things within one person. Don't try to arrange a hierarchy of things that are virtuous to your character."[14] Perhaps, this was why Wright felt at home in Tangier. He was not a joiner, he was sexually fluid or bisexual, and he believed in few imposed labels and categories, which are forms of epistemic violence.

By the fall of 1981, all of Wright's published novels were out of print. When he asked Strachan about acquiring the three "original manuscripts," she told him they "would have been sent to you six months after their publication. . . . Let's hope you stashed them away safely, and that they'll turn up soon."[15] Straus concurred, telling Wright he had "searched our old files and f[ound] nothing about your manuscripts."[16] Wright insisted that he had "absolutely no recollection of receiving the three original manuscripts. And though I've led a gypsy type of existence—memory, notebooks have no records of it."[17] But as he had done with earlier manuscripts, he had obviously lost the originals.

In March 1982, Wright was living in his own studio apartment in the Village and was relatively financially secure. People and institutions still seemed to be interested in his work. For instance, Charles Harris, the executive director of Howard University Press, wrote that his press was planning to "launch a series of reprints" that might include Wright: "Tentatively titled The Afro-American Literature Book Shelf . . . [the series] will consist mainly of works that received wide critical acclaim when they were published, mainly during the 1960s. While these works . . . were widely reviewed, they never received the public attention that they deserved."[18] But Manor Books now held the license to Wright's novels; therefore, Farrar, Straus could not give reprint permission. The critic Joe Weixlmann had several telephone interviews with Wright as he prepared to write an entry about him in the Black American Writers Series of *The Dictionary of Literary Biography*. Likewise, Russell C. Brignano published an entry on Wright in *Black Americans in Autobiography*.

Chris Willerton, the director of the Texas Reading Circuit at Abilene Christian University, contacted Farrar, Straus about inviting Wright to tour and read at five colleges in the circuit; but when the publisher forwarded the letter to Wright's last address, it was marked "moved, not forwardable, return to sender."[19] By 1986, all of Wright's published novels had been out of print for some time, and he was homeless and destitute. He needed money desperately, and he wrote to Strachan about publishing a novella, *Caroline's Book*, focused on the experiences of a young American niece of Jean Rhys in Paris.[20] She asked for a copy of the manuscript-in-progress, but nothing came of the project.[21] In 1987, he sent Strachan another proposal, this time for a novel tentatively titled *Fade In, Fade Out*. It was a *The Messenger* type of book, he told her:

Story of a drunk with low-life scenes and flashbacks—Robert Blakes encounters with the upper class (basically English) the arrangement of marriages, ex-hippies, basically middle class now and striving. Keeping up with the Joneses isn't dead. I'm trying to get say 75 pages—the beginning to the end, which could be expanded without padding. But I need to be alone and refuse the gas light charms of Park Slope [where the Hodenfields lived.]"[22]

Strachan expressed an initial interest, but nothing came of this project either. Unlike Vursell, she would not take charge of nurturing Wright's fiction into a finished manuscript, and thus he never published another book with Farrar, Straus.[23]

However, in 1986, Wright did publish a short story in *Black American Literature Forum*. Like "Sonny and the Sailor," "Mr. Stein" was set in New Franklin, Missouri. It tells of a German Jew who moves there in 1939 to escape the troubles in Germany. A bachelor, he buys a farm from an out-of-state owner who inherited it in the 1920s. But Mr. Stein is different, even from the other four Jewish families who live in the town. He is isolated, dignified, and wealthy, and the community leaves him alone. He does not take part in the town's social life, though he behaves like a gentleman among the men and tips his hat to the ladies. Then he hires Mamie and Cody Estill, "of New Franklin's old colored family fabric."[24] He becomes friends with Cody and is kind to their daughter Mary Ella and nephew Sonny, giving them money for the movies. Nonetheless, the children lead a group of their friends to Mr. Stein's haystacks and set a fire in his barn.

Mr. Stein refuses to press charges, which surprises the community, and the Estill family continues to work for him. Though he remains what he has always been, the townspeople come to accept him. Like the community in "Sonny and the Sailor," it expands and becomes more tolerant of difference: "Mr. Stein . . . became nothing more than another successful farmer. A good fellow, even a jolly fellow. But he had invested heavily in solitude and remained so until his premature death in the spring of 1952."[25]

It is interesting that, in many of Wright's short stories, which are well organized and tightly structured, the author was ultimately concerned with compassion and empathy for the other, for difference, just as he was in his novels. This probably had something to do with the fact that he had spent his entire life as an outsider. And because almost everything Wright wrote was ultimately about him and his search for himself, the purpose of these stories could be interpreted as his attempt to locate a social and psychological space for himself, a "path to freedom."[26]

CHAPTER NINE

Forgotten in the 1990s

By 1989, Charles Wright felt completely forgotten by the literary world, although he continued to be active. One day in the early 1990s, he visited the public library in Brooklyn to borrow one of his own books, and the librarian said, "Oh, I remember Charles Wright. Isn't he dead?"[1] It was a painful moment in a difficult period of his life. As he told Roger Straus, "breathless, aching, inch by inch, [I've] been climbing out of hell. Glaucoma . . . . Severe depression. And I'm not afraid of Virginia Woolf. After all, she only had a stone in her pocket." Yet despite his personal hardship, he was still somewhat optimistic and upbeat. He concluded the description of himself to Straus with "nevertheless—[I] feel young. Hopeful as an Ellis Island arrival. At the present moment."[2] Galvanized by recent racial unrest, Wright, along with Clarence Major and Ishmael Reed, were making plans to start the African American Society. He told Straus he was eager to edit a book of African American voices, which would include up to twenty essays by living and dead writers focusing on how race had affected their lives. Once again, however, this book never materialized.

These were trying times for Charles Wright. His books were out of print, and he was destitute. Yet critics, scholars, and publishers still had an interest in his work. Professors around the nation were teaching his novels in contemporary literature and creative writing classes.[3] As late as 1995, he was still listed in the newest edition of *Who's Who Among Black Americans*.[4] Wright struggled with this seesaw of neglect and admiration and made a stab at solving the problem by finding a new literary agent, Charlotte Sheedy.

At first this seemed like a useful move. Sheedy made a reprint deal with HarperCollins to release his three previously published novels in a single paperback volume. The deal would include a $7,500 advance for Wright.[5] Straus told him, "I'm glad that your old books will have a new and deserved life."[6] But trouble ensued. Because the books had been out of print for fifteen years, Sheedy had assumed that the copyrights had reverted to the author. Actually, one of the editors at Farrar, Straus had agreed to revert the rights of his three novels to the author and let HarperCollins publish them, providing HarperCollins paid Farrar, Straus the final advance payment of $2,500. Roger Straus was aware of the deal. But this was not the first time that Wright, with Farrar, Straus's cooperation, had tried to get his three novels published in a single volume. As I have mentioned, as early as 1977, at Wright's prompting, Eugene Brissie, who worked in subsidiary rights at the publisher, wrote to the Quality Paperback Book Club "wonder[ing] if it wouldn't be possible to [put a pair of titles together in one volume] . . . with two of these not-overly-large Wright books."[7]

But, in the course of Wright and Sheedy's early 1990s move to package his novels, the situation changed when director Michael Hathaway of Farrar, Straus rushed a letter off to Straus, informing him "we didn't license any titles by Wright to HarperCollins. We still control three."[8] This action created an animated internal discussion among editors and the publisher to discern if the contracts with Farrar, Straus were still valid and if the press had "pending reversion notices anywhere in [its] files."[9] In a letter to Sheedy, Hathaway insisted that he could "find nothing to indicate that rights to *Absolutely Nothing to Get Alarmed About*, *The Messenger*, and *The Wig* [had] ever reverted to the author":

> If you have some paperwork that suggests otherwise, please let me know. It seems clear, however, that these are still under contract to FSG, with all subsidiary rights controlled by us, and you should not have licensed paperback rights to HarperCollins. As a first step to straightening this out, please send me a copy of the contract with HarperCollins. And do let me know if you have made any other subsidiary rights sales.[10]

Obviously, Farrar, Straus was trying to keep its finger in the pie. In an internal memo, a press staff member wrote, "Can't believe we'd ask for anything—books have been op [out of print] for 15 yrs, author has been on skid row. If ask for 50% will make a fuss."[11] In another memo, Hathaway wrote, "Not planning on screwing Charles Wright, but not planning on letting go of the books. Want to see [a] contract and want to know what payments still to come."[12]

When Sheedy told Wright that Farrar, Straus had decided not to allow the copyrights to revert to him, he exploded with anger. In a letter to an editor at Farrar, Straus, he wrote, "Ms. Sheedy informed. I passed out. Twenty years ha[ve] passed. The world wasn't interested in Charles Wright and his old books. In fact, Ms. Sheedy saved the books. The copyright was about to expire. Did you know that? If so, why in the hell didn't you renew it?"[13] Wright made it clear that he would prefer to have Farrar, Straus publish his books. But if that press did not want to reissue them, it should let HarperCollins publish them.

Farrar, Straus responded, telling Sheedy that "Wright's titles . . . are in the red by some $2,500 . . . . [If] you pay us the final advance payment from HarperCollins . . . we will stand aside and revert the three works to the author. I'm sure you'll agree this is a fair solution for all."[14] Nevertheless, in an internal memo, Hathaway said, "I must admit I'm losing my stomach for this battle—i.e. I'm tempted to recommend to RWS that we just drop."[15] In the end, Sheedy rejected the offer, and Farrar, Straus agreed "to revert the rights immediately to the author on these three titles."[16]

In 1993, the HarperCollins imprint HarperPerennial published *The Complete Novels of Charles Wright: "The Messenger," "The Wig," and "Absolutely Nothing to Get Alarmed."* The cover featured an old blurb by James Baldwin: "A very beautiful job. Charles Wright is a terrific writer." Steve Cannon and other members of a Gathering of the Tribes hosted a book party to celebrate the reissue. At the party, Cannon noticed that Wright had gained weight and lost the exuberance he had displayed during their visit at the Hotel Albert in the mid-1960s. Wright read from his work, and afterward he joined Cannon and the poet John Farris at a nearby bar, where he quietly sipped a drink as Farris interviewed him.[17] This was another coming-out party for Wright as he and his fiction continued to evolve and become.

In the early 1990s Wright was working on two absurdist, black-humor novels. In a letter to Straus, he described the plot:

A young Harlem man is imprisoned at the North Pole. He had embezzled $1,000,000. He want[s] Reagan to lead a posse to Death Valley. Then on April 14, 1989, page three of the *New York Times*, [there is] a photograph of Bush and Thatcher meeting in Bermuda. Occasionally Reagan and Thatcher met on an unnamed Caribbean Island. Most of the dialogue would be taken from their public comments. Of course, I'd put words in. But you'd need a Philly lawyer.[18]

Straus did not express an interest.

At the same time Wright was working on a novella about his child-hood, an idea that came to him after rereading Marguerite Duras's novel *The Lover*. He apparently also shopped this one to Straus, who wrote back, "requesting pages from a novel you are working on. . . . It's a funny idea and if you really work on it, I would love to read it in progress."[19] Charles was excited: "If Mr. Straus says: 'It's a good idea'—I don't give a damn what anyone else says."[20] But nothing came of this proposal either.

In 1991, in the middle of recovering from glaucoma surgery, Wright was wrestling with a manuscript titled *On My Black Facts*, which he had been working on since 1976. Though nothing came of this book either, he did finish several short stories, one of which was eventually published in *Shade: An Anthology of Fiction by Gay Men of African Descent*. "Tom and Brock" a poignant, touching story, tells of two middle-aged men who meet periodically in a park in Chinatown. They are connected by the Vietnam War, an interest in sports, and drinking. Brock, who is Black, is a "reclu-sive, homebound in Park Slope," while Tom, who is white, is a "golf pro in Westchester County." They sit together in Roosevelt Park, drinking beer and watching Chinese American boys play basketball. As the men talk, we learn that they have different attitudes about sex. Tom is eager for it, but Brock redirects his urges into drink, dope, and pills. Nonetheless, he is bothered by the obsession of "Anglo Saxon men" with "the myth of Black sexual prowess," and he tells Tom that he is "celibate and basically happy."[21]

Eventually, Tom gets up and walks away toward Grant Street. For a while, Brock stays where he is, but then he, too, moves off in that direc-tion. He turns onto Allen Street, encountering "men and women . . . lobot-omized by the past. . . . These strangers were part of his world of drugs and alcohol. He understood them, listened to them, offered advice, spared cigarettes and change, but kept his distance."[22] As in Wright's other fiction, the story portrays these outcasts compassionately, allowing readers to understand that the sensitive and aware protagonist belongs to this com-munity yet is also alienated from it. His intellect allows him to rise above the group and assess it.

Stopping at a liquor store, Brock buys a large bottle of cheap scotch and returns to the park, where he feels grateful to be alone among the crowd. Taking a long drink, he readies himself to escape "misery, anger and loneli-ness." As therapist van der Kolk writes, those suffering from trauma are "on sensory overload." As a result, they attempt to shut themselves down through self-medication or "develop tunnel vision and hyperfocus."[23] Brock's drinking would have started as an attempt at self-soothing to cope with or numb a trauma from the past, but clearly the effects are disastrous in part because it keeps him from integrating the trauma into his consciousness and beginning steps toward recovery. Instead, the drinking becomes part of his life, becomes who he is. Over time, trauma in a person can look like personality. With the scotch to help him, he tells himself he "will be serene until morning."[24] But then, at the end of the story, Tom returns with beer.

Here, Charles Wright has written a story in which one of the two protagonists is lost to the world and who knowledgeably and existentially accepts the misery, anger, and loneliness in his life. This life has become a niche that he knows, and he has become comfortable with it. Like Charles Stevenson in *The Messenger*, Brock fully understands that he is using alcohol not to escape but to suppress and numb this misery and anger, the chaotic, absurd world around him. More importantly, he wants to do it alone.

In 1995, Wright left the Hodenfields, apparently because of a disagreement. With his glaucoma worsening, he moved into a shelter. He still wanted to write; but according to Phelonise Willie, his "nerves [were] bad," and he complained that "the people in the shelters [were] so boring" they gave him "writer's block."[25] He had long been alcoholic and depressed, and now his health was failing, and he was trapped in dismal living. Yet he still managed to laugh, which gave him the courage to continue, and his black humor startled and amused his listeners. He was as unsentimental about life as he was about pain. Talking to him, you would never guess that he was homeless and on the verge of going blind.

The shelter management was trying to find Wright an apartment in a retirement complex. But he refused anything uptown in Harlem or downtown near Avenue D and the East River. "The East Village is home," he told Willie:

> I've lived here ever since I arrived from St Louis. Even when I was washing dishes in the Catskills, I hiked back on my days off. Even when I was sleeping in those Bowery Fleabags, they were always lower East side fleas. . . . I'm not worried about getting a pad; something will turn up. It's the stuff around the bend worrying me. My Socialized Security if I go blind.[26]

Wright was convinced that he needed the solitude of his own place if he were ever to be able to write again. Willie tried to help, publishing an article in the local journal *Vice Versa* about his homelessness. But Wright himself did not reach out to the people who could have helped him. Larl Becham, for instance, was not aware that Wright was homeless, though his friend Abba Elethea was sure that he would have invited Wright to live with him and his partner.[27] In Maine, Mary Jacobs and Charles Robb also did not know that Wright was homeless. Most likely the Hodenfields were aware, but their response is unknown.

In 1997, Robb died, and Wright traveled to Maine, spending two days there to pay his respects. The two had been estranged, and Robb, who had inherited some money, left amounts to Jacobs and his sister but not to Wright. Of course, Wright was not happy. Nonetheless, he was concerned about Robb's journals, which the family wanted to be destroyed. To prevent that, he and Jacobs broke into Robb's apartment and retrieved the journals, which remained in Jacob's possession until her death in October 2019.

By now Wright was wrangling with nearly everyone. According to Jacobs, he "thought he was superior intellectually," and even she stopped talking to him.[28] Fighting had long been a pattern in his life—arguing with friends and mentors as well as physical aggression. As I have discussed earlier, Wright had internalized a disempowering narrative from his early childhood where he became aware of power dynamics, of not having power. In these fights, he was trying to overcome his feelings of powerlessness. Rather than drink at the well of healing and self-recovery, he acted out his trauma, never making the journey to self-love where he could value his self-worth.

Yet now the quarreling had as much to do with his health as it did with his sense of superiority. Not only was he drinking even more heavily, which was changing his personality and altering his state of consciousness, but he had also been diagnosed with lupus. "I think when Charles realized his body was betraying him," said Willie, "it set him adrift on an island. Charles never obeyed any rules except his own but suddenly even those must have seemed absurd."[29] He was failing to take responsibility for his existence, which was something he had always done.

When he returned to New York City, Wright moved into a small, inexpensive apartment. Jacobs recalled that he was "hypersensitive" in the new place: "[He said] everything that goes on beyond the walls impacts him, and he follows it, and he would kind of either laugh at it or confess that it annoyed the hell out of him."[30] As always, he thrived on human connection, but he missed his youth; he missed casing the bars and having money to spend for books. Willie said:

He could be so gentle and caring. So wise. But the part of him [that] was deeply human was also deeply complicated. Time changed him. Time changes everyone but most of us wear masks to hide our angst. Charles did not believe in masquerade. His pain was public domain. But in the end his rage became his mask. In the end I'm not sure even Charles could see Charles.[31]

Nor could he get started on a writing project. "I remember he told me once," said Jacobs of these years, that "he felt he was somewhere between purgatory and hell."[32]

Yet Wright was not consumed with his problems and issues. Despite his bouts with depression, anxiety, and subsequent drinking, he was respectful to and generous with his friends. He used what clout he had at Farrar, Straus to get his friends, if not published, at least considered. He sent an outline and chapters of Jacobs's book to the press for consideration.[33] It was returned because of its erotic nature. "It isn't right for us," replied Pat Strachan, "due to its fantastic elements."[34] While in Tangier, he sent a short story by Roess, "The Firefly," to Farrar, Straus for consideration. Vursell was impressed by her writing talent and encouraged her to continue.[35] Wright also offered to send Vursell a copy of Chester's unpublished novel.[36] He sent Clemson Brown's poems to Vursell, asking if the press was interested in publishing them. Vursell responded, "While we agreed there were many fine things in the manuscript, on the whole it didn't seem to add up to something we were dying to publish."[37] In 1974, Wright tried to get his friend Marian's two-character play published at Farrar, Straus, saying she was better than Carlene Hatcher Polite, whose books the press had published.[38]

Wright was compassionate, and he gave advice to others. Almost twenty years after visiting Boulder, he reconnected with Clarence Major, telling him about "a brilliant idea for a Clarence Major novella."[39] He once told Vursell, "All I want out of this world is money and fame and to do whatever I am able to do for people who I think are worthy."[40]

In 1998, Wright began to receive Social Security checks, and with help from the Hodenfields he moved to Casa Victoria, an elder housing complex in the Village, where he lived for several years until he was admitted to the hospital.

CHAPTER TEN

The Death and Rediscovery of Charles Wright and His Fiction

The turn of the twenty-first century found Charles Wright still restless and erratic, and in declining health. In 2000, Charles Wright wrote to Clarence Major: "I have been on the move. Moving here and there. Desperately, fortunately, a mile ahead of the motherfuckers who have been trying for years to place me in hell. Their hell." He returned to his grandfather's saying: "'This world is not my home.' If the latter is true, then what a trip. What a hell of a vacation."[1] As always, Wright was trying to laugh in the face of life and death. Laughter was one of the ways he handled the pain, suffering, and hardship of his life and this absurd world. Laughter and humor were essential to his existence. Without humor, he once told Major, he would be "a goner. . . . [Facing] the most terrible thing . . . I can always laugh about it, [and] that sort of reinforces me or gives me the courage to go on." Always, he protected "that private part that I keep to myself, to maintain my sanity and my serenity."[2]

But even with his declining health, Wright was still trying to write. He was still interested in his influence and legacy. In a letter to Major in 2003, he wrote about the reissue of *The Wig*, saying that he was happy that the novel would reach a new generation. He also talked to Major about his health, taking a blues attitude and being existential about his "failing eyesight. So I want to ride that horse. Fast and well before the whatever."[3] As he recovered from eye surgery, he wrote forty to fifty pages of a nonfiction manuscript titled *The Black Book* and sent it to Toni Morrison at Random House. He was hurt that her two-sentence reply did not even acknowledge him as a fellow writer. He told Major about the manuscript and Morrison's "rejection note."[4] We now know that she had "two . . . common reasons for rejecting a submission": either the "writing is poor" or "the book's topic is too specialized or narrow." We also know that Morrison had her own "personal vision of Black literature," and perhaps she saw Wright's manuscript as either poorly written or unable to fit into that vision.[5] *The Black Book* became another book by Wright that did not materialize.

But Charles Wright was still interested in Charles Wright, still wanting to know what the world thought of him. He was still trying to justify his existence in a world that was not his home. He was still reaching out to people, his friends, trying to get assistance for his writing:

> I talked about a grant with Ish [Ishmael Reed]. He was jetting for Paris. Others: TalkTalkTalk. I wrote Miss Maya A. Asked help in securing a grant. Stating that I didn't want to rattle pencils in Tompkins Square Park or go deep into the valley of bottles & cans. I guess she wasn't entertained. . . . Pleased with the first drafts I'd show the world. Securing a grant. Meanwhile: Hustling.[6]

The problem with the trauma of separation, substance abuse, mental illness, and alcoholic addiction was that, in addition to radically changing the personality, they also impaired memory by altering the brain's chemical makeup. In *Trauma and Recovery*, Judith Herman wrote, "The dialectic of trauma gives rise to complicated, sometimes uncanny alterations of consciousness."[7] These bodily changes made it impossible for Wright to have the mental stability, discipline, patience, memory, and comfort to write and create in a sustained way.

Mary Jacobs and her daughter Sarah visited him at the Casa Victoria in about 2003. His apartment was a small one-bedroom with a big picture window, overlooking a construction site. Wright was an old man now, very economical and compulsively neat, prone to complaining about the construction noise outside. Jacobs said, "I'm trying to find the words that describe [his life at this time]. . . . It's minimalist, I guess, in terms of his use of anything. He just used a straight chair, a wooden chair. No you never found him slouched in a soft chair. . . . He was always very energetic sitting in a wooden chair. . . . He thought . . . he was tough."[8]

In his last years, Wright still loved to watch people, and often did this at Lynn Hodenfield's dinner parties, where he would have drinks but not eat, as he had done in Tangier.[9] He said to Major "there is . . . a part of me that always is operating as the observer." He thought of observation as "this little pocket that I always keep for myself, and, also, I remember more by being an outsider . . . than in a group." It was, he noted, a "technique that writers sort of instinctively [use]," maybe without "even being conscious of it." As a child he had been forced to "entertain" white people. Now "I'm an old hand at that," and he would let the white people "perform" for him.[10]

In 2003, Mercury House published a new edition of *The Wig*, with an introduction by Ishmael Reed. Steve Cannon and the Gathering of the Tribes again hosted a book party, with Norman Douglas reading the first chapter aloud and Reed introducing Wright and the novel to the small but racially diverse crowd. In Reed's view, "[the] novel marked a change in African American fiction . . . . The fact that . . . [it] was ignored tells a lot about how African American fiction has been kept in its place. But, a classic refuses to remain in its place."[11] Attendees noticed that Wright was frail, wearing his trademark black hat as well as a pair of dark glasses to hide his glaucoma. Nonetheless, he was eager to talk about *The Wig*, discussing its conception and mentioning that, when he reread it fourteen years after it first appeared, he was surprised by the book's anger. Upon reflection, he said, he realized that this anger had been inside him since childhood.[12]

By 2008, Wright had no relationship with Farrar, Straus. Everyone he had known there was dead or had left the company. Vursell, Wright's biggest supporter, had died in 1977. After Roger Straus had promoted Jonathan Galassi to editor-in-chief over her, Pat Strachan, who was simply promoted to associate publisher, had moved on to another job in the late 1980s. Roger Straus had died in 2004 at the age of eighty-seven.[13] The house that built Wright was no longer there.

We must understand that Wright had developed an unusual relationship with Farrar, Straus, establishing a dependent, family type of relationship with the press. Farrar, Straus was his publisher and it successfully processed, advertised, and printed his books. And by all indications press personnel were very supportive of Wright, particularly Straus and Vursell. When Wright was feeling intellectually insecure about speaking at the Literary Society of the State University of New York's college of Fredonia, Vursell offered "to look at [his] notes."[14] When Wright was working on *The Messenger*, Farrar, Straus "supplement[ed] his income with option money, so much per page as he turn[ed] it in."[15] With the publication of *The Messenger*, the press established an account for his advances and royalties. Many times, he would overdraw that account or would ask for money when the account was empty. Occasionally, Vursell would ask the business office for money for Wright. Other times, realizing that the business office had no right to give Wright money, he would give him the money himself.

The press adjusted to Wright's bohemian lifestyle, his lack of money, buying and sending him books as he requested. As the librarian Richard Peek explained, "Charles's best days were when he was being celebrated as one of the rising stars in Roger Straus's stable which at the time included Mailer and Sontag, heady days for him that proved to be much too much."[16] Wright considered it an honor to be published by the most admired press in the United States in the twentieth century. Yet I am not sure Farrar, Straus fully understood Wright's traumatic life, his damaged personality, or his psychic injuries. Instead, I think, the publisher accounted for his behavior by "seeking flaws in [his] personality or moral character," not in something that could be attributed to trauma.[17]

In 2008, with help from Phelonise Willie, Wright began negotiations with Peek, who worked at the University of Rochester Library, about selling his papers to the institution. Peek recalled, "Charles and I had meetings and conversations for about a three-year period up until his death."[18] The two men became "fast friends," and Peek could see that Wright was struggling through "plenty of dark days," though "we tended to skirt around the rough times during our talks."[19] The university did agree to buy Wright's papers, apparently with the understanding that he would eventually furnish them with the original documents . In the end, however, the archive remained thin. Peek said, "There's not much there. Charles wasn't one to save a lot of things. His lifestyle didn't lend itself to that sort of personal responsibility."[20] Willie concurred: "Charles had a genius for losing stuff. For a while he [would] borrow his novels from me because he didn't have copies."[21] Peek did note that Wright's papers included

a typescript to *The Highest Tension*, his first work, a Korean War novel written while at the Handy Writers' Colony while Charlie was very much standing in the shadow and influence of James Jones. It's a good sophomoric effort but it's not very interesting. Charles explained that "it was more of a writing exercise" for him. It's certainly not on the creative level of *The Messenger* or *The Wig*. Other than that, Charlie had what could be politely called sketches of pieces, extended ideas scrawled on paper but there's not much there and nothing that holds together. And there's no correspondence and no photographs or videos. Pity.[22]

Without any originals, the university eventually returned Wright's papers to him. They remain in the possession of Phelonise Willie, a co-executor of his estate.

In early October 2008, Wright was admitted to the hospital; and Willie, along with Lynn and Hallie Hodenfield, was at his side when he died on October 8 of heart failure. When Willie returned to his apartment, she found that someone had been rummaging through his papers and other belongings, probably looking for money; therefore, she gathered up what was left and took them home with her.[23] I have not been able to examine those papers and belongings.

Since Wright's death, a community of readers and critics has worked to reestablish his stature in the public arena, critically and aesthetically rereading and reinterpreting his work. In addition to Ishmael Reed, other voices have chimed in with glowing reassessments, particularly of *The Wig*. As Joe Weixlmann has written, that novel "encapsulates a familiar theme within an unaccustomed covering, an easily decodable message within an unusual form." Yet he admits that, "while this is, undeniably, the principal reason for the novel's being so well-regarded today, one can imagine that the book might have produced no small amount of consternation among those introduced to it in 1966."[24]

By the early twenty-first century, the institutions within the ideological state apparatus had moved beyond the strictures of New Criticism that had marginalized Wright in the 1960s and 1970s. Maybe this renewed interest in Wright had something to do with changes in the literary and publishing industries, which were opening up and becoming more inclusive of different tastes, ideas, values, and perspectives. In 2014, the Paris publishing house Le Tripode brought out a French translation of *The Messenger*. In 2017, Dwight Garner offered a reconsideration of *Absolutely Nothing to Get Alarmed About*, arguing that "it's time to exhume Wright's novels. . . . Reading Wright is a steep, stinging pleasure." In his view, Wright's fiction remains highly relevant in contemporary America: "The comedy comes back loaded with pain. The laughter . . . confront[s] America's shattered promises regarding race and progress and, as often as not, [readers] end up grinning and shaking their heads in disbelief."[25]

There were other becomings, reevaluations, and reassessments of Wright's literary work. In 2019, HarperPerennial reissued *The Collected Novels of Charles Wright* with a new foreword by Reed. That same year John Lingan reviewed Wright's fiction in *Slate*, along with James Alan McPherson's *Hue and Cry* and George Cain's *Blueschild Baby*, focusing on how he and other geniuses of the 1960s and 1970s had been lost or ignored.[26] Like Garner, he believed such works still spoke to the contemporary moment. Gene Seymour agreed, writing in *Bookforum*:

> Through the dedication and (even) fervor of his steadfast readers, Wright's sardonic, lyrical depictions of a young Black intellectual's odyssey through the lower depths of mid-twentieth century New York City have somehow materialized in another country. . . . Even at his most marginalized, Wright wrote with a sense of style and intensity of vision that allowed me to believe I could live, grow, and strain for enlightenment within the isolation the book evokes. That's why, I suppose, Wright's meager literary output won't go away: As much as his Fitzgeraldian dreams were atomized by life, he never stopped taking it all down, turning it into art, and being true to his calling.[27]

For Seymour, Wright's fiction successfully translated into "another country," another generation. Charles Wright gambled, took risks, and accepted the consequences because, for him, there was no tomorrow. For Charles Wright, life was an existential journey and a hell of a vacation.

Lastly, in retrospect and in terms of African American fiction, we can see how Charles Wright's satirical novel *The Wig* was proceeded by the work of George Schuyler (*Black No More*) and Rudolph Fisher (*The Walls of Jericho*), and anticipated the satirical works of Ishmael Reed, Steve Cannon, Fran Ross, Paul Beatty, and Darius James. In the modern era, Reed credited Wright with breaking "Black writers out of the aesthetic prison that critics had placed around them. . . . [He] began the jailbreak."[28] Wright was a trailblazer who charted his own path, regardless of the consequences. He was a maverick who chose to go it alone against the grain.

Finally, I wish I could say that I hoped that Charles Wright could have gotten professional help that would have allowed him to manage his traumatic and conflicted life in a way that would have allowed him to finish many of the novels and short stories he began. Those works were unfinished and lost because he was unable to overcome his addictions and traumas, because he could not establish the financial security that would have allowed him to develop the discipline to create a full, mature body of work. Yet wishing for change in Wright would be like wishing that the great jazz musicians Thelonious Monk, Billie Holiday, and Charlie Parker could have conquered their demons and thus have lived longer and produced more great music. Wright's talent and innovations, his gusto for life, were inseparable from his addictions and his psychic injuries. Even as they damaged him, they were the engine behind his writing. Charles Wright and his fiction never resisted life. Maybe Wright was aware that he lived what I perceived as a conflicted, contradictory and destructive life, and he was just fine with it. With all of this said, he was a unique modern American writer.

NOTES

PREFACE

1. Bruce Weber, "Charles Wright, Novelist, Dies at 76," *New York Times*, October 8, 2008.
2. Lynn Hodenfield, personal communication, May 14, 2014.
3. Phelonise Willie, personal communication, April 26, 2013.
4. Phelonise Willie, personal communication, April 25, 2013.
5. Quoted in Frances S. Foster, "Charles Wright: Black Black Humorist," *CLA Journal* 15, no. 1 (1971): 44–53, 52.
6. Joseph Henry, "A *MELUS* Interview: Ishmael Reed," in *Conversations with Ishmael Reed*, ed. Bruce Dick and Amritjit Singh (Jackson: University Press of Mississippi, 1995), 205–18, 213.
7. Mel Watkins, "An Interview with Ishmael Reed," in ibid., 253.
8. Michel Foucault, *The Archaeology of Knowledge & The Discourse on Language*, trans. A. M. Sheridan Smith (New York: Pantheon, 1971), 24.

CHAPTER ONE: A TUMULTUOUS, TRAUMATIC MISSOURI CHILDHOOD

1. Melissa Harris-Perry, *Sister Citizen: Shame, Stereotypes, and Black Women in America* (New Haven, CT: Yale University Press, 2011), 72.
2. Missouri State Board of Health, Bureau of Vital Statistics, certificate of death for Anna Rose Hughes, filed October 23, 1931.
3. Missouri State Board of Health, Bureau of Vital Statistics, certificate of death for Nannie Hughes, filed September 13, 1920.
4. U.S. Department of Commerce and Labor, Bureau of the Census, State of Missouri, Franklin Township, April 29, 1940.
5. James Dallas Parks folder, Department of Library and Information Studies, Lincoln University, Jefferson City, MO.

6. Missouri State Board of Heath, Bureau of Vital Statistics, certificate of death for Henry Hughes, filed April 6, 1953.

7. Charles Wright, letter to Lowney T. Handy, July 19, 1951, Handy Writers' Colony Collection, Norris L. Brookens Library, University of Illinois, Springfield (hereafter cited as Handy Collection).

8. Phelonise Willie, personal communication, May 14, 2013.

9. Carol Garhart Mooney, *Theories of Attachment: An Introduction to Bowlby, Ainsworth, Gerber, Brazelton, Kennell, and Klaus* (St. Paul, MN: Redleaf, 2010), 18.

10. Ibid., 18, 28.

11. Clarence Major, "A Conversation with Charles Wright," Clarence Major Papers, Elmer L. Anderson Library, University of Minnesota, Minneapolis, 1–26, 1 (hereafter cited as Major Papers).

12. Bruce Weber, "Charles Wright, Novelist, Dies at 76," *New York Times*, October 8, 2008.

13. Wright, letter to Handy, July 19, 1951.

14. Mooney, *Theories of Attachment*, 23.

15. Wright, letter to Handy, July 19, 1951.

16. Ibid.

17. Charles Wright, letter to Lowney T. Handy, April 23, 1961, Handy Collection.

18. Judith Herman, *Trauma and Recovery* (New York: Basic Books, 2015), 56.

19. Although the school superintendent in New Franklin claimed that the elementary school must have been integrated because it was the only one in town, all of Wright's later references indicate that it was segregated. In the short story "Mr. Stein," it is referred to as a "colored school." In his *Village Voice* column, Wright refers to the students as "colored."

20. Ishmael Reed, "Introduction," in *The Collected Novels of Charles Wright: "The Messenger," "The Wig," and "Absolutely Nothing to Get Alarmed About,"* by Charles Wright (New York: HarperPerennial, 2019), ix–xx, xix.

21. Major, "A Conversation with Charles Wright," 10.

22. James Dallas Parks folder. In a letter to Clarence Major, Wright referred to James Parks as "my cousin's husband" (February 7, 2000, Major Papers).

23. Florence Parks's obituary, *Jefferson City Post Tribune*, March 6, 2003.

24. Wright, letter to Major, February 7, 2000.

25. Charles Wright, letter to Harold Vursell, May 22–23, 1965, Farrar, Straus, and Giroux Records, Manuscripts and Archives Division, New York Public Library, Astor, Lenox, and Tilden Foundations (hereafter cited as FSG Records).

26. GerShun Avilez, *Black Queer Freedom: Spaces of Injury and Paths of Desire* (Urbana: University of Illinois Press, 2020), 11.

27. Wright, letter to Handy, July 19, 1951.

28. Charles Wright, "Welfare: Easy Living & Christmas Tree Light," *Village Voice*, December 17, 1970, 17.

29. Wright, letter to Handy, July 19, 1951.
30. Ibid.
31. Rhonda Chalfant, personal communication, August 19, 2014.
32. Major, "A Conversation with Charles Wright," 2.
33. Ibid.
34. Mooney, *Theories of Attachment*, 10.
35. Avilez, *Black Queer Freedom*, 12.
36. Major, "A Conversation with Charles Wright," 25.
37. Wright, letter to Handy, July 19, 1951.
38. Weber, "Charles Wright, Novelist, Dies at 76."
39. Major, "A Conversation with Charles Wright," 25–26.
40. Reed, "Introduction," xiv–xv.
41. Joe Weixlmann, "Charles Stevenson Wright," in *Afro-American Writers after 1955: The Dictionary of Literary Biography*, vol. 33, ed. Thadious Davis and Trudier Harris (Farmington Hills, MI: Gale Research, 1984), 3.
42. Wright, letter to Handy, July 19, 1951.
43. Ibid.
44. Major, "A Conversation with Charles Wright," 22.
45. Wright, letter to Handy, July 19, 1951.
46. Ibid.
47. Vincent Tubbs, "Writer's Colony: Two Negro Writers in Downstate Illinois Camp Turn Out Novels under Whiplash of Tyrannical Mentor," *Sepia* (December 1957): 36–40, 38.
48. Ibid., 36.
49. George Hendrick, *James Jones and the Handy Writers' Colony* (Carbondale: Southern Illinois University Press, 2001), 121.
50. Tubbs, "Writer's Colony," 38.
51. Ibid., 38.
52. Charles Wright, letter to Lowney T. Handy, September 6, 1951, Handy Collection.
53. Charles Wright, letter to Lowney T. Handy, August 18, 1952, Handy Collection.
54. Louis Althusser, "Ideology and Ideological State Apparatuses," in *Lenin and Philosophy* (New York: Monthly Review Press, 1971), 127–18, 142–43.
55. Ibid., 143.
56. Raymond Williams, *Marxism and Literature* (New York: Oxford University Press, 1977), 48.
57. Richard Jean So, *Redlining Culture: A Data History of Racial Inequality and Postwar Fiction* (New York: Columbia University Press, 2021), 9.
58. Helen Howe, Don Sackrider, and George Hendrick, eds., *Writings from the Handy Colony* (Urbana, IL: Tales Press, 2001), 1.
59. Hendrick, *James Jones and the Handy Writers' Colony*, 3

60. Ibid., 137.
61. Tubbs, "Writer's Colony," 39, 38.
62. Ibid., 39.
63. Hendrick, *James Jones and the Handy Writers' Colony*, 2.
64. Ibid., 4.
65. Tubbs, "Writer's Colony," 36.
66. "Writers' Colony: Woman Who Trained James Jones Is Tutoring Two Negro Authors," *Ebony* 23 (November 1957): 114.
67. Charles Wright, "Vietnam: Freak In or Freak Out?," *Village Voice*, December 28, 1967, 7.
68. John O'Brien, "Charles Wright," in *Interviews with Black Writers* (New York: Liveright, 1973), 245–57, 254.
69. Ibid.
70. Wright, "Vietnam: Freak In or Freak Out?," 7.
71. Ibid., 22.
72. O'Brien, "Charles Wright," 254.
73. Mary Jacobs, personal communication, February 13, 2015.
74. Weixlmann, "Charles Stevenson Wright."
75. Charles Wright, letter to Lowney T. Handy, December 17, 1954, Handy Collection.
76. Weixlmann, "Charles Stevenson Wright," 3.
77. Lowney T. Handy, letter to Charles Wright, February 4, 1955, Handy Collection.
78. In 1957 and 1958, the editor Harold Vursell repeated talked to Wright and his agent about writing a novel about "Negroes in St. Louis" (Harold Vursell, letter to Candida Donadio, March 8, 1966, FSG Records).
79. Charles Wright, letter to James Jones, October 29, 1955, James Jones Papers, Harry Ransom Center, University of Texas, Austin (hereafter cited as Jones Papers).
80. Ibid.
81. Ibid.
82. Charles Wright, letter to Lowney T. Handy, January 9, 1955, Handy Collection.
83. Lowney T. Handy, letter to Charles Wright, January 11, 1956, Handy Collection.
84. Lowney T. Handy, letter to Charles Wright, n.d., Handy Collection.
85. Ibid.
86. Wright, letter to Handy, January 9, 1955.
87. Ibid.
88. Handy, letter to Wright, January 11, 1956.
89. Wright, letter to Handy, January 9, 1955.
90. Ibid.
91. Handy, letter to Wright, January 11, 1956.
92. Ibid.
93. Lowney T. Handy, letter to Charles Wright, February 2, 1956, Handy Collection.

94. Karen Horney, *Our Inner Conflicts: A Constructive Theory of Neurosis* (New York: Norton, 1945, 1992), 32.

CHAPTER TWO: THE STRUGGLE TO BECOME
A WRITER IN NEW YORK CITY

1. Charles Wright, letter to James Jones, October 3, 1956, Jones Papers.
2. Charles Wright, letter to Lowney T. Handy, July 13, 1961, Handy Collection.
3. Lowney T. Handy, letter to Charles Wright, September 11, 1956, Handy Collection.
4. Clarence Major, "A Conversation with Charles Wright," 1–26, 1, Major Papers.
5. Ibid., 1.
6. Charles Wright, letter to James Jones, October 19, 1956, Jones Papers.
7. Samuel R. Delany, *Times Square Red, Times Square Blue* (New York: New York University Press, 2019), 141.
8. Elise Czyzowska, "Allen Ginsberg's 'Sunflower Sutra' (1955)—A Vision for Counter Culture America," November 29, 2020, https://thecultural.me.
9. Major, "A Conversation with Charles Wright," 1–2.
10. Charles Wright, letter to Clarence Major, February 7, 2000, Major Papers.
11. Charles Wright, letter to Harold Vursell, August 12, 1966, FSG Records.
12. Phelonise Willie, personal communication, May 5, 2013.
13. Ozzie Rodriguez, personal communication, n.d.
14. Robert F. Reid-Pharr, "Foreword," in Delany, *Times Square Red*, xvi.
15. Phelonise Willie, email to author, May 14, 2013.
16. "Writers' Colony: Woman Who Trained James Jones Is Tutoring Two Negro Authors," *Ebony* 23 (November 1957): 118.
17. Helen Howe, Don Sackrider, and George Henrick, eds., *Writings from the Handy Colony* (Urbana, IL: Tales Press, 2001), 188.
18. Vincent Tubbs, "Writer's Colony: Two Negro Writers in Downstate Illinois Camp Turn Out Novels under Whiplash of Tyrannical Mentor," *Sepia* (December 1957): 36.
19. Ibid.
20. Charles Wright, letter to Lowney T. Handy, January 9, 1955, Handy Collection.
21. Major, "A Conversation with Charles Wright," 21, 22, 23.
22. Tubbs, "Writer's Colony," 114.
23. Ibid., 36.
24. Ibid., 40.
25. Ibid.
26. Ibid., 114.
27. Aijaz Ahmad, *In Theory: Classes, Nations, Literatures* (New York: Verso, 1992), 56.

28. Jeffrey R. Di Leo, "A New American Canon," *American Book Review* 42 (March–April 2021): 11–13, 12.

29. Ibid., 12.

30. Judith Herman, *Trauma and Recovery* (New York: Basic Books, 2015), 42.

31. Charles Wright, letter to James Jones, March 6, 1958, Jones Papers.

32. Charles Wright, *The Messenger*, in *The Complete Novels of Charles Wright* (New York: HarperPerennial, 1993), 113.

33. Bessel van der Kolk, *The Body Keeps the Score: Brain, Mind, and Body in the Healing of Trauma* (New York: Penguin, 2014), 21.

34. Wright, letter to Jones, March 6, 1958.

35. Ibid.

36. Lowney T. Handy, letter to Charles Wright and Charles Robb, August 18, 1959, Jones Papers.

37. Wright, letter to Jones, March 6, 1958.

38. Ibid.

39. Charles Robb, letter to Lowney T. Handy, June 4, 1960, Handy Collection.

40. Charles Wright, letter to James Jones, May 14, 1961, Jones Papers.

41. Wright, letter to Jones, March 6, 1958.

42. Wright, letter to Handy, January 9, 1955.

43. Ibid.

44. Charles Wright, letter to Lowney T. Handy, July 7, 1959, Handy Collection.

45. Charles Wright, letter to Lowney T. Handy, October 2, 1957, Handy Collection.

46. Charles Wright, letter to Lowney T. Handy, April 23, 1961, Handy Collection.

47. Wright, letter to Handy, July 7, 1957.

48. Wright, letter to Handy, April 23, 1961.

49. Charles Wright, letter to Lowney T. Handy, n.d., Handy Collection.

50. Wright, letter to Handy, April 23, 1961.

51. Ibid.

52. Wright, letter to Jones, May 14, 1941.

53. Ibid.

54. Ibid.

55. Abba Elethea (also known as James W. Thompson) recalled visiting Wright in the 1960s with Becham after the publication of *The Wig*. He noticed that Wright was enthusiastic about the new book and was warm and generous, yet he remained distant and did not show signs of being a joiner (personal communication, December 29, 2014).

56. Charles Robb, letter to Norman Mailer, May 10, 1961, Norman Mailer Papers, Harry Ransom Center, University of Texas, Austin (hereafter cited as Mailer Papers).

57. Norman Mailer, letter to Charles Robb, May 17, 1961, Mailer Papers.

58. Joe Weixlmann, "Charles Wright," http://www.answers.com.

59. Norman Mailer, letter to Charles Wright, June 27, 1961, Mailer Papers.

60. Charles Wright, letter to Norman Mailer, n.d., but before September 20, 1961, Mailer Papers.

61. Karen Honey, *Our Inner Conflicts: A Constructive Theory of Neurosis* (New York: W. W. Norton, 1945, 1992), 13.

62. Norman Mailer, letter to Charles Wright, October 14, 1961, Mailer Papers.

63. Charles Wright, letter to Norman Mailer, October 17, 1961, Mailer Papers.

64. Norman Mailer, letter to Charles Wright, October 23, 1961, Mailer Papers.

65. Charles Wright, letter to Norman Mailer, December 19, 1961, Mailer Papers.

66. Norman Mailer, letter to Charles Wright, January 13, 1962, Mailer Papers.

67. Norman Mailer, letter to Charles Wright, January 24, 1962, Mailer Papers.

68. Norman Mailer, letter to Charles Wright, March 3, 1962, Mailer Papers.

69. Norman Mailer, letter to Charles Wright, March 26, 1962, Mailer Papers.

70. Norman Mailer, letter to Charles Wright, April 19, 1962, Mailer Papers.

71. Norman Mailer, letter to Charles Wright, March 26, 1962, Mailer Papers.

72. Charles Wright, letter to Norman Mailer, November 26, 1965, Mailer Papers.

73. Phelonise Willis, "Who's Who in Black America and Homeless?," *Vice Versa* 49 (July–August 1995): 5.

74. Charles Wright, letter to Kay Boyle, December 25, 1972, Kay Boyle Papers, Special Collection Research Center, Morris Library, Southern Illinois University, Carbondale.

75. Boris Kachka, *Hothouse: The Arts of Survival and the Universal Art at America's Most Celebrated Publishing House, Farrar, Straus & Giroux* (New York: Simon and Schuster, 2013), 9.

76. Richard Jean So, *Redlining Culture: A Data History of Racial Inequality and Postwar Fiction* (New York: Columbia University Press, 2021), 33.

77. Kachka, *Hothouse*, 9, 6, 27, 47, 13.

78. In a letter to Handy, Wright admitted that *No Regrets* had been rejected by several publishers but told her that it would be out in the summer, published by Brett Associates: "a new, small offbeat publishers are bringing it out. . . . It tells about the end of a Greenwich Village love affair and is told in the first person by the young Negro hero, who is not me, though everyone thinks Joey is me" (March 14, 1963, Handy Collection).

79. Roger Straus, letter to Charles Wright, February 5, 1963, FSG Records.

80. "A statement is never individual, they argue, but always collective. Forces, bodies, objects, and territories form temporary assemblages fuelled by desire and with a particular function. These forces form an assemblage when its set of components becomes machinic. The notion of machinic is important because it indicates that the assemblage is active while stressing its nonpersonal and nonhuman dimension. It functions not because of an individual but because of a combination of movements" (Frida Beckman, *Gilles Deleuze* [London: Reaktion, 2017], 12).

81. Charles Wright, letter to Norman Mailer, August 3, 1962, Mailer Papers.
82. Harold Vursell, letter to Charles Wright, January 21, 1963, FSG Records.
83. Harold Vursell, letter to Charles Wright, November 20, 1962, FSG Records.
84. Herman, *Trauma and Recovery*, 44.
85. Vursell, letter to Wright, January 21, 1963.
86. Kachka, *Hothouse*, 11.
87. Harold Vursell, letter to Herbert Gold, April 8, 1963, FSG Records.
88. Norman Mailer, letter to Roger Straus, January 16, 1963, FSG Records.
89. Roger Straus, letter to Norman Mailer, January 21, 1963, FSG Records.
90. Harold Vursell, letter to Charles Wright, March 14, 1963, FSG Records.
91. Herbert Gold, letter to Harold Vursell, April 7, 1963, FSG Records.
92. Philip Roth, letter to Roger Straus, January 12, 1963, FSG Records.
93. Lillian Smith, letter to Harold Vursell, April 5, 1963, FSG Records.
94. Harold Vursell, letter to Lillian Smith, April 11, 1963, FSG Records.
95. So, *Redlining Culture*, 42.
96. Kachka, *Hothouse*, 46, 163.
97. Harold Vursell, letter to Charles Wright, June 12, 1963, FSG Records.
98. James Baldwin, letter to Harold Vursell, April 6, 1963, FSG Records.
99. Kay Boyle, letter to Harold Vursell, April 23, 1963, FSG Records.
100. Lucy Freeman, letter to Harold Vursell, March 24, 1963, FSG Records.
101. Harold Vursell, letter to Gerald Pollinger, April 22, 1963, FSG Records.
102. Edith Kiilerich, letter to Paula Diamond, May 13, 1963, FSG Records.
103. Harold Vursell, letter to Charles Wright, April 11, 1963, FSG Records.
104. Hendrick, *James Jones and the Handy Writers' Colony*, 133, 134.
105. Charles Wright, letter to Lowney T. Handy, April 15, 1957, Handy Collection.
106. Harold Vursell, letter to Charles Wright, June 17, 1963, FSG Records.
107. David McCullough, letter to Charles Wright, May 22, 1963, FSG Records.
108. "Books Noted," *Negro Digest* 12 (October 1963): 51.
109. L. M. Meriwether, "From Cover to Cover," *Los Angeles Sentinel*, June 13, 1963, A6.
110. Charles Wright, letter to Lowney T. Handy, June 27, 1964, Handy Collection.
111. "Charles Wright's *The Messenger*," *Atlantic* 212 (August 1963): 121–22.
112. Milton Byam, *Library Journal* (July 1963): 2730.
113. Whitney Balliett, "Books," *New Yorker*, November 2, 1963, 206.
114. Nat Hentoff, "Neo Beat," *Reporter*, July 4, 1963, 40.
115. David Littlejohn, *Black on White: A Critical Survey of Writing by American Negroes* (New York: Viking, 1966), 149; Noel Schraufragel, *The Black American Novel* (Deland, FL: Everett/Edwards, 1973), 122; Jerome Klinkowitz, "The New Black Writer and the Old Black Art," *Fictional International* 1 (1997): 123.
116. Harold Vursell, letter to Charles Wright, August 21, 1963, FSG Records.

117. Rupert Croft-Cooke, *The Caves of Hercules* (London: Allen, 1974), 90.
118. Langston Hughes, letter to Charles Wright, August 25, 1963, Langston Hughes Papers, ser. 1, Personal Correspondence, JWJ MSS 26, box 174, folder 3191, Beinecke Library, Yale University (hereafter cited as Hughes Papers).
119. Ernest Hecht, letter to Paula Diamond, April 7, 1964, FSG Records.
120. Unknown writer, letter to Paula Diamond, June 24, 1963, FSG Records.
121. Leona Nevler, letter to Paula Diamond, September 23, 1963, FSG Records.
122. Farrar, Straus, and Giroux, memo, n.d., FSG Records.
123. Leslie Smith, letter to Farrar, Straus, and Giroux, September 17, 1965, FSG Records.
124. Peter Hinzmann, letter to Gabriella Drudi, August 13, 1970, FSG Records.
125. Akira Takasawa, letter to Henry Robbins, , August 10, 1974, FSG Records.
126. Harold Vursell and Charles Wright, signed agreement, July 1, 1963, FSG Records.
127. Harold Vursell, letter to Charles Wright, July 8, 1963, FSG Records.

CHAPTER THREE: AN EXISTENTIAL READING OF *THE MESSENGER*

1. Clarence Major, "A Conversation with Charles Wright," 1–26, 17, Major Papers.
2. GerShun Avilez, *Black Queer Freedom: Spaces of Injury and Paths of Desire* (Urbana: University of Illinois Press, 2020), 152.
3. John O'Brien, ed., "Charles Wright," in *Interviews with Black Writers* (New York: Liveright, 1973), 251, 252.
4. Ibid., 252.
5. Several critics did mention existentialism in their reviews, but they had problems balancing their notion of Wright as purveyor of "racial artefacts" versus Wright as poetic artist. Noel Schraufragel acknowledges "the influence of such French writers as Sartre and Camus" on Wright and *The Messenger* and admits that Charles Stevenson is portrayed as an existential hero who "merely drift[s] along in a world that seems devoid of meaning" (*The Black American Novel* [Deland, FL: Everett/Edwards, 1973], 122). Yet he ultimately defines *The Messenger* as racial accommodationist fiction. Likewise, David Littlejohn briefly defines *The Messenger* as an existential text—"What we have here is a pure, calm existentially true bit of self awareness by a very genuine, very sad, very lonely human being"—but does not develop an existential reading of *The Messenger* (*Black or White* [New York: Viking, 1966], 149).
6. A. Robert Lee, "Making New," in *Black Fiction: New Studies in the Afro-American Novel Since 1945* (London: Vision, 1980), 222–50, 240.
7. Charles Wright, *The Messenger*, in *The Complete Novels of Charles Wright* (New York: HarperPerennial, 1993), 10.
8. Ibid., 4.

9. Albert Camus, *The Myth of Sisyphus and Other Essays*, trans. Justin O'Brien (New York: Vintage, 1955), 16.

10. Wright, *The Messenger*, 106, 21.

11. Dominick La Capra, *Writing History, Writing Trauma* (Baltimore: Johns Hopkins University Press, 2001), 57.

12. Wright, *The Messenger*, 22, 25, 26.

13. Ibid., 110.

14. Ibid., 112.

15. Ibid., 116–17.

16. Camus, *The Myth of Sisyphus*, 13.

17. Wright, *The Messenger*, 35.

18. *Ibid.*, 26, 6, 70.

19. Ibid., 7.

20. Edward W. Said, *Representations of the Intellectual* (New York: Random House, 1994), 53.

21. Camus, *The Myth of Sisyphus*, 5.

22. Wright, *The Messenger*, 79.

23. Barbara Hernstein Smith, *Contingencies of Value: Alternative Perspective for Critical Theory* (Cambridge, MA: Harvard University Press, 1988), 168.

24. Said, *Representations of the Intellectual*, 59.

25. Julia Kristeva, *Desire in Language*, trans. Thomas Gora and Alice Jardine (New York: Columbia University Press, 1980), 269, 268–69.

26. Wright, *The Messenger*, 22, 102–3, 29.

27. Ibid., 33.

28. Ibid., 16, 87.

29. Ibid., 42–43.

30. Ibid., 58.

31. Ibid., 25.

32. Ibid., 127.

33. Ibid., 8–9, 124, 130.

34. Jean-Paul Sartre, "Self-Deception," in *Existentialism from Dostoevsky to Sartre*, ed. Walter Kaufman (New York: New American Library, 1956), 299–328.

35. Wright, *The Messenger*, 51.

36. Schraufragel, *The Black American Novel from Apology to Protest*, 122.

37. Jean-Paul Sartre, "Existentialism Is a Humanism," in *Existentialism from Dostoevsky to Sartre*, 345–369, 353.

38. Major, "A Conversation with Charles Wright," 22.

39. Handy did not want Charles to write about racial oppression, and other writers at the colony such as Tom Chamales, James Jones, and Jerry Tschappat were angered by his writing about sex. See Lowney T. Handy, letter to Charles Wright, February 17, 1956, Handy Collection.

40. Wright, *The Messenger*, 85, 84.

41. Ibid., 52, 53.

42. Ibid., 54, 55.

43. Albert Murray, *The Omni-Americans* (New York: Avon, 1970), 90.

44. Albert Murray, *Stomping the Blues* (New York: Da Capo, 1976), 250–51.

45. Wright, *The Messenger*, 62, 77, 104, 124.

46. Murray, *Stomping the Blues*, 251.

47. James H. Cone, *The Spirituals and the Blues: An Interpretation* (New York: Seabury, 1972), 112.

48. Wlad Godzich, "Foreword," in *Heterologies: Discourse on the Other*, by Michel de Certeau, trans. Brian Massumi (Minneapolis: University of Minnesota Press, 1986), vii–xxi, ix, viii.

49. Jean-Paul Sartre, "Existentialism Is a Humanism," in *Existentialism from Dostoevsky to Sartre*, ed. Walter Kaufman (New York: New American Library, 1956), 353.

50. Wright, *The Messenger*, 131.

51. Smith, *Contingencies of Value*, 94.

52. Charles Wright, letter to Harold Vursell, May 21, 1963, FSG Records.

53. Charles Wright, "Happy Birthday" note, April 16, 1963, Jones Papers.

54. Charles Wright, "To Nathanael West on Memorial Day," *Village Voice*, June 3, 1971, 13.

55. Charles Wright, letter to Harold Vursell, January 13, 1964, FSG Records.

56. Charles Wright, letter to Harold Vursell, January 13, 1964, FSG Records.

57. Charles Wright, letter to Lowney T. Handy, June 27, 1964, Handy Collection.

58. George Hendrick, *James Jones and the Handy Writers' Colony* (Carbondale: Southern Illinois University Press, 2001), 122–23.

59. Charles Wright, "Nobody Knows His Name," *Village Voice*, October 12, 1967, 8.

60. Harold Vursell, letter to Charles Wright, July 9, 1964, FSG Records.

CHAPTER FOUR: THE YEARS IN TANGIER AND
THE FINDING OF A HOME

1. Claude McKay, *A Long Way from Home* (New York: Furman, 1937), 236.

2. Ibid., 236–37.

3. Rupert Croft-Cooke, *The Caves of Hercules* (London: Allen, 1974), 14.

4. Greg A. Mullins, *Colonial Affairs: Bowles, Burroughs, and Chester Write Tangier* (Madison: University of Wisconsin Press, 2002), 3.

5. Ibid., 3, 4.

6. Croft-Cooke, *The Caves of Hercules*, 140, 164.

7. Michelle Green, *The Dream at the End of the World: Paul Bowles and the Literary Renegades in Tangier* (New York: HarperCollins, 1991), xi.

8. Mullins, *Colonial Affairs*, 7, 5.

9. Ibid., 7. In *History of Sexuality*, Michel Foucault puts forth a similar argument: "sexuality is a cultural product that cannot be regarded as a simple extension of a biological process" (quoted in Tamsin Spargo, *Foucault and Queer Theory* [New York: Torem, 1999], 45).

10. Abba Elethea, personal communication, December 29, 2014.

11. Mary Jacobs, personal communication, February 13, 2015.

12. Croft-Cooke, *The Caves of Hercules*, 165.

13. Green, *The Dream at the End of the World*, 46.

14. Harold Vursell, letter to Leona Nevler, August 4, 1964, FSG Records.

15. Mullins, *Colonial Affairs*, 14, 17.

16. Jacobs, personal communication, February 13, 2015.

17. Ibid.

18. Charles Wright, "Hassan of Morocco: A King's Courage." *Village Voice*, July 29, 1971, 13.

19. Charles Wright, "Nobody Knows His Name," *Village Voice*, October 12, 1967, 8.

20. Clarence Major, "A Conversation with Charles Wright," 12, Major Papers.

21. Jacobs, personal communication, February 13, 2015.

22. Charles Wright, letter to Harold Vursell, October 3, 1964, FSG Records.

23. Wright, "Nobody Knows His Name," 8.

24. Wright, "Hassan of Morocco," 13.

25. Ibid.

26. Wright, letter to Vursell, October 3, 1964.

27. Jacobs, personal communication, February 13, 2015.

28. Ibid.

29. Ibid.

30. Ibid.

31. Wright, "Nobody Knows His Name," 8.

32. Mary Jacobs, personal communication, August 14, 2016.

33. Charles Wright, letter to Charles Robb, April 9, 1965, Jones Papers.

34. Jacobs, personal communication, February 13, 2015.

35. Wright, letter to Robb, April 9, 1965.

36. Charles Wright, letter to Charles Robb, May 27–28, 1965, Jones Papers.

37. Jacobs, personal communication, February 13, 2015.

38. Alfred Chester's letter to Norman Glass, January 3, 1965, box 1, folder 2, Alfred Chester Papers, Collections and Archives, Kent State University Libraries.

39. Jacobs, personal communication, February 13, 2015.

40. Edward Field, *The Man Who Would Marry Susan Sontag: And Other Intimate Portraits of the Bohemian Era* (Madison: University of Wisconsin Press, 2005), 130, 131, 132, 139.

41. Quoted in Green, *The Dream at the End of The World*, 301.

42. Albert Chester, letter to Edward Field, August 6, 1964, in *Letters from Morocco,* by Alfred Chester, 202, unpublished manuscript, private collection.

43. Ibid., 200.

44. Alfred Chester, letter to Edward Field, September 11, 1964, in Chester, *Letters from Morocco.*

45. Alfred Chester, letter to Edward Field, November 24, 1964, box 340, folder 19, Edward Field and Alfred Chester Archive, Special Collections, Morris Library, University of Delaware.

46. Charles Wright, remarks about *The Wig* at a book party hosted by the Gathering of the Tribes, February 16, 2003, video in Gathering of the Tribes Archives (MSS 198, Tribes 1), New York University Special Collections.

47. Major, "A Conversation with Charles Wright," 26.

48. Frank Campenni, "Charles (Stevenson) Wright Biography—Charles Wright Comments," https://biography.jrank.org.

49. Mary Jacobs, personal communication, January 23, 2015.

50. Harold Vursell, letter to Charles Wright, July 24, 1964, FSG Records.

51. Jacobs, personal communication, February 13, 2015.

52. Harold Vursell, letter to Candida Donadio, November 2, 1964, FSG Records.

53. Karen Horney, *Our Inner Conflicts: A Constructive Theory of Neurosis* (1945; reprint, New York: Norton, 1992), 34.

54. Charles Wright, telegram to Harold Vursell, December 29, 1964, FSG Records.

55. Harold Vursell, telegram to American consul general, Tangier, December 30, 1964, FSG Records.

56. Alfred Chester, letter to Norman Glass, January 3, 1965, box 1, folder 11, Alfred Chester Papers, 1963–65, Kent State University Libraries, Special Collection and Archives (hereafter Chester Papers).

57. Alfred Chester, letter to Norman Glass, n.d., Chester Papers.

58. Campenni, "Charles (Stevenson) Wright Biography."

59. Phelonise Willie, personal communication, May 13, 2013.

60. Horney, *Our Inner Conflicts,* 13.

61. Green, *The Dream at the End of the World,* 301.

62. Wright, letter to Vursell, October 3, 1964.

63. Charles Wright, letter to Norman Mailer, November 26, 1965, Mailer Papers.

64. John O'Brien, ed., "Charles Wright," *Interviews with Black Writers* (New York: Liveright, 1973), 251.

65. Major, "A Conversation with Charles Wright," 13.

66. Charles Wright, letter to Harold Vursell, May 22–23, 1965, FSG Papers.

67. Ibid.

68. Wright, letter to Robb, May 27–28, 1965.

69. Roger Straus, letter to Charles Wright, September 10, 1965, FSG Records.

70. Wright, letter to Robb, May 27–28, 1965.

71. Wright, letter to Robb, April 9, 1965.

72. Charles Wright, letter to Rupert Croft-Cooke, January 7, 1966, Mailer Papers.

73. Wright, letter to Robb, May 27–28, 1965.

74. Rupert Croft-Cooke, letter to Charles Wright, February 16, 1966, Mailer Papers.

75. Jacobs, personal communication, February 13, 2015.

76. Ibid.

77. Croft-Cooke, *The Caves of Hercules*, 90.

78. Charles Wright, letter to Harold Vursell, July 5, 1965, FSG Records.

79. Jacobs, personal communication, August 14, 2016.

80. Charles Wright, letter to Harold Vursell, December 12, 1966, FSG Records.

81. Wright, letter to Vursell, July 5, 1965.

82. Harold Vursell, letter to Charles Wright, May 16, 1965, FSG Records.

83. Chester, letter to Glass, n.d.

84. Alfred Chester, letter to Edward Field, March [?], 1965, in Chester, *Letters from Morocco*, 263.

85. Alfred Chester, letter to Edward Field, March 19, 1965, in ibid., 266.

86. Alfred Chester, letter to Norman Glass, May 22, 1965, in ibid., 289.

87. Alfred Chester, letter to Norman Glass, August 2, 1965, box 1, folder 21, Chester Papers.

88. Alfred Chester, letter to Edward Field, August 18, 1965, in Chester, *Letters from Morocco*, 311.

89. Harold Vursell, letter to Charles Wright, May 26, 1965, FSG Records.

90. Ibid.

91. Florence Roess, letter to Harold Vursell, July 16, 1965, FSG Records.

92. Harold Vursell, letter to Florence Roess, July 21, 1965, FSG Records.

93. Wright, letter to Vursell, May 22–23, 1965.

94. Ibid.

95. Charles Wright, letter to Rupert Croft-Cooke, January 27, 1966, Mailer Papers.

96. Charles Wright, letter to Rupert Croft-Cooke, November 28, 1965, Mailer Papers.

97. Harold Vursell, letter to H. Worthington-Smith, October 15, 1965, FSG Records; Charles Wright, letter to Harold Vursell, October 20, 1965, FSG Records.

98. Rupert Croft-Cooke, letter to Charles Wright, December 10, 1965, Mailer Papers.

99. Rupert Croft-Cooke, letter to Charles Wright, January 7, 1966, Mailer Papers.

100. Rupert Croft-Cooke, letter to Charles Wright, February 16, 1966, Mailer Papers.

101. Charles Wright, letter to Rupert Croft-Cooke, June 14, 1966, Mailer Papers.

102. Charles Wright, letter to Rupert Croft-Cooke, July 8, 1966, Mailer Papers.

103. Major, "A Conversation with Charles Wright," 8.

104. Charles Wright, "Notes of a Circular Man: The Seeds of Violence." *Village Voice*, July 27, 1967, 5, 6.

105. Croft-Cooke, *The Caves of Hercules*, 90–91.

106. Ibid., 90.

CHAPTER FIVE: PUBLICATION OF *THE WIG*

1. John O'Brien, ed., "Charles Wright," *Interviews with Black Writers* (New York: Liveright, 1973), 252.

2. Joe Weixlmann, "Charles Stevenson Wright," in *Afro-American Writers after 1955: The Dictionary of Literary Biography*, vol. 33, ed. Thadious Davis and Trudier Harris (Farmington Hills, MI: Gale Research, 1984), 3.

3. Rupert Croft-Cooke, *The Caves of Hercules* (London: Allen, 1974), 90.

4. Charles Wright, letter to Norman Mailer, November 26, 1965, Mailer Papers.

5. Roger Straus, letter to Norman Mailer, October 22, 1965, FSG Records.

6. Norman Mailer, letter to Roger Straus, November 8, 1965, FSG Records.

7. O'Brien, "Charles Wright," 251.

8. Charles Wright, *The Wig* (1966; reprint, San Francisco: Mercury House, 2003), dedication page.

9. Steven Weisenburger, *Fables of Subversion: Satire and the American Novel, 1930–1980* (Athens: University of Georgia Press, 1995), 155, 3.

10. Clarence Major, "A Conversation with Charles Wright," 1–26, Major Papers.

11. Max F. Schulz, *Black Humor Fiction of the Sixties: A Pluralistic Definition of Man and His World.* (Athens: Ohio University Press, 1973), 6.

12. Martin Esslin, "The Theater of the Absurd Reconsidered," in *Reflections: Essays on Modern Theatre* (New York: Doubleday, 1969): 84–109.

13. Schulz, *Black Humor Fiction of the Sixties*, 6.

14. At the 2003 book party hosted by the Gathering of the Tribes, Wright stated that Lester Jefferson was based on the men of the Charles Wright family, who were businessmen. Mr. Fishback was based on a Korean buddy he encountered on 5th Avenue in New York City (video in Gathering of the Tribes Archives (MSS 198, Tribes 1), New York University Special Collections. Also see Schulz, *Black Humor Fiction of the Sixties*, 7, 96, 97.

15. A. Robert Lee, "Making New," in *Black Fiction: New Studies in the Afro-American Novel Since 1945* (London: Vision, 1980), 241.

16. Schulz, *Black Humor Fiction of the Sixties*, 7.

17. Wright, *The Wig*, 7.

18. George S. Schuyler, "Book Shelf," *Pittsburgh Courier*, April 16, 1966, 9B.

19. Wright, *The Wig*, 21.

20. Ibid., 22.

21. Frances S. Foster, "Charles Wright: Black Black Humorist," *CLA Journal* 15, no. 1 (1971): 48.

22. Wright, *The Wig*, 98.

23. Ibid., 14.

24. Ibid., 16.

25. Conrad Knickerbocker, "Laughing on the Outside," *New York Times*, March 5, 1966, 25.

26. Ishmael Reed, "Introduction," in *The Collected Novels of Charles Wright*, by Charles Wright (New York: HarperPerennial, 2019), xii.

27. Major, "A Conversation with Charles Wright," 12.

28. Reed, "Introduction," xii.

29. Wright, *The Wig*, 41.

30. Ibid., 106, 141.

31. Schulz, *Black Humor Fiction of the Sixties*, 97–98.

32. Wright, *The Wig*, 7.

33. Ibid., 7, 23.

34. Lee, "Making New," 241.

35. Albert Memmi, *The Colonizer and the Colonized* (New York: Vintage, 1973), 121.

36. Wright, *The Wig*, 8.

37. Valerie Babb, *A History of the African American Novel* (New York: Cambridge University Press, 2017), 138.

38. Wright, *The Wig*, 12.

39. Reed, "Introduction," xi.

40. Babb, *A History of the African American Novel*, 138.

41. Schuyler, "Book Shelf."

42. Wright, *The Wig*, 23.

43. Ibid., 17.

44. Ibid., 28, 18.

45. Ibid., 38–39.

46. Ibid., 49, 61, 67.

47. Ibid., 71.

48. Weisenburger, *Fables of Subversion*, 155.

49. Wright, *The Wig*, 85.

50. Ibid., 89.

51. Ibid., 111.

52. Ibid.

53. Ibid., 112, 113, 115, 116.

54. Ibid., 116.

55. Robert P. Sedlack, "Jousting with Rats: Charles Wright's *The Wig*," *Satire Newsletter* 7, no. 1 (1969): 37–39.

56. Wright, *The Wig*, 137–38.

57. Ibid., 148, 147.

58. Foster, "Charles Wright: Black Black Humorist," 46.

59. Wright, *The Wig*, 152, 154.

60. Ibid., 165.

61. Weisenburger, *Fables of Subversion*, 155.

62. Eberhard Kreutzer, "Dark Ghetto Fantasy and the Great Society: Charles Wright's *The Wig*," in *The Afro-American Novel Since 1960*, ed. Peter Bruck and Wolfgang Karrer (Amsterdam: Gruner, 1982), 151.

63. Ibid., 151, 148.

64. Memmi, *The Colonizer and the Colonized*, 125.

65. Schulz, *Black Humor Fiction of the Sixties*, 111, 101.

66. Wright, *The Wig*, 125, 68.

67. Foster, "Charles Wright: Black Black Humorist," 49.

68. Weixlmann, "Charles Stevenson Wright," 12.

69. Lee, "Making New," 241.

70. "Charles Wright: Almost Victim to Censorship of Black Writers," *New York Amsterdam News*, April 17, 1993, 28.

71. Loyle Hairston, review of *The Wig*, *Freedomways* 6, no. 3 (1966): 274.

72. Ibid.

73. Major, "A Conversation with Charles Wright," 7, 14.

74. Richard Jean So, *Redlining Culture: A Data History of Racial Inequality and Postwar Fiction* (New York: Columbia University Press, 2021), 69.

75. Victor S. Navasky, "With Malice toward All," *New York Times Book Review*, February 27, 1966, 4.

76. William James Smith, review of *The Wig*, *Commonweal*, April 29, 1966, 182.

77. "Fiction," *Kirkus*, December 15, 1965, 1241–42.

78. Weixlmann, "Charles Stevenson Wright," 9.

79. Irv Goodman, letter to Lila Karpf, October 7, 1965, FSG Records.

80. Rachel Dranow, letter to unknown recipient, May 3, 1966, FSG Records.

81. Phelonise Willie, "Who's Who in Black America and Homeless?," *Vice Versa* 49 (July–September 1995): 5–6.

82. Harold Vursell, letter to Charles Wright, May 10, 1966, FSG Records.

83. "East-West Sons of Huck Finn," *Nation*, April 18, 1966, 467–68.

84. Untitled review, *Books and Bookmen* 12 (May 1967): 34.

85. Conrad Knickerbocker, review of *The Wig*, *New York Times Book Review*, March 5, 1966, 25.

86. Willie, "Who's Who in Black America and Homeless?," 6.

87. J. F. Yanez, letter to Paula Diamond, April 20, 1964, FSG Records; Gerald Pollinger, letter to Paula Diamond, November 11, 1963, FSG Records; Lila Karpf, letter to Mundy, January 7, 1966, FSG Records; Ursula Bender, letter to E. Whitby, March 29, 1966, FSG Records; Lila Karpf, letter to Herbert Lottman, March 25, 1966, FSG Records.

88. Ursula Bender, letter to Arabel Porter, March 31, 1966, FSG Records.

89. Foster, "Charles Wright: Black Black Humorist," 44.

90. Charles Wright, letter to Harold Vursell, January 10, 1966, FSG Records.

91. John Peck, letter to Charles Wright, October 6, 1966, FSG Records.

92. Sales memo, n.d., FSG Records.

93. Harold Vursell, letter to Candida Donadio, June 1, 1966, FSG Records.

94. Harold Vursell, letter to Charles Wright, May 10, 1966, FSG Records.

95. O'Brien, "Charles Wright," 248.

96. Charles Wright, letter to Harold Vursell, August 12, 1966, FSG Records.
97. "Charles Wright: Almost Victim to Censorship of Black Writers," 28.
98. Charles Wright, letter to Langston Hughes, December 12, 1966, Hughes Papers.
99. Charles Wright, letter to Langston Hughes, December 20, 1966, Hughes Papers.
100. Quoted in Willie, "Who's Who in Black America and Homeless?," 6.
101. Michael di Capua, letter to Carolyn Kizer, July 18, 1968, FSG Records.
102. Wright, letter to Vursell, August 12, 1966.
103. Charles Wright, letter to Harold Vursell, July 5, 1965, FSG Records.
104. Charles Wright, to letter Rupert Croft-Cooke, July 8, 1966, Mailer Papers.
105. Harold Vursell, letter to Candida Donadio, March 6, 1966, FSG Records.
106. Mary Jacobs, personal communication, February 13, 2015.
107. Charles Wright, "A New Day," in *The Best Short Stories by Negro Writers: An Anthology from 1899 to the Present,* ed. Langston Hughes (Boston: Little, Brown, 1967), 341–46, 342.
108. Ibid., 342.
109. Ibid., 345.
110. "Ibid., 345, 346.
111. Reed, "Introduction," xix, vii, ix.
112. Steven Cannon, personal communication, June 24, 2014.
113. Ibid.
114. Phelonise Willie, personal communication, summer 2013.
115. Babb, *A History of the African American Novel,* 138.
116. Willie, "Who's Who in Black America and Homeless?," 6.
117. Charles Wright, letter to Harold Vursell, August 12, 1966, FSG Records.
118. Barbara Hernstein Smith, *Contingencies of Value: Alternative Perspective for Critical Theory* (Cambridge, MA: Harvard University Press, 1988), 94.
119. Jerome Klinkowitz, "A World's Wrongs Made Wright," *Village Voice,* May 17, 1973, 41.
120. Ursula Bender, letter to Bernard Shir-Cliff, May 20, 1966, FSG Records.
121. Rhoda F. Gamson, letter to Donald A. Scrader, August 28, 1973, FSG Records.
122. Jerome Klinkowitz, letter to Charles Wright, September 27, 1977, FSG Records.
123. Kirsten Jannene-Nelson, letter to Roger Straus, November 5, 2002, FSG Records.
124. Willie, "Who's Who in Black America and Homeless?," 6.
125. Charles Wright, "Sonny and the Sailor," *Negro Digest,* 17, no. 10 (1968): 63–67, 64.
126. Ibid., 64, 65.
127. Ibid., 66–67.
128. H. Worthington-Smith, to Farrar, Straus, and Giroux, Office of Public Relations, October 12, 1965, FSG Records.
129. Charles Wright, letter to Harold Vursell, October 16, 1966, FSG Records.
130. Lila Kerpf, letter to Michael Myer, August 18, 1970, FSG Records.

131. Jay Martin, letter to Charles Wright, February 4, 1969, FSG Records.

132. Jay Martin, letter to James Jones, March 5, 1969, Jones Papers.

133. James Jones, letter to Jay Martin, April 29, 1969, Jones Papers.

134. Harold Vursell, letter to Jay Martin, April 8, 1969, FSG Records.

135. Ibid.

136. Howard B. Gotlieb, letter to Charles Wright, January 8, 1971, FSG Records.

137. Harold Vursell, letter to Charles Wright, January 12, 1966, FSG Records.

138. GerShun Avilez, *Black Queer Freedom: Spaces of Injury and Paths of Desire* (Urbana: University of Illinois Press, 2020), 3.

CHAPTER SIX: WRITING IN THE 1970S AND THE *VILLAGE VOICE*

1. John O'Brien, ed., "Charles Wright," *Interviews with Black Writers* (New York: Liveright, 1973), 245–57, 256. There is only one editor.

2. Clarence Major, "A Conversation with Charles Wright," 3, Major Papers.

3. Nancy Fraser, *The Old Is Dying and the New Cannot Be Born: From Progressive Neoliberalism to Trump and Beyond* (New York: Verso, 2019), 44–45.

4. Major, "A Conversation with Charles Wright," 4–5, 11–12.

5. Ibid., 5.

6. "Charles Wright: Almost Victim to Censorship of Black Writers," *New York Amsterdam News*, April 17, 1993, 28.

7. Major, "A Conversation with Charles Wright," 17.

8. Harold Vursell, letter to Charles Wright, November 9, 1967, FSG Records.

9. Harold Vursell, letter to Charles Wright, August 22, 1967, FSG Records.

10. O'Brien, "Charles Wright," 256.

11. Lynn C. Goldberg, letter to Clarence Major, October 16, 1972, Major Papers.

12. Clarence Major, letter to Lynn C. Goldberg, October 22, 1972, Major Papers.

13. Quoted in Lynn C. Goldberg, letter to Peter Bailey, October 25, 1972, FSG Records. s

14. Kay Boyle, letter to Andree Conrad, October 14, 1972, FSG Records.

15. Richard Huett, letter to Peter Hinzmann, March 7, 1973, FSG Records.

16. Roger Straus, letter to John Bright-Holmes, March 12, 1973, FSG Records.

17. Charles Wright, letter to Barbara Holler, September 25, 1963, FSG Records.

18. Charles Wright, letter to Kay Boyle, December 25, 1072, Kay Boyle Papers, Special Collection Research Center, Southern Illinois University, Carbondale.

19. Andree Conrad, letter to Douglas Turner Ward, January 11, 1973, FSG Records.

20. Charles Wright, letter to Lynn C. Goldberg, November 20, 1072, FSG Records.

21. Lynn C. Goldberg, letter to H. H. Pritchard, October 25, 1972, FSG Records.

22. Charles Wright, "Mexico in White, Red, and Black," *Village Voice*, August 31, 1972, 6.

23. Charles Wright, "Mucho and Upward with El Presidente," *Village Voice*, September 14, 1972, 17.

24. Charles Wright, letter to Roger Straus, July 8, 1974, FSG Records.

25. Charles Wright, "The Act of Surrender," *Yardbird Reader* 2 (1973): 173–77, 174, 175, 176, 175.

26. Phelonise Willie, personal communication, May 14, 2013.

27. Mary Jacobs, personal communication, February 13, 2015.

28. Boris Kachka, *Hothouse: The Arts of Survival and the Universal Art at America's Most Celebrated Publishing House, Farrar, Straus & Giroux* (New York: Simon and Schuster, 2013), 3.

29. Roger Straus, letter to Carter Burden, May 26, 1972, FSG Records.

30. Roger Straus, letter to Charles Wright, June 28, 1972, FSG Records.

31. Major, "A Conversation with Charles Wright," 17–18.

32. Charles Wright, *Absolutely Nothing to Get Alarmed About*, in *The Complete Novels of Charles Wright*, by Charles Wright (New York: HarperPerennial, 1993), 316.

33. Jerome Klinkowitz, *Literary Disruptions: The Making of a Post-Contemporary American Fiction*. (Urbana: University of Illinois Press, 1975), 180.

34. A. Robert Lee, "Making New," in *Black Fiction: New Studies in the Afro-American Novel Since 1945* (London: Vision, 1980), 222–50, 242.

35. Wright, *Absolutely*, 336.

36. Klinkowitz, *Literary Disruptions*, 180.

37. Albert Camus, *The Myth of Sisyphus and Other Essays*, trans. Justin O'Brien (New York: Vintage, 1955), 13.

38. Wright, *Absolutely*, 257, 258.

39. Lee, "Making New," 242.

40. Gene Seymour, "The Margins Will Not Hold: Reconsidering Cult Novelist Charles Wright," *Bookforum* 26, no. 3 (2019): 25.

41. Wright, *Absolutely*, 291.

42. Lee, "Making New," 243.

43. Miles A. Smith, "Street People Are Featured in New Book," *Daily Times* (Salisbury, MD), April 12, 1973, 9.

44. Wright, *Absolutely*, 285, 286, 287.

45. Barbara Hernstein Smith, *Contingencies of Value: Alternative Perspective for Critical Theory* (Cambridge, MA: Harvard University Press, 1988), 168.

46. Wright, *Absolutely*, 269.

47. Ibid., 259, 270.

48. Major, "A Conversation with Charles Wright," 5–6.

49. Wright, *Absolutely*, 270.

50. Ibid., 271.

51. Ibid., 307, 289.

52. Simone de Beauvoir, *Ethics of Ambiguity*, trans. Bernard Frechtman (New York: Open Road, 2018), 28.
53. Wright, *Absolutely*, 313.
54. Ibid.
55. Ibid., 305.
56. Samuel R. Delany, *Times Square Red, Times Square Blue* (New York: New York University Press, 2019), 148–49.
57. Ibid., xxviii.
58. Wright, *Absolutely*, 314, 314.
59. Ibid., 259.
60. Ibid., 324.
61. Nancy Fraser and Rahell Jaeggi, *Capitalism: A Conversation in Critical Theory*, ed. Brian Milstein (Medford, MA: Polity, 2018), 175.
62. Klinkowitz, *Literary Disruptions*, 182.
63. Wright, *Absolutely*, 324.
64. Ibid., 326.
65. Ibid., 327.
66. Ibid., 332.
67. Ibid., 335.
68. Ibid.
69. Major, "A Conversation with Charles Wright," 9.
70. Wright, *Absolutely*, 336.
71. Ibid., 337.
72. Ibid., 343, 344.
73. Ibid., 349, 351.
74. Ibid., 353.
75. Ibid., 355.
76. Ibid., 356.
77. Ibid.
78. Ibid., 358.
79. Ibid.
80. Ibid.
81. Ibid., 362.
82. Ibid., 369.
83. Ibid., 373.
84. Klinkowitz, *Literary Disruptions*, 182.
85. Wright, *Absolutely*, 375.
86. Ibid., 387.
87. Memo about *Absolutely*'s print run, n.d., FSG Records.
88. Sussman and Sugar, advertising schedule, memo to FSG, February 19, 1973, FSG Records.

89. Roger Straus, letter to Robert Kotlowitz, February 8, 1973, FSG Records.

90. Lynn C. Goldberg, letter to Keith Darby, January 12, 1973, FSG Records.

91. Barbara H. Neilson, letter to Leona Nevler, February 2, 1973, FSG Records.

92. Linda B. Schweikardt, letter to Barbara H. Neilson, February 1, 1973, FSG Records.

93. Peter Hinzmann, letter to Roberta Hellman, October 16, 1972, FSG Records. Additional letters were sent to the other clubs mentioned in the text.

94. Richard Jean So, *Redlining Culture*, 103.

95. David Freeman, "Absolutely Nothing to Get Alarmed About," *New York Times*, March 11, 1973, 410.

96. Review of *Absolutely*, *Publishers Weekly*, January 29, 1973, 257.

97. Phoebe Adams, "Short Reviews: Books," *Atlantic* 232 (April 1973): 128.

98. Review of *Absolutely*, *New Yorker*, March 17, 1973, 131.

99. Bernette Golden, "Wright Diagnoses the Urban Malady, Finds 'Nothing to Get Alarmed About,'" *National Observer*, March 31, 1973, 23.

100. Anthony Burgess, letter to Andree Conrad, October 21, 1972, FSG Records.

101. Al Young, letter to Lynn C. Goldberg, February 3, 1973, FSG Records.

102. Peter Hinzmann, letter to Robert Hellman, October 16, 1972, FSG Records.

103. Harold D. Cohen, letter to Farrar, Straus, and Giroux's subsidiary rights department, March 13, 1973, FSG Records.

104. Jerome Klinkowitz, letter to Andree Conrad, January 22, 1973, FSG Records.

105. Andree Conrad, letter to Roger Straus, January 25, 1973, FSG Records.

106. So, *Redlining Culture: A Data History of Racial Inequality and Postwar Fiction* (New York: Columbia University Press, 2021), 123.

107. Quoted in Frances S. Foster, "Charles Wright: Black Black Humorist," *CLA Journal* 15, no. 1 (1971): 53.

108. Darryl Dickson-Carr, *African American Satire: The Sacredly Profane Novel* (Columbia: University of Missouri Press, 2001), 2.

109. Foster, "Charles Wright: Black Black Humorist," 53.

110. "A Survey: Black Writers' Views on Literary Lions and Values," *Negro Digest* 17, no. 3 (1968): 10–44, 15.

111. Kinoshi Nishikawa, "The Book Reads You: William Melvin Kelley's Typographic Imagination," *American Literary History* 30, no. 4 (2018): 730–55, 732, 733.

112. Joe Weixlmann, "Charles Stevenson Wright," in *Afro-American Writers After 1955: The Dictionary of Literary Biography*, vol. 33, ed. Thadious Davis and Trudier Harris (Farmington Hills, MI: Gale Research, 1984), 9–10.

113. Lee, "Making New," 239.

114. Darryl Pinckney, *Out There: Mavericks of Black Literature* (New York: Basic Civitas, 2002), x–xiii.

115. GerShun Avilez, *Black Queer Freedom: Spaces of Injury and Paths of Desire* (Bloomington: University of Illinois Press, 2020), 6.

CHAPTER SEVEN: LIFE AFTER *ABSOLUTELY* AND THE HODENFIELDS

1. Quoted in Richard Jean So, *Redlining Culture: A Data History of Racial Inequality and Postwar Fiction* (New York: Columbia University Press, 2021), 37.
2. Ishmael Reed, "Introduction," in *The Collected Novels of Charles Wright: "The Messenger," "The Wig," and "Absolutely Nothing to Get Alarmed About,"* by Charles Wright (New York: HarperPerennial, 2019), xiii.
3. Charles Wright, "Note to a Dead Poet," *Village Voice*, October 12, 1967, 5.
4. Tamsin Spargo, *Foucault and Queer Theory* (New York: Torem, 1999), 31.
5. So, *Redlining Culture*, 107, 123.
6. Ibid., 108, 43.
7. Ibid., 8.
8. Harold Vursell, letter to Charles Wright, June 7, 1965, FSG Records.
9. Ibid. These four stories were never published and have been lost from Wright's oeuvre.
10. Charles Wright, letter to Roger Straus, n.d., FSG Records.
11. Hy Cohen, letter to Andree Conrad, August 29, 1972, FSG Records. In August 1972, Donadio decided to stop handling Wright's work, and Georges Borchardt became his agent (Andree Conrad, letter to Georges Borchardt, August 31, 1972, FSG Records).
12. Charles Wright, letter to Roger Straus, September 1, 1982, FSG Records.
13. Charles Wright, letter to Pat Strachan, August 30, 1981, FSG Records; Charles Wright, letter to Roger Straus, September 1, 1982, FSG Records.
14. John O'Brien, "Charles Wright," in *Interviews with Black Writers* (New York: Liveright, 1973), 26.
15. Karen Horney, *Our Inner Conflicts: A Constructive Theory of Neurosis* (New York: W. W. Norton, 1945, 1992), 227.
16. Charles Wright, letter to Thomas Stewart, July 31, 1974, FSG Records.
17. TAS, memo to Roger Straus, August 22, 1974, FSG Records.
18. Charles Wright, "The Orgy of Hesitation," *Scene* 1 (November 1969): 21–22, 52, 21.
19. Ibid., 21.
20. Ibid., 21.
21. Ibid., 22.
22. Ibid., 52.
23. Ibid.
24. Bruce Weber, "Charles Wright, Novelist, Dies at 76," *New York Times*, October 8, 2008.
25. Mary Jacobs, personal communication, February 13, 2015.
26. Ibid.

27. Weber, "Charles Wright, Novelist, Dies at 76."

28. Jacobs, personal communication, February 13, 2015.

29. Ibid.

30. Fisher would often not answer Wright's letters or phone calls and would be late in sending his checks. He took to complaining to Farrar, Straus, which meant that somebody there would have to call her. See Tom Stewart, letter to Roger Straus, January 28, 1974, FSG Records; Diane Fisher, letter to Andree Conrad, August 21, 1972, FSG Records.

31. Charles Wright, letter to Roger Straus, March 15, 1976, FSG Records.

32. Roger Straus, letter to Charles Wright, March 17, 1976, FSG Records.

33. Eugene Brissie, letter to David Godine, January 17, 1977, FSG Records.

34. Clarence Major, letter to Charles Wright, October 17, 1978, Major Papers.

35. Charles Wright, letter to Clarence Major, October 26, 1978, Major Papers.

36. Faculty members Wilfred Samuels, Clarence Major, and Charles Nilon hosted Wright (Wilfred Samuels, personal communication, January 21, 2015).

37. Ibid.; Wilfred Samuels, personal communication, January 11, 2015.

38. Samuels, personal communication.

39. Pat Strachan, letter to Charles Wright, April 26, 1978, FSG Records.

40. Internal memo, Farrar, Straus, and Giroux editorial department, April 4, 1978, FSG Records.

41. Charles Wright, letter to Pat Strachan, n.d., FSG Records.

42. Gary Stuart, letter to Charles Wright, February 22, 1979, FSG Records.

43. Charles Wright, letter to Pat Strachan, August 9, 1979, FSG Records.

44. Ibid.

45. Charles Wright, letter to Roger Straus, September 1, 1982, FSG Records.

CHAPTER EIGHT: STALLED IN THE 1980S

1. Mary Jacobs, personal communication, February 13, 2015.

2. Ibid.

3. Mary Jacobs, personal communication, August 14, 2016.

4. Jacobs, personal communication, February 13, 2015.

5. Pat Strachan, letter to Charles Wright, May 1, 1980, FSG Records.

6. Boris Kachka, *Hothouse: The Arts of Survival and the Universal Art at America's Most Celebrated Publishing House, Farrar, Straus & Giroux* (New York: Simon and Schuster, 2013), 60, 117.

7. Pat Strachan, letter to Charles Wright, October 1, 1980, FSG Records; Charles Wright, letter to Pat Strachan, September 18, 1980, FSG Records.

8. Wright, letter to Strachan, September 18, 1980.

9. Pat Strachan, letter to Ron Bernstein, February 20, 1981, FSG Records.

10. Charles Wright, letter to Lowney T. Handy, April 23, 1961, Jones Papers.

11. Charles Wright, letter to Norman Mailer, September 20, 1961, Mailer Papers.

12. Charles Wright, letter to Norman Mailer, November 28, 1965, Mailer Papers.

13. Reed, "Introduction," The Collected Novels of Charles Wright, xi.

14. Ron Simmons, "*Tongues Untied*: An Interview with Marlon Riggs," in *Brother to Brother: New Writings by Black Gay Men*, ed. Essex Hemphill (Boston: Alyson), 191.

15. Pat Strachan, letter to Charles Wright, October 2, 1981, FSG Records.

16. Roger Straus, letter to Charles Wright, September 15, 1982, FSG Records.

17. Charles Wright, letter to Pat Strachan, March 5, 1982, Manuscripts and Archives Division, NYPL.

18. Charles Harris to Roger W. Straus, April 23, 1981, FSG Records.

19. Chris Willerton, letter to Peggy Miller, August 27, 1984, FSG Records; Peggy Miller, letter to Chris Willerton, September 7, 1984, FSG Records.

20. Charles Wright, letter to Pat Strachan, August 7, 1986, FSG Records.

21. Pat Strachan, letter to Charles Wright, August 19, 1986, FSG Records.

22. Charles Wright, letter to Pat Strachan, July 13, 1987, FSG Records.

23. In response to my query about an interview to discuss her relationship with Wright, Pat Strachan said, "I'm afraid I have no memory of working directly with Charles Wright. His last novel was published in 1973, and I was still an editorial assistant then. I may later have helped to reissue paperback editions of his books, but remember no details" (personal communication, July 23, 2020).

24. Charles Wright, "Mr. Stein," *Black American Literature Forum* 23, no. 2 (1989): 379.

25. Ibid., 380.

26. Gershun Avilez, *Black Queer Freedom: Spaces of Injury and Paths of Desire* (Urbana: University of Illinois Press, 2020), 17.

CHAPTER NINE: FORGOTTEN IN THE 1990S

1. Phelonise Willie, personal communication, May 5, 2013.

2. Charles Wright, letter to Roger Straus, November 25, 1989, FSG Records.

3. This included Mary Mebane, University of South Carolina; W. Lawrence Hogue, University of Houston; Clarence Major, University of Colorado; Kay Boyle, San Francisco State University; and Jerome Klinkowitz, Northern Illinois University.

4. Phelonise Willie, "Who's Who in Black America and Homeless?," *Vice Versa*, no. 49 (1995): 5.

5. Michael Hathaway, memo to Roger Straus, November 12, 1992, FSG Records.

6. Roger Straus, letter to Charles Wright, August 3, 1992, FSG Records.

7. Eugene Brissie to David Godine at Quality Paperback Book Club, January 1977, Manuscripts and Archives Division, NYPL.

8. Michael Hathaway, memo to Roger Straus, August 11, 1992, FSG Records.

9. Michael Hathaway, memo to AS/LY, August 13, 1992, FSG Records.

10. Michael Hathaway, letter to Charlotte Sheedy, October 9, 1992, FSG Records.

11. Farrar, Straus, and Giroux, internal memo, August 25, 1992, FSG Records.

12. Michael Hathaway, memo to Roger Straus, October 21, 1992, FSG Records.

13. Charles Wright, letter to Michael Hathaway, n.d., FSG Records.

14. Michael Hathaway, letter to Charlotte Sheedy, November 12, 1992, FSG Records.

15. Michael Hathaway, memo to JLK, November 17, 1992, FSG Records.

16. Michael Hathaway, memo to Farrar, Straus, and Giroux contracts department, November 18, 1992, FSG Records.

17. Steve Cannon, personal communication, June 24, 2014.

18. Charles Wright, letter to Roger Straus, June 16, 1992, FSG Records.

19. Roger Straus, letter to Charles Wright, August 3, 1992, FSG Records.

20. Charles Wright, letter to Michael Hathaway, [early August 1992], FSG Records.

21. Charles Wright, "Tom and Brock," in *Shade: An Anthology of Fiction by Gay Men of African Descent,* ed. Bruce Morrow and Charles Rowell (New York: Avon, 1996), 160, 162.

22. Ibid., 163.

23. Bessel van der Kolk, *The Body Keeps the Score: Brain, Mind, and Body in the Healing of Trauma* (New York: Penguin, 2014), 70.

24. "Tom and Brock," 264.

25. Willie, "Who's Who in Black America and Homeless?," 5.

26. Ibid., 6.

27. Abba Elethea, personal communication, December 29, 2014.

28. Mary Jacobs, personal communication, February 13, 2015.

29. Phelonise Willie, personal communication, May 10, 2013.

30. Jacobs, personal communication, February 13, 2015.

31. Willie, personal communication, May 10, 2013.

32. Jacobs, personal communication, February 13, 2015.

33. Charles Wright, letter to Pat Strachan, July 13, 1987, FSG Records.

34. Pat Strachan, letter to Charles Wright, December 16, 1987, FSG Records.

35. Harold Vursell, letter to Charles Wright, June 25, 1965, FSG Records.

36. Charles Wright, letter to Harold Vursell, May 16, 1965, FSG Records.

37. Harold Vursell, letter to Charles Wright, January 16, 1970, FSG Records.

38. Charles Wright, letter to Tom Stewart, February 11, 1974, FSG Records.

39. Charles Wright, letter to Clarence Major, January 20, 2000, FSG Records.

40. Charles Wright, letter to Harold Vursell, July 5, 1965, FSG Records.

CHAPTER TEN: THE DEATH AND REDISCOVERY OF
CHARLES WRIGHT AND HIS FICTION

1. Charles Wright, letter to Clarence Major, February 7, 2000, Major Papers.
2. Clarence Major, "A Conversation with Charles Wright," Major Papers, 20.
3. Charles Wright, letter to Clarence Major, April 8, 2003, Major Papers.
4. Ibid.
5. Richard Jean So, *Redlining Culture: A Data History of Racial Inequality and Postwar Fiction* (New York: Columbia University Press, 2021), 36, 38.
6. Wright, letter to Major, April 8, 2003.
7. Judith Herman, *Trauma and Recovery* (New York: Basic Books, 2015), 1.
8. Mary Jacobs, personal communication, February 13, 2015.
9. Phelonise Willie, personal communication, June 14, 2013.
10. Major, "A Conversation with Charles Wright," 3, 10.
11. Ishmael Reed, "Introduction," in *The Collected Novels of Charles Wright*, by Charles Wright (New York: HarperPerennial, 2019), ix.
12. Video of a book party for Charles Wright, February 16, 2003, Gathering of the Tribes Archives (MSS 198, Tribe 1), New York University Special Collections.
13. Boris Kachka, *Hothouse: The Arts of Survival and the Universal Art at America's Most Celebrated Publishing House, Farrar, Straus & Giroux* (New York: Simon and Schuster, 2013), 4, 221.
14. Harold Vursell, letter to Charles Wright, October 25, 1966, FSG Records.
15. Harold Vursell, letter to Candida Donadio, March 8, 1966, FSG Records.
16. Richard Peek, personal communication, April 25, 2013.
17. Herman, *Trauma and Recovery*, 115.
18. Ibid.
19. Ibid.
20. Ibid.
21. Phelonise Willie, personal communication, May 5, 2013.
22. Peek, personal communication, April 25, 2013.
23. Ibid.
24. Joe Weixlmann, "Charles Stevenson Wright," in *Afro-American Writers After 1955: The Dictionary of Literary Biography*, vol. 33, ed. Thadious Davis and Trudier Harris (Farmington Hills, MI: Gale Research, 1984), 10.
25. Dwight Garner, "The Pleasures of a Writer Who Was 'Richard Pryor on Paper,'" *New York Times*, February 23, 2017.
26. John Lingan, "The Long, Familiar Obscurity of Charles Wright," *Slate*, September 13, 2019.
27. Gene Seymour, "The Margins Will Not Hold: Reconsidering Cult Novelist Charles Wright," *Bookforum* 26, no. 3 (2019): 25.
28. Reed, "Introduction," xix.

INDEX

Page numbers in *italics* indicate a figure.

W. LAWRENCE HOGUE (PhD, Stanford University; MA, University of Chicago) is the John and Rebecca Moores Distinguished Professor of English, Emeritus, at the University of Houston. He is the author of many books, including *The African American Male, Writing, and Difference* (2003), *Postmodern American Literature and Its Other* (2009), *Postmodernism, Traditional Cultural Forms, and African American Narratives* (2013), and *A Theoretical Approach to Modern American History and Literature* (2020).